CONTENTS

Tables and Illustrations

Dedication

This book is dedicated to Alyna and Brenan Wyatt for all the hours I didn't spend with them.

Acknowledgments

THIS BOOK COULD NOT HAVE BEEN WRITTEN without the assistance and encouragement of the Canadian Association of Financial Planners. Financial planning is a relatively young profession that embraces the disciplines of the investment world, insurance, tax planning, estate planning, family law and sound money management. It's a holistic approach to managing your money that brings together the individual aspects of your finances in a package that fits your unique needs.

The CAFP, founded in December 1982, has become the leading voice of that new profession in Canada. Although the association does have a strict code of ethics, the most convincing step toward true professionalism was taken in the fall of 1988 with the creation of the new designation, the Registered Financial Planner. But the profession remains completely untouched by any sort of government legislation. The provincial chapters of the CAFP are fighting hard to convince the provincial legislatures to bring in some sort of government regulations that will protect the public and maintain the integrity of the profession itself.

There are many people within the CAFP who deserve to be recognized for their contribution to this book. Unfortunately, I have the space to mention only a few. I'd like to thank Leslie Mezei, vice-president of The Alexander Consulting Group, who sparked the idea of writing this book through his conviction that many people can be their own financial planner if they will only make the effort. It was Leslie and Tim Egan, president of T.E. Financial Consultants Ltd. in Toronto and former president of the CAFP, who offered the assistance and encouragement of the CAFP and its members in the research and writing of this book.

My research began in Winnipeg in the head office of Investors Group where Wayne Walker, a senior vice-president of Investors, gave me the unique opportunity to take part in a week-long

financial planning training session. I'd like to thank Doug Macdonald, of Macdonald, Shymko & Company Ltd. in Vancouver who
endured eight hours of questions and prodding during a marathon
of interviews. There are many other individuals who patiently answered questions no matter how often I called – Jim Rogers and
David Chalmers at the James E. Rogers Group Ltd. in Vancouver;
George Swan, Bank of Montreal Private Client Services in Toronto;
the people at Royal Trust from Vancouver to Saint John, New Brunswick; Michael Nairne, and the staff at The Equion Group in
Toronto; Chris Snyder at ECC Financial Planning Group in Toronto;
Barry Teague, manager of mortgage marketing, Bank of Montreal,
and Stephen Smith, president of Yorkminster Insurance Brokers
Ltd., in Port Hope, Ontario. Rob Kerr, president of Kerr Financial
Consultants Inc. in Montreal, a former president and 1991 chairman
of the CAFP, is a planner who played a unique role in the writing of
this book. He too endured hours of interviews and took the time to
read the finished manuscript for accuracy.

There are several people to whom I owe a special thanks: Barbara
Tar, a planner with Kerr Financial in Toronto; Jennifer Osther, a
librarian and researcher of rare skill; and Bob Barney, president of
Compulife Software Inc.. June Yee, Janice Small and Jeff Preboy
worked hard to publish the 1993 editions of the Financial Times
Personal Finance Library and I appreciate their endurance and soft
spirits. I find it professionally rewarding and a personal pleasure to
work with such special people.

Finally, I'd like to thank Alyna and Brenan, my children, and
Charles, my colleague and husband. Charles edited, proofed and de-
bated every word in this book. He remains my most valued critic
and partner.

Elaine Wyatt
September 1992

CHAPTER 1

Not All the Best Things in Life Are Free

WE LIVE IN A WORLD OF temptation. We can buy fine leather shoes from Italy, gold watches from Switzerland, silk from China. We can decorate our homes with tapestries from France and carpets from Persia. We can float in hot air balloons over the Serengeti Plain, hike with Nepalese sherpas deep into the Himalayas and laze on beaches in the Caribbean. The luxuries of the world that were once the privilege of the aristocracy are now within everyone's grasp.

Even the mundane has become exotic. A bewildering array of kitchen appliances can chop, grate, purify, liquefy and cook our food. We can install Blaupunkt stereo systems in our cars or 18-jet whirlpools in our bathrooms. We can clothe our children in designer togs at $150 for a pair of bib overalls – perfect for a trip to finger painting class. We can spend every cent we earn without stepping out of our own home just by flipping through catalogues or watching home-shopping television.

A world of comforts and trinkets can be ours with the chunk-chunk of an imprinter over a well-worn credit card. We can draw on a personal line of credit or borrow against the equity in our home with a simple signature on a cheque.

But this veneer of prosperity has been tarnished. Since April 1990 Canada has suffered through a recession that has left us with 1,606,000 people unemployed, 11.6 percent of the labour force. Economists tell us that the economy is strengthening – the number of personal and business bankruptcies has begun to recede – but in one month alone, July 1992, 129,000 full-time jobs were lost across the country and full-time employment fell to a five-year low. On Bay Street and Main Street, memories linger of Meltdown Monday, the day in October 1987 when stock markets around the world crashed. Even prophecies of invigorating competition arising from new laws giving bankers, stockbrokers and insurance companies the freedom to encroach upon each other's turf are stale and slightly ridiculous. The pillars of the financial world have crumbled, but they didn't fall gracefully. Nor, did the tumble bring any real benefits to consumers.

The damage that can be done to your financial well-being by a bank failure, the collapse of a trust company or upheaval in the financial markets is obvious. But managing your money is more than protecting yourself in a cruel world. If you indulge your passions without restraint, you risk living a life that drifts with the tug of advertising and the promises of avaricious salesmen.

It's a crude carrot and stick, but the moral remains: if you don't look after your money, it's unlikely that your life will unfold as you would like. Financial planning may seem tedious, but if you make the effort you can weave your spending and saving into a sweeping plan that will give you control over your financial destiny.

Think of financial planning as a voyage and this book as your companion. Not only will *The Money Companion* guide you through the financial marketplace, it will help you discover where you are now, where you want to go and how you can get there.

Part One, Your Financial Framework, will help you establish your personal financial goals and avoid the most common money mistakes. You'll be guided through Canada's income tax system – and end up reducing the taxes you pay. Finally, you'll learn how to protect yourself and your family against the financial damage that can be caused by life's crises.

Part Two, Your Investment Strategy, will show you how to invest wisely and profitably so you can achieve financial independence. Part Two also looks at the wisdom of buying your own home and the most practical ways to save for your children's future education.

Part Three, Will This Never End?, covers those aspects of your financial plan most people often ignore – estate planning and the critical decisions you will have to make as you approach retirement.

If financial planning sounds vaguely confining, remember that there can be embellishments to your plan as you travel through life. But if you don't take the time to map out a route, or at least a vague goal, you could end up in Patagonia when you really wanted to go to Istanbul. And you can't be an armchair traveller – you must act. Don't procrastinate. As you begin to make decisions, your financial skills will mature. As the nickels and dimes you save become dol-

Your Assets

WHAT YOU OWN	VALUE
Personal possessions	
House	
Car	
Furniture	
Cottage	
Collectibles	
Others	
Savings and investments	
Bank accounts	
Canada Savings Bonds	
Term deposits and GICs	
Employee savings plan	
Life insurance cash value	
Stocks	
Bonds	
Mutual funds	
Real estate	
Other investments	
Retirement savings	
Registered retirement savings plans	
Savings accounts	
GICs	
Stocks	
Bonds	
Mutual funds	
Pension plan	
TOTAL OWNED	

WORKSHEET I

lars, momentum will build. Time is money, and wasting it will only erode your ability to fulfill your dreams.

Do you know how much you're worth?

To begin your financial voyage, take a few minutes to see where you stand. By tallying everything you own and subtracting everything you owe, you'll arrive at your net worth. By creating a personal fi-

Your Liabilities

WHAT YOU OWE	VALUE
Personal debts	
Mortgage on home	
Car loan	
Credit card balances	
Personal loan	
Mortgage on cottage	
Unpaid bills	
Income tax owing	
Other debts	
Investment debts	
Investment loans	
Business loans	
Other debts	
TOTAL OWED	

WORKSHEET II

Your Net Worth

What you own	
Less what you owe	
YOUR NET WORTH	

WORKSHEET III

nancial snapshot you have a starting point; without it you're just drifting in the dark. Don't be tempted to skip this step for fear of bad news. Most people discover they're wealthier than they think.

For an accurate picture, pinpoint exact values wherever you can. Where you must estimate, try for a compromise between a professional appraisal and a seat-of-the-pants guess by checking the prices of items in newspaper classified ads. Your insurance company can give you the cash value of your life insurance policy. If you keep an eye on the price of houses selling in your neighbourhood, you'll know the value of your home. For your car, take the mid-range price from the classified ads for cars of the same model and year. Don't get caught on the wrong side of the market when pricing your collectibles – their value is not the price you saw on a similar doll or rocking chair at an auction last week, it's what you would get if you sold them today.

Determining the value of your wealth should be straightforward, but for a sharper picture, separate the value of your pension or investments in your RRSP from those held outside a tax shelter. When listing your interest-bearing securities, show the interest rate and maturity dates. Their current value consists of principal, plus interest that hasn't yet been paid to you, less the tax you will have to pay.

If you own more than you owe, you're already ahead of the game. If you owe more than you own, you needn't despair but you do have to take the time to probe the spending and saving habits that have so far spoiled your ability to create a solid financial foundation in your life. Whether behind or ahead, you should look at your net worth every year. If you've taken control of your money you should see a steady building of wealth. Set a target for growth, say 3 or 4 percent more than inflation, and decide how you're going to achieve it. Keep score to see if you can make yourself richer by this time next year.

Setting your financial priorities

Knowing your financial worth is your groundwork; it provides a foundation that you can use to understand and analyse your finances and to set goals. If you continue to live and save as you do now, will you be able to satisfy your ambitions? Do you even know what your ambitions are? Do you know where you're going or what you really want? At the core of financial planning is knowing your financial aspirations and creating a plan to make them a reality. You might have a hazy notion of what you want, but until you write it down it will remain nebulous and beyond your grasp. If you're married or have children, this soul-searching should be done as a family.

Before you begin, each family member must understand the difference between needs and wants. It's the distinction between needs and wants that is the true reflection of ourselves. One person might want to take a vacation to Europe or the Far East but can't because he *needs* a new car every couple of years; another will be

Your Family's Wish List

Husband's Goals	Cost	Achievement Date

Wife's Goals	Cost	Achievement Date

Children's Goals	Cost	Achievement Date

Family's Goals	Cost	Achievement Date

willing to take public transit to work because he *needs* an exotic vacation every year. One family will make any sacrifice for music lessons for the children, another will skip the music lessons for a VCR. Give each person in your family a piece of paper and a few days to make a list of needs and wants.

The more specific your goals, the easier it will be to design a strategy and to keep track of how you're performing. Do you want to take an ocean cruise through the South Pacific? Do you want a cottage in the country? A sports car? Early retirement? Your own business? Once each member of your family has compiled a wish list, sit down and fill out your family wish list.

Obviously, you can't have everything you want. You should pace yourself, set priorities, understand the sacrifices of not having one thing so you can have another. Just as your children must realize you can't afford both horseback riding lessons and supper in a restaurant every night, you should realize you probably won't be able to retire at age fifty-five and buy all the widgets and gadgets and trinkets that you might want.

Get tough with your dream world. Put a price tag and a time frame on each wish. If you want a $1,200 debt paid in six months, realize you will have to pay your banker more than $200 a month. If you want a VCR within the next couple of months, start saving $100 a week and assign a member of your family the task of reading consumer reports and comparing prices. Be realistic. Don't commit more money to your dreams than you can squeeze out of your daily budget or you'll soon quit in despair. You're also more likely to be successful if you keep track of the money you're setting aside. For big dreams – perhaps early retirement, a home or your own business – this could mean a separate bank account or pre-authorized cheques for a savings account or mutual fund. For less expensive dreams, if you don't set up a separate bank account, at least keep a record of the funds being set aside so the money isn't swallowed by day-to-day expenses or something bought on an impulse.

Warning! The thirteen worst money mistakes

Everyone makes mistakes with money. We have personal debts at the same time as we have savings, we can't be bothered to change our investment strategy when we know we should, we stick to a broker we don't even like because we don't want to hurt his feelings, we lose the receipts for tax-deductible expenses.

You may not be guilty of all of these financial bloopers, but you can learn to recognize and avoid the chronic pitfalls. Here are a few of the most damaging offences:

1. Not enough insurance.
Most families have at least some life insurance, although it's seldom enough and often the wrong kind. But fewer than half of all working adults have disability insurance. You're twice as likely to be disabled for at least ninety days as you are to die before age sixty-five. How will you pay your living expenses and your medical expenses if you can't work? You need enough coverage to provide 60 to 70 percent of your family income if you're disabled yet this is probably not what you'll receive if your employer is paying your disability premiums.

2. Too many debts.
It's easy to fall into debt, especially if you use credit cards. You can pay so little each month and fall deeper into a hole without a whisper of recrimination from your banker. Try to stop using credit indiscriminately. For personal expenses, use only one credit card and charge no more than you can pay off every month. Most people not only have too many debts, the interest rates they pay are excessive. If you do have credit card debts, don't leave them on your card where you'll pay as much as 28 percent interest; pay them off with a personal loan at 10 percent. Try to avoid any personal debt, but if you can't, shop the banks, trust companies and credit unions for the best rate and haggle with lenders for better terms.

3. Sloppy investing.
Too many people allow their investment decisions to be driven by fear, flashy ads and laziness instead of an intelligent investment strategy. The worst offence is improper diversification. People tend to invest in just one thing – investment certificates, real estate and gold are among the favourite indulgences – but there are those who scatter investments so haphazardly they create chaos. Other common goofs are ignoring investments altogether or constantly shuffling them in a greedy race for the best return. Either way, you end up losing.

4. Accepting advice without questioning its wisdom.
No one cares as much about your money as you do. Even if you consult a stockbroker, accountant, investment counsellor or financial planner, you need enough knowledge to judge the advice you're given. You don't have to be a financial whiz, and you should never hesitate to ask questions. If you're made to feel dumb or you're told the investment is too complicated for you to understand, find another advisor.

Although these money goofs can have an immediately damaging impact on your financial well-being, there are other, more insidious, errors of omission that can distort your ability to build your financial health over a lifetime. These can be difficult and time-consuming to correct, but you ignore them at your peril:

5. Not knowing what you want your money to do.
You work hard for your money. Do you know why? What do you want your money to do for you? Do you want to take a vacation in Europe, send your children to college or university, start your own business, retire with financial security? Most people put the cart before the horse, saving and investing their money in hopes that everything will work out in the end. Instead, you must decide what you want in life. Write it down, figure out what your dreams will cost and then handle your money so you'll get what you want.

6. Not knowing how you spend.
Financial planners tend to whisper the word "budget" because it raises so many red flags. A budget feels constraining. It feels too much like work. Most people don't know how much they spend or how they spend it – and they're afraid to know. But if you don't have a grip on your income and expenses, you won't know what money is flowing through your hands and what's being kept for the future, if anything.

7. Not knowing how much you're worth.
You can't plan with confidence if you don't know where you are today. Don't be afraid to sit down and figure out your net worth. You may be pleasantly surprised.

8. Procrastinating.

Whether because of fear or laziness, people are plagued by an inability to act. It's the bane of financial advisors. Even after a financial strategy has been created and the necessary steps carefully mapped out, often nothing happens. People forget, they can't be bothered, they procrastinate until it's too late. Start your financial plan today.

9. Failing to keep financial records.

Tossing your financial papers into shoe boxes and drawers can only breed frustration and faulty decisions. You won't be able to find receipts at tax time or make intelligent investment decisions. If you should die or fall ill, your family will have to fit together the fragments of their financial lives from the bits of papers and notes you'll have left scattered around. Keep a list of your investments, bank accounts, insurance policies and credit card numbers. Write out the names of your financial advisors and the locations of your will and safe-deposit box. Finally, keep your past income tax returns in one place. Keeping records gives your financial life order. It's quite possible this is all you'll have to do to give yourself a feeling of control.

10. Knowing too little about employer-sponsored benefit plans.

Your employer may offer health and counselling plans, financial advice or savings plans that you might be missing out on. Even if these benefits are taxable, it will always be less expensive for you to receive them from your employer than to buy them with money out of your own pocket.

11. Making too little effort to reduce your tax burden.

Most people wait until the last minute to file their income tax returns, swear softly at Revenue Canada as they drop their returns in the mailbox and then forget about taxes for another year. Take the time to understand the tax system and you can reduce your tax burden.

12. Waiting too long to begin saving for retirement.

Don't float along, hoping the future will take care of itself. Establish a structured savings plan using the tools the government gives you for saving efficiently. Anyone who is not putting as much as legally possible into an RRSP had better look hard at his financial affairs.

13. Refusing to probe the way we feel about money.
We're all creatures of habit, at the mercy of influences that can distort our ability to manage money. If you don't probe your psyche for the emotional reasons why you buy on impulse, pinch pennies or stash all your money in Canada Savings Bonds, you'll wind up handling your money just as you have in the past. No matter how many books you read, financial satisfaction could remain elusive.

A framework for achieving financial freedom

Creating a personal financial plan takes knowledge, time and a strategy for action. That strategy can be developed through these nine steps:

1. Generate a picture of where you stand now. Get all your papers together and create a personal financial record. Work out your net worth and track your income and spending for at least a couple of months so you'll know how you make, spend and save your money.

2. Make sure you and your family are protected by up-to-date wills as well as adequate life, disability and property insurance.

3. Decide what you want your money to do for you. Sit down with your family and discuss your dreams for the future.

4. Look at the legal contracts in your life: your will, the beneficiary designation on your RRSPs and life insurance and the impact of family law reforms on your marriage.

5. Pay off your debts and build a cushion of money for emergencies.

6. Create a savings and investment strategy that will let you fulfill your dreams. You can begin simply; pay yourself first by putting 10 percent of your income into a savings account when you cash your pay cheque.

7. Understand the tax system so you can pay as little tax as possible. Make sure you're taking full advantage of all credits and deductions and that you're using every tax planning tool, including RRSPs and income splitting, to reduce your taxes.

8. Act immediately. Don't procrastinate or you'll waste time and money.

9. As each year passes, sit down and look at your progress. Make changes if necessary and get on with life, knowing your finances will unfold as you wish.

Creating a financial plan is hard work. But once you've taken care of the future and the unexpected, the confusion and anxiety

will be gone. You'll be able to spend the rest of your money in un-
fettered pleasure. You'll also have the peace of mind that comes
from knowing that in a world that seems to be slipping into chaos,
you can control your financial destiny.

CHAPTER 2

Where Does All the Money Go?

MOST OF US HAVE, AT ONE time or another, experienced a sense of bewilderment as we've stared into our wallets. A pitifully slim stack of bills is stashed untidily where only a few days before had rested enough money to last all week. A blur of cash is flowing through our mind – $28 for groceries, $8 for a movie, $6 at the drugstore, $8.50 for dry cleaning and $5 for magazines. But that's only $55.50 and we'd started with $100. Where did the rest of it go? Why doesn't the money last all week?

There are a few people who are comfortable with their spending, people who never feel pinched, never experience a twinge of uncertainty. Most of us find ourselves at least once in a while shaking our heads, wondering where the money went, resolving to spend less and save more.

In fact, most people do live within their means. And although the word "budget" may conjure up the image of a cramped life of deprivation, it shouldn't. Budgeting gives you an insight into your spending habits that will allow you to make informed, intelligent decisions. It reduces the uncertainties in your life so that you may never again hear yourself say, "Where on earth did all the money go this month?"

It sounds trite, but to spend well you have to know the value of a dollar, that spending ninety cents for a cup of coffee twice each working day comes to $9 a week, $37.50 a month, $450 a year – the price of a round trip airline ticket from Toronto to Bermuda. That's budgeting.

Budgeting doesn't mean you can't go for coffee. Nor does it mean you can't go to Bermuda if you don't cut out coffee breaks. Budgeting means going for coffee once a day and flying to Bermuda every other year. It means being in control of your money instead of your money being in control of you. A budget is putting your dollar down when and where you want, not where serendipity takes it. A budget turns spending into a conscious act.

Budgeting is a state of mind. Sure, brown-bagging makes you feel cheap. After all, executives, doctors and newspaper publishers don't take their lunches to work, do they? Besides, you don't like making sandwiches. What's the solution? Brown-bag it for three days a week and go for lunch twice. Don't deprive yourself every day, but muster a little discipline. There are sacrifices you can make that aren't as painful as you might believe. Budgeting is also a frame of mind. Don't tell your friends you can't afford a coffee or a muffin if you're saving for an exotic trip. Tell them you've decided not to buy the goodies off the office coffee wagon. No one can buy everything they want; there's no need to apologize or feel sorry. Who's going to be wistful at the end of the year – you for all the muffins you didn't eat or your friends for the trip they can't afford to take?

It's irritating, but Mom was right: take care of the pennies and the dollars will take care of themselves. Or at least the dollars will be there for you to invest. For just a little while, carry a pencil and a small notebook everywhere and jot down everything you buy. You'll be shocked by the results. Most people lose track of 10 percent to 20 percent of their money.

Your budget is the foundation of your financial plan. You have to know how much money is coming into your hands and how much is flowing out. You have to know what you spend every day before you can know what you will spend tomorrow. Ask yourself what you will spend next September when the kids start school or this spring when the boat has to be put back in the water. How much do you *really* spend on vacation? If you need $12 to pay a bill, and you get $20 from an automatic teller, where does the other $8 go?

Creating a budget you can live with

There are a zillion ways to budget. But this adaptation of the method used by one Toronto financial planner is simple, reasonably painless to establish and easy to stick to over time. There isn't a budgeting system around that can promise financial bliss, but this one will do at least seven things for you:

  • Tell you how much money is coming in and when it's coming,
  • Ensure you can pay for all of the necessities of life and avoid the panic that sometimes arises with the arrival of a heating or telephone bill,

• Tell you how much is left over for comforts and luxuries,
• Set up a plan to get you out of debt and keep you out,
• Establish a savings plan to help you achieve your lifetime dreams,
• Create a method for keeping tidy financial records,
• Give you a sense of control.

It can be done in a few easy steps. You'll look first at your income, then at your unavoidable expenses. The money left over can be juggled to cover your savings, clothing, food and day-to-day expenses. All of this will be done with the help of Worksheet V on the following pages, a three-ring binder, an accordion file and two small change purses.

What do you earn and when do you earn it?

Do you even know how much money you're working with? How much of your salary are you actually able to take home and spend? Maybe you were hired at $36,000 a year but as much as $9,000 could be taken to pay income taxes and $647 to cover Canada Pension Plan. Another $1,850 goes toward the company pension plan, $893 for unemployment insurance premiums, $200 for life insurance and your dental plan, and $720 for union dues. It's like Popeye peeling potatoes – you end up with baby spuds. A $36,000 salary can be quickly whittled down to about $24,000, or less. If you spend the full $36,000, you're going to run yourself into the ground. Don't laugh – many people do it unwittingly.

After you look at how much income you have, look at how it comes in. Money can come into your home in a steady stream or it can come in dribs and drabs. Salaries can be monthly, twice monthly, weekly or every other week. Interest on corporate bonds can be paid twice a year, but stock dividends quarterly. Interest from Canada Savings Bonds (CSBs) and most bonuses are paid once a year. List everything and, although it can be difficult, list it after all of the benefits and taxes have been taken out. If you're in doubt, keep your estimates low. You don't want any painful surprises.

You can either use the income statement provided on page sixteen or create a similar worksheet on the first page of your three-ring binder to record your flow of income and when you receive it. (There are also computer programs available that can help you budget and keep track of your investments.)

Where the Money Comes From

	Jan.	Feb.	Mar.	Apr.	May	June	July	Aug.	Sept.	Oct.	Nov.	Dec.	Annual
Husband's salary													
Wife's salary													
Bonuses													
Pensions													
Investments Dividends													
Interest													
Rent													
Other													
Alimony													
Child support													
Other													
TOTAL													

Expenses That Are Difficult to Change

	Jan.	Feb.	Mar.	Apr.	May	June	July	Aug.	Sept.	Oct.	Nov.	Dec.	Annual
Housing Mortgage or rent													
Telephone													
Heat													
Electricity													

WORKSHEET V

	Jan.	Feb.	Mar.	Apr.	May	June	July	Aug.	Sept.	Oct.	Nov.	Dec.	Annual
Housing (continued) Water													
Property taxes													
Property insurance													
Health care Provincial insurance													
Medicine													
Dentist													
Life insurance													
Disability insurance													
Income tax													
Transportation Vehicle licence													
Insurance													
Maintenance													
Parking													
Train and bus fares													
Child care													
Christmas													
Other													
TOTAL													

WORKSHEET V (continued)

Where does your money go?

You have control over all your expenses, but many are difficult to change – not impossible, just difficult. Some expenses, such as life insurance or property taxes, do not come up often. But they do surface regularly and you can plan for them. To avoid getting caught without the money to pay a bill, spread these expenses over the year. If your insurance premium is $480 a year, put aside $40 every month. If you spend $1,000 to celebrate Christmas and New Year's, put aside $85 a month. Don't dip into this money for any other reason.

You can use the worksheet on pages sixteen and seventeen or transfer the worksheet to the second page of your binder to record those expenses that are difficult to change and when they must be paid.

Expenses you can juggle

Now determine how much you have to spend or save each month by deducting your expenses from your take-home pay.

Your annual disposable income $ _____
Your annual unavoidable expenses $ _____
The money left to spend or save each year $ _____
If you divide this last number by 12, you'll know
how much money you'll have left each month to
spend on expenses such as food and clothing $ _____

Juggling the money left over after the unavoidable expenses are paid is tough; the money just seems to disappear.

The next step in creating a budget mixes reality and fantasy. You may not spend your money as you think you do, or as you would like. A budget should tell you the truth and help you to spend your money as you wish. Your cheque book and credit card receipts can help dredge up past expenditures, but unless you've kept detailed records in the past, you'll have to do some guessing. Keep records for at least a month to get a good grip on how you spend money day to day.

In planning your budget, put your consumer debts at the top of your list; pay these off or you'll never get off the treadmill. If you have a debt that doesn't have a fixed repayment schedule – perhaps a car loan on your personal line of credit – set your own schedule for repaying that debt. If you have a $10,000 loan at 8 percent interest, you could decide to pay it off at $483 a month over two years or

Monthly Expenses that You Can Juggle

	Reality	The Way You Would Like It To Be
Savings		
Retirement		
Dreams		
Loans		
Credit cards		
Car		
Personal		
Line of credit		
Food and household expenses		
Clothing		
Laundry and dry cleaning		
Pocket money		
Transportation		
Oil and gas		
Parking		
Train and bus fares		
Entertainment		
Books and magazines		
Movies		
Performing arts		
Club fees		
Hobbies		
Cable television		
Vacations		
Gifts		
Charities		
Household repairs		
TOTAL		

at $433 a month over three years. Taking a year longer to pay your loan may keep your monthly payments down, but over the life of the loan you'll pay $800 more in interest.

Unfortunately, you really can't start to save until you've paid off your debts. It's a mistake to buy CSBs yielding 7.5 percent a year while you're racking up debts on your credit card at 18 percent or more. If you aren't in debt, but your savings plan is catch-as-catch-can, jot in 10 percent. Don't try saving money that's left over, there won't be any. The key to successful saving is not to save a lot of money, but to save regularly. Look upon saving as a bill that must be paid every month.

Turn to the third page of your binder and write the name of the current month at the top. Sharpen your pencil, find a fat eraser and list all of the expenses that you can easily control. By the time you're finished with this you'll have eraser streaks across the page and rubber crumbs scattered across the table.

If your calculations would have you believe you have hundreds of dollars left over at the end of every month and reality leaves you broke by the end of the second week, you know you are spending more than you think. A hint: the culprits are usually pocket money, entertainment and clothes. You may have forgotten a few things. Did you count the vet bills and the garden supplies?

It can be easier to watch your cash if you put the money for a week's household and grocery expenses into an envelope or purse and your pocket money into another. If you think you spend only $5 a day, put $5 in your pocket before you leave home in the morning. How does it feel? Terrible! Maybe $5 isn't enough. If you want more pocket money you'll have to take it from somewhere else – you'll have to spend less on vacations, clothes, books, something. You can't spend more than you earn.

If you just can't seem to make ends meet, let alone overlap, maybe you should take another look at expenses that are difficult to change. Are you carrying an expensive whole life policy when term insurance would meet your needs? Are you spending too much on gifts? Are you trying to pay down your mortgage too quickly?

Juggle, juggle, juggle. Give yourself time. Tracking your money for only a month really isn't enough – you'll cheat, everyone does. You won't buy as many magazines or muffins because it won't look good on the budget record. There's nothing wrong with that – after all, your goal is to control spending – but if you only do it for a month you'll fall back into old habits as soon as you quit tracking. If you track your money for six months or a year you'll have an accurate record of your spending habits and a workable budget that you really are able to live with comfortably.

Using your bank accounts to control your money

This painstaking budget, wrung from the core of your financial soul, is still just a piece of paper with scribbles on it. To prevent it from disintegrating, you need to control your financial flow by creating a personal banking system.

In their competitive frenzy, banks, trust companies and credit unions have unleashed a flood of different kinds of chequing, savings and foreign currency accounts. Some of us avoid the confusion by having too few accounts and pass up the chance to earn more interest. Others use too many and drown in a sea of passbooks, cheque books, statements, and service charges.

Instead, you want to use your bank accounts to separate your spending responsibilities. There are many different ways of doing this to suit your own needs, but you could start with these four accounts:

• A master chequing account into which you deposit every cent you get. From here, money is moved into other accounts, each with its own purpose. The remaining money is used for day-to-day expenses – mortgage or rent, groceries, the cleaning lady, pocket money and entertainment. At the end of the month, the balance in this account should always be zero. All of the money will have been spent or saved.

• A daily-interest chequing account to hold the money you'll need to pay unavoidable expenses that pop up occasionally – property taxes, insurance premiums, magazine subscriptions, gifts and utility bills.

• A savings account in which your savings can build until you have enough to invest. You could have a savings account into which you deposit your registered retirement savings plan (RRSP) contribution every month. Just make sure you don't let the money languish there. It can also hold the money you'll use to pay your income tax, take a vacation or make house repairs.

• Another daily-interest chequing account to hold the money you can spend on impulse. If you're an electronics buff or can't resist a seat sale to Bangkok, you can control your spending by indulging your urges to spend with money in this account. This account should be a family affair. Decide along with your husband or wife how much money can be spent impulsively. Once the money is gone, it's gone. If there isn't enough left for a weekend fling to New York or a CD player or another pair of Gucci shoes, then you can't have them. No one ends up the grinch, refusing to open the purse strings to satisfy the other's spending urge.

As a couple or family, your banking will be more complicated than that of someone on his or her own. Money can stir up unpleasant emotions, and every family member should have some financial privacy. Each person must have something he or she is free to spend without explanation or justification. One way to establish this privacy is through an account for each person from which cash can be taken for clothing, entertainment and pocket money.

Keep it simple

Your goal is to create a banking system that helps keep your money under control. But a word of warning: make it as simple as possible, especially if you deal with only one financial institution. In this age of computers, technical glitches and clerical errors can create chaos if money starts moving in and out of the wrong accounts. Because it's important that your savings be untouched and the paper trails of your investments be clean, it is wiser still to open your savings or investment account at a different institution. Not only is this efficient, it can blunt the temptation to dip into your savings.

Whatever you do, just be sure you don't get muddled. Write the purpose of each account on the front of your passbook or cheque book. Husbands and wives should also be careful to keep investment transactions distinct or you could risk running into trouble with Revenue Canada.

Choosing the right bank account from the jumble can seem daunting but in reality there are only a few typical accounts:
• Chequing accounts,
• Savings accounts,
• Chequing/savings accounts,
• Premium rate savings accounts paying high interest rates for balances that usually must exceed $5,000. Often, top rates are paid only on balances that exceed $100,000, an amount that exceeds your protection by the Canada Deposit Insurance Corporation.

• U.S. dollar accounts.

A chequing account is straightforward. It doesn't pay any interest and you incur charges for cheques, withdrawals, transfers, deposits and sometimes just for maintaining the account.

Chequing-savings and savings accounts have become more complicated. With a chequing-savings account, your interest is usually calculated daily and you may not be charged for cheques if you maintain a specified minimum balance. Savings accounts, and some chequing-savings accounts, can pay interest in one of a variety of ways. Some institutions calculate interest daily, some on the lowest daily balance during the past month and others on the average balance for the month. To complicate matters further, some chequing-savings and savings accounts pay increasingly higher interest rates on increasingly higher balances.

The competition among financial institutions for your business is hot, but don't chew your pencil into a stub fussing over it. Your money should never languish in any bank account. Premium treasury bill accounts may pay 2 percent more than a regular savings account, but if you have enough money to earn the premium rate perhaps you should consider buying T-bills or investing in a money market mutual fund.

When choosing a financial institution, you should also consider the charges levied by that institution. Bank bashing, long a national sport, spun into a furor several years ago as the public balked at being hit by mounting charges for everything from cancelled cheques to closing accounts. The federal government has promised to protect consumers from unfair bank service charges by requiring banks to explain their fees, provide at least thirty days' notice of changes and give customers time to complain. The banks have agreed it's unfair to charge for correcting errors they've made, and competition will undoubtedly keep other fees in flux. Still, you shouldn't switch institutions just for cut-rate charges, especially if you're self-employed or an investor who needs to develop a history of banking with a particular institution and an understanding banker.

If you have a good reason to switch from one institution to another, look hard at the bank services you do use and ignore others. Ask questions. At what level does the interest rate change on tiered accounts? How long will the institution hold a cheque before cashing it? How much does it charge for cheque writing? What will it charge for a certified cheque? How much will you be charged for using your overdraft protection? When you compare financial institutions, make sure you look at them all within a week to keep comparisons fair. And don't put all your eggs in one basket. It never hurts to forge financial relationships with more than one institution.

Finally, you should be aware of the limits and coverage of the Canada Deposit Insurance Corporation. The CDIC was created in 1967 to protect the money you deposit in member financial institutions. Members include banks, trust companies and loan companies but membership is not mandatory; look for the CDIC sign, especially if you're dealing with a smaller, regional company.

CDIC insurance covers savings and chequing accounts, term deposits such as guaranteed investment certificates (but only those payable within five years), debentures issued by loan companies, money orders, drafts, certified cheques and traveller's cheques. These deposits must be payable in Canadian currency. It does not cover foreign currency deposits, deposits that are locked in for longer than five years, nor the debentures issued by a chartered bank.

CDIC coverage is limited to $60,000 (principal and interest) at any one member, not any one branch. However, CDIC also insures joint deposits, trust deposits and deposits held in RRSPs and in RRIFs – each to the $60,000 maximum. For example, if you have an account in your name and a joint account with your husband or wife, both accounts are insured separately for $60,000. If you have money in an RRSP, you will have another $60,000 protection; if you also have a RRIF, your combined protection on all of your accounts will be $240,000. (Remember, the RRSP funds must be invested in savings accounts or term deposits that meet the CDIC's requirements.) Funds which you deposit into a spousal RRSP are combined with your spouse's funds; not yours.

Keeping track of your papers

The final step in setting up your budgeting system is to impose control over the flood of papers, bills and receipts that make up your financial documents. To tame the deluge of paper, you need an accordion file. Label the different sections with the name of each month and save all your bills and receipts – insurance premiums, mortgage or rent receipts, tax bills, automated teller transaction re-

ceipts and cancelled cheques. Keep all your credit card purchase receipts and compare them with your monthly statement.

In a separate section, keep all of your receipts that will be used in
calculating your income tax such as income statements, charitable
and political donations, medical expenses, moving expenses and
child care receipts.

Take the next eleven pages from your three-ring binder and write
the name of the next eleven months at the top. (Remember, you
tackled the current month when exploring the possibilities of juggling your money.) Reproduce Worksheet VI. When you receive a
bill, attach it with a paper clip to the binder. Once it's paid and re-
corded in the binder, drop the bill in your accordion file. If you're
tracking your spending on food, entertainment and pocket money,
enter those numbers in your binder as well.

You'll also need a waterproof, fireproof box in which to store im-
portant documents that must be kept safe and readily accessible.
These will include:
- Your insurance policies,
- Bank books and a list of bank accounts,
- Income tax files from past years,
- A copy of your will,
- A list of all your credit card numbers,
- An inventory of everything in your home or photographs of
each room and the insides of cupboards and closets,
- Warranties on any appliances or equipment you purchase,
- A list of what's in your safety-deposit box and where the key
can be found,
- The names of professionals you deal with, including your doc-
tor, dentist, lawyer, accountant, financial planner, investment ad-
visors and insurance agent.

In your safety deposit box, keep your certificates of birth,
marriage, divorce and adoption, as well as your immigration or citi-
zenship papers, CSBs and any documents that prove ownership of
your home, cottage or investments. Don't put your will or your insurance policy in a safety deposit box. The box could be sealed
upon your death and the settlement of your estate might become
unnecessarily complicated if these documents are inaccessible.

Keeping both monthly records and a box in your home for important documents will eventually pay off in both time and money. Insurance documents will be easy to locate if there's an accident, theft

or fire. You'll find it easier to file your income tax return when your receipts and statements are in one place. Should Revenue Canada decide to audit your income tax returns, your record-keeping will ease the strain. Deductions that didn't require inclusion of receipts with your tax return may be probed and disallowed if you can't prove your claims. You should keep your files for at least six to seven years, but if the auditors are suspicious they can ask for records as far back as they want. If you want to throw them away, get permission from Revenue Canada before you toss them, especially if you own a business or your investments are complicated.

Making sure your budget doesn't fail

Budgeting is a skill you must cultivate. Most budgets fail because they're too tight and the temptation to slash savagely at our vices – cigarettes, a drink after work – is so satisfying. Don't kid yourself. Don't try to reform a lifetime of habits by the stroke of a pencil across a piece of paper.

If impulse spending is a problem, ask some tough questions whenever temptation strikes. Do I really need this or am I being indulgent? What terrible things will happen if I don't buy it? Why didn't I need this yesterday? You may also have to take a close look at the emotional underpinnings of your financial habits. Your budget will fail if:

• It's too complicated. A binder, an accordion file and a banking strategy are all you need to keep it straight.

• It's too rigid. Don't be too hard on yourself or you'll shatter your good intentions. You'll have a better shot at taming indulgences if you leave yourself a little breathing space.

• You get caught by time. You might forget to send your aunt a birthday card and have to phone her in Inuvik. Or old friends may drop by on their way through town, so you invite them for supper and make a quick dash to an expensive delicatessen. Or you might leave work late, miss the bus and take a cab home. Plan for crises – hide $50 or $100 under a rock.

• You succumb to a burst of generosity and buy a gift, a drink or lunch for someone else. If not being able to indulge in a spontaneous gesture of generosity will make you feel poor, budget for it.

• You become bored and frustrated. Don't aim for castles in Spain or $1 million in savings by the end of the next decade. Set realistic targets you can hit within a couple of years. Anything more than three years away is often just a dream. Tell yourself over and over: "I don't have to do this forever." Within twelve months you'll have a working budget and you'll be able to relax.

• Your spending troubles mask unhappiness and loneliness. Many compulsive shoppers go shopping when depressed or anxious. Spending can ease emotional hurts – but not effectively and not for long. Debt will only make your troubles worse.

• You keep your credit cards in your pocket. No one's perfect. One day you'll get frustrated and you'll binge. Forgive yourself for your indiscretion, but don't forget it. If you blow this month's MasterCard payment on tickets to the opera, you'll have to cut back on something else. It might even mean that next month you won't be able to afford to go out at all. But don't give up easily. Pat yourself on the back for knowing you've fallen off the budget wagon and get back on as quickly as possible.

Using credit cards wisely

If you have problems controlling credit card spending, try giving your credit cards the cold shoulder. Take your cards out of your wallet and put them in a plastic container. Fill the container with water. Now put it in the freezer.

Can't do it? Maybe these statistics will help convince you. On October 31, 1991, Canadians owed $11.2 billion on their Master-Card and Visa cards alone, $1.9 billion more than they owed in the fall of 1989.

It's a mother lode of debt but it shouldn't surprise you. Credit cards are seductively convenient. There's a certain mood associated with spending with plastic, a feeling of immaculate consumption, as if real money weren't involved. But every time you use your credit card you're borrowing someone else's money – and if you don't pay it off each month you're borrowing at usurious rates. A debt on your Eaton's card will cost you 28.8 percent a year, on your Visa or MasterCard around 16.75 to 18.5 percent. Dalmys charges 34.8 percent – $34.80 a year on a $100 debt!

Sometimes you can't avoid debt. You may suddenly need cash when the fridge conks out in the middle of the summer or the furnace seizes up in the dead of winter. Unfortunately, credit cards also make it irresistibly easy to spend money you don't have on things you don't need – not just once in a while but day after day.

And spending room on your credit card can be deceptive, masking serious financial difficulties. You know you're in trouble if you:
- Can afford to pay only the minimum payment each month on your credit cards and department store accounts,
- Juggle creditors by sinking deeper into debt with one creditor in order to keep another at bay,
- Are never out of debt,
- Aren't sure how much you owe,
- Tend not to open any piece of mail you think is a bill or answer the phone for fear of a creditor's call,
- Take out cash advances on your charge cards to pay for ordinary expenses such as rent or food.

If you're swamped by bills and bits of paper, move all of your debts and loans into a consolidation loan or onto your personal line of credit where you can at least cut your interest expenses. If you're paying 10 percent instead of 18 percent you'll cut your interest rate by 8 percent. On $2,500, that's $200 a year. Be aware, though, that a consolidation loan is a red flag. If you can't even keep track of your debts, then you are having trouble controlling your spending. Destroy the temptation to use a consolidation loan just to free up your credit card limit. Get the cards out of reach – put them in your freezer. Or if that doesn't appeal to you, put them in your safe-deposit box, snip them in half or send them back to the issuer.A cash-only existence may be humbler, but there is a certain satisfaction in knowing that when you buy something, it's paid for.

Of course, taking such a step could create problems if you travel for work and must reserve a hotel room or rent a car. You'll have to decide how best to control your spending without interfering with your ability to earn a living. If you're sinking further into debt as each month passes you will have to change your lifestyle. Cut back a little on everything. Spend a little less on clothes and not quite as much on eating out, vacations and entertainment. If you've sunk into unmanageable debt, go to your creditors and explain your difficulties or go to a community credit counselling bureau and get help before you severely damage your financial health.

Not everyone sinks into debt just by having credit cards but you will find it easier to stay out of trouble if you have only one card. Carrying a stack of them makes it that much more difficult to tame or to track your spending. One way to track your spending is to write a credit card charge into your cheque book (just as you would a cheque) and deduct it from the balance in your account. Of course, it's not a cheque but it will alert you to any spending beyond your ability to pay your credit card bill at the end of the month – which should be paid in full. Sound impossible? It's not. Between 54 and 56 percent of all credit card holders do pay off their balance every month.

You should also check your credit card bills thoroughly. Keep every charge slip and check every entry on your monthly statement. If there are any discrepancies, call the card issuer immediately. You normally have ten or fifteen days to make your complaint. Jot down the date and time of your complaint, as well as the person to whom you spoke. Follow your call with a letter.

Don't buy your car on time

Car loans are killers, even though they've become as acceptable as a mortgage on a house. If you can save enough money to pay cash for your cars instead of buying them on credit, you'll save thousands of dollars over a lifetime.

Look at the difference in your out-of-pocket cost for just one car. Let's say you're willing to pay $10,000 for a car every three years. For three years you could save $274 a month in a savings account earning 1.5 percent and then buy the car. Or, you could borrow $10,000 at 11.75 percent and repay the loan at $326.83 a month for the next thirty-six months. If you save, your out-of-pocket cost for the car will be $9,432. If you borrow, the real cost of the car will be $11,765, $2,200 more than the real cost if you save.

It's hard to get ahead if you're already strapped with a loan. But there may be a way out. It's not uncommon for people to have CSBs or guaranteed investment certificates (GICs) stashed away earning 7 or 8 percent interest while they're scrimping to pay a 12 or 13 percent car loan. You shouldn't take all of your savings and leave yourself without a financial cushion, but it would be better to pay for the car with the bonds and rebuild your savings as quickly as possible. If you find it hard to discipline yourself to write a cheque to your savings account instead of the finance company, you could peg your monthly savings to match the payments you would have made on your loan. If you're aggressive, you could borrow to make an investment and at least your interest payments will be tax deductible.

How are other people doing?

If you're feeling squeezed, you're not alone. Over the past decade, it hasn't been easy for Canadians to get ahead. In all but two of the past ten years wage gains have trailed inflation. By 1990 the average family income had climbed to $51,633 but there were wide differences across the country. The average income was highest in Ontario, at $57,027, and lowest in Prince Edward Island, at $39,701. Families headed by university graduates had average incomes of $75,440, but almost one in five of those families had incomes of $100,000 or more. How do you stack up?

Are you wealthy?

The wealthiest 20 percent of Canadian families earn more than $72,394 a year and together pull in 39.3 percent of all personal income earned by Canadians. These families are well educated and often headed by a doctor, a business executive, a dentist or a lawyer.

Are you affluent?

A notch down the prosperity ladder, the next wealthiest 20 percent of Canadian families earn between $53,247 and $72,394. Together they take home 24 percent of our personal earnings.

Are you average?

Across the country 40 percent of Canadian families earn $24,647 to $53,246 a year, 30.3 percent of the national personal income. If you earn $46,069 you sit in the centre of Canadian income – half of all families earn more, half earn less.

Or are you falling behind?

The poorest 20 percent of Canadians have family incomes of less than $24,647 a year. Together they account for only 6.4 percent of all personal income earned in Canada. It is here you find the elderly, the widowed, single parents and those with below-average education. Many are the working poor – those who work long hours at tough jobs yet don't earn enough to live in comfort. But the poverty line is not straight: a farm family in Saskatchewan can live comfortably on less money than a family in Montreal. In Toronto, families with income below $29,661 fall into what Statistics Canada

How Canadians Spend Their Money

Item	Families Earning $35,000 to $39,000	Families Earning over $85,000
Food bought in stores	$4,563	$ 6,261
Restaurants	1,213	3,421
Shelter	7,601	13,049
Transportation	5,326	10,552
Household goods and furniture	2,945	6,688
Clothing	2,021	5,564
Life insurance premiums	212	616
Recreation	2,025	5,056
Education	350	1,102
Tobacco and alcohol	1,253	1,838
Personal care	866	1,421
Health care	793	1,410
Pet care	185	330
Personal taxes	5,765	31,278
Pensions and RRSPs	770	2,617
Gifts and charity	1,984	3,948
Lottery tickets	154	152

SOURCE: STATISTICS CANADA, FAMILY EXPENDITURES IN CANADA, 1990

TABLE I

calls "low income". In Lloydminster, families with less than $23,200 find it hard to live comfortably.

How do we spend our money?

The way you spend your money is intimately mingled with your philosophy of life and your aspirations for the future. Every family spends its money in a unique way, and the typical spending pattern compiled by Statistics Canada is no more than a titillating peek at "the average family", an entirely fictitious group created by statisticians. But curiosity is only human. You can see how Canadians spend their money in the table above.

These typical family spending patterns are interesting only as a bench mark. If your life's pleasure is gourmet cooking, you may feel comfortable spending $1,000 a month on food when other families are spending $300 or $400. But if your food bill is high and you don't know why, you might want to take a closer look at the groceries you're putting in your cart or the food you're tossing into the garbage.

A nation of consumers

Money has power, but it can also cause confusion and grief. We're like children with noses pressed against the candy store window. The candies within our grasp are so tempting and so easy to have. We've lost the ability to delay gratification. Gadgets that were luxuries a few years ago have become commonplace. At the end of 1991, 73.5 percent of Canadians had microwave ovens, 20.9 percent had compact disc players and 68.5 percent had video recorders.

To perpetuate this lifestyle, Canadians are getting deeper in debt. Our incomes may have been ravaged by inflation, but our spending has been uninhibited, exceeding inflation every year for the past five years. In 1982 we saved $17.80 of every $100 we made. By 1991 that figure had been chopped in half to a slim $10.30. On the other hand, the total household debt has almost doubled, rising from $186,567 million in 1984 to $388,139 million – five times as much as the cost of living. The pace at which our debt rose in those seven years was between 5.9 percent and 15.2 percent a year while inflation hovered between 3.9 percent and 5.6 percent.

The dangers of debt are not new. As Charles Dickens' Mr. Micawber told David Copperfield: "Annual income twenty pounds, annual expenditure twenty pounds ought and six, result misery." There is a remedy for this misery, although it may seem inconvenient and tedious: careful budgeting and a touch of discipline.

CHAPTER 3

So You Think You Pay Too Much Tax

DAY AFTER DAY, THROUGH-
out the summer and fall of 1987, the members of the House of Commons finance committee dug through the details of tax reform legislation that had been tabled by Prime Minister Brian Mulroney's Progressive Conservative government. The minutiae of tax are tedious, but the criticisms of committee chairman Don Blenkarn and his troops were often accompanied by biting humour. Their look at the potential impact of tax reform on an elderly woman giving money to her church was an occasion for the following conversation between Blenkarn and David Dodge, a finance department assistant deputy minister of tax policy.

Mr. Blenkarn: "Let's discuss the situation of a lady who gives $375.14 to her favourite church. She, of course, deducts $250 and calculates that at 17 percent and then deducts the $250 from the $375.14. She calculates that by 29 percent and adds the two together. That is her credit."

Mr. Dodge: "That is correct."

Mr. Blenkarn: "Right. Now, she is entitled to deduct $375.14. Will you please tell me why you have to make it so hideously complicated for her? What did you want to do to her? Do you want to drive her up the wall? Why do you not just let her deduct the damn $375 from her income? You allow somebody giving to an RRSP to deduct it from his income. You allow somebody paying babysitting payments to deduct it from his income. Why do you not let people deduct their charities from their income? What is the big deal? Why do we have to be ultimately fair or ultimately confusing or ultimately maddening? Why do you want to drive people to H & R Block? Do you guys have an interest in H & R Block or something?"

Exchanges like these have been heard in Canada and throughout the world as governments tackle the complex issue of tax reform. The changes to the Canadian tax structure embody the essence of

tax philosophy that has captured the imaginations of the governments of many countries over the past decade. The complexity of
tax reform is borne of taxpayers' ruses to keep their money in their
own pockets and the governments' frantic attempts to stem the
escape of funds from the tax net. International tax reform of the late
1980s is cloaked in an aversion to government interference. As the
world moved through the 1970s, persistent economic problems
made it obvious that governments could not effectively manipulate
economic growth or solve the social ills of the world through income taxes alone. Cleverly contrived tax systems led only to distortion of the economy and an unending flow of wasted money as the
attempts by the governments to manipulate their economies failed.
The tower of tax began to topple as incentives and grants and credits piled higher. Some individuals and corporations were able to
avoid paying their share of taxes. Perhaps more damaging was the
distortion of investment decisions by the accompanying tax implications.

At the same time as tax dollars were slipping through loopholes,
government revenues were failing to keep up with spending and
massive national deficits became suffocating. In Canada, former Lib-
eral Finance Minister Allan MacEachen launched a politically inept
1981 assault on the tax system that met with howls of protest. It was
only the first halting step.

Worldwide reforms actually started two years earlier when
British Prime Minister Margaret Thatcher laid out her blueprints for
tax reform and took the first tentative steps by cutting personal tax
rates and raising Britain's value-added tax. Meanwhile, wrangling
began in Japan over reforms that would shift the tax burden from income taxes to a value-added tax. This wrangling led to the eventual
toppling of the government of Japanese Prime Minister Yasuhiro
Nakasone in 1987, and the Japanese Diet was finally persuaded to
adopt a value-added tax in early 1988.

New Zealand, Australia, France and West Germany are among
the many countries that have reformed their tax systems to ensure
they are not out of step with those of their major trading partners.
Reforms in the U.S. in 1986 were both sweeping and unexpectedly
swift as tax rates declined for both individuals and corporations and
virtually all tax shelters were eliminated.

When the elephant rolled over, the mouse had to move too. In
Canada, the Tories swept into power in 1984 promising tax changes

and moved quickly to lower corporate taxes. Abolishing the antiquated manufacturers' sales tax was one item on the agenda, but when the U.S. passed its version of tax reform in May 1986, Canadian Finance Minister Michael Wilson began working feverishly to reduce personal and corporate taxes instead. Close to 30 percent of the Canadian economy is related to trade, and 80 percent of that trade is with the U.S. If the two countries' tax structures were to become radically different, jobs, people, investment dollars and profits could flow south. Canada became even more vulnerable with the signing of the Canada-U.S. free trade agreement.

In step with the reforms around the world, Canada reduced top personal tax rates from 34 percent to 29 percent (not including provincial taxes or surtaxes), chopped the number of tax brackets from ten to three and lowered top corporate rates from 46 percent to 38 percent. But don't count your pennies yet. With the elimination of tax breaks such as the $1,000 investment income deduction, the $500 employment expense deduction and the investment incentive tax credit, more of your income is being swept into the tax net. In the end, despite lower tax rates, Ottawa will collect as much tax as it did in the past – with only a modest shift of the burden from individuals to corporations.

Every Canadian can easily pay less tax

Despite rumours of its demise under reform, tax planning is still alive. The pickings may be slim, but if you take the time to plan you can reduce the taxes you pay. Despite reform, many traditional strategies stand. To reduce your tax bill you should:
- Claim every deduction and credit you legally can.
- Tap the company benefits your employer offers you.
- Postpone some of your tax bill until future years through the use of tax shelters such as RRSPs.
- Split your income with your husband or wife and children to reduce the taxes you pay as a family.
- Be tax efficient in the way you save and invest.

Tax planning isn't an esoteric privilege of the rich and it needn't be complicated. The most powerful tax planning tool is your RRSP, yet fewer than 23 percent of taxpayers have one. There many strategies that will nibble at your tax burden, but only a few will be useful to any one taxpayer. You can reduce your tax load, but it takes planning, discipline, careful record-keeping and time. If you wait until the end of the year to look for ways to cut your tax bill, it will be too late.

Saving the last dollar you make

On September 10, 1988, the hefty 500-page tax reform bill first proposed more than a year before was passed by Parliament. Despite exhortations from a few tax philosophers for a flat tax, the government has created three tax brackets. In the 1992 tax year, your federal tax bill is 17 percent of the first $29,590 you earn, 26 percent on your income between $29,591 and $59,180, and 29 percent on every dollar over $59,591. To feed provincial government coffers you must add another 44 to 60 percent to your federal tax, a significantly higher percentage than in the past. These brackets increase each year according to a formula tied to inflation.

Tiered tax levels are the essence of a progressive tax system – the more money you make, the more tax you pay on the last dollar you earn. That rate of tax on your last dollar is known as your marginal tax rate. It's also the rate at which you save tax if you reduce your taxable income. If you're in a 39.2 percent tax bracket and you receive a $1,000 bonus, you would have to give Ottawa $392. But if you contribute $1,000 to an RRSP, you can deduct $1,000 from your income and save $392 in tax. For someone in a 51.2 percent tax bracket, the tax bite or tax saving would jump to $512. Tax planning is essentially any strategy that will keep the last dollars you earn in your own pocket and your marginal tax bracket as low as possible.

Understanding the shift to credits

The change in tax rates is only half of the tax reform story. The other half stems from the conversion of many deductions and exemptions to tax credits. While financial experts scoff at any intimation that the new tax system is simpler, most agree that the switch to credits does make it fairer. Exemptions and deductions create greater tax savings for the rich than for the poor because they're deducted from net income, and the tax saved depends on your marginal tax rate. If you're in a 50 percent tax bracket, a $1 deduction will save you fifty cents; if you're in a 25 percent tax bracket a $1 deduction will save you only twenty-five cents. Credits, on the other hand, are deducted directly from the tax you owe. If you claim a $1 credit you'll receive $1, whether you pay tax at your marginal tax rate of 50 percent or 25 percent.

Tax rules regarding children are an excellent example of the difference between deductions and credits. Under the old system a deduction was available for each child, but there was no social or economic justification for a rich family with children to get a more generous tax break than a poor family with children. Under the credit system, all parents will receive the same tax relief for their children.

Unfortunately, the new system is confusing because it's a mix of old deductions and new credits. To further confuse matters, not all credits work the same way. Most of the old exemptions have become credits of a certain dollar value – such as the personal exemption and married status exemption. Others are a percentage of your expenses, usually 17 percent (20 percent in Quebec). For instance, in the past you could deduct your contribution to the Canada Pension Plan or Quebec Pension Plan. Now you can claim a credit for 17 percent of your contribution.

There are at least twenty tax credits. A few can be transferred from one person to another and only two are refundable, meaning you'll receive a "refund" even if you don't owe any tax. The rest can be used only to reduce tax – if you don't owe any tax, you can't claim the credit.

The power of deductions

Credits cover normal and recurring expenses, while deductions tend to cover more discretionary expenses such as alimony, RRSP contributions, financial counselling fees and other expenses not seen on every tax return. It's not clear why these items weren't changed to credits, but that doesn't make them any less critical to your tax planning strategies. First, let's examine the deductions you can use.

Contributions to your pension plan or RRSP

Few changes to the Income Tax Act have caused as much confusion and frustration as the delays in introducing new limits governing contributions to RRSPs. Finally, on June 27, 1990 Bill C-52 received royal assent, bringing into law virtually all the changes to RRSPs which Ottawa had been promising for several years. The reforms are now in place and for the 1992 tax year, you can contribute 18 percent of the income you earned in 1991 – not your 1992 earned income – up to $12,500. The same $12,500 limit applies in 1993 but limits are then scheduled to increase by $1,000 a year until 1996 when you'll be able to contribute $15,500. After 1996, the limits will rise with the national rise in wages.

If you're a member of a defined benefit pension plan, the contributions you can make to your RRSP will be reduced by what the federal government calls a pension adjustment. The pension adjustment calculation promises to be so complicated that Revenue Canada will obtain pension information from your employer and let you know how much you can contribute to your RRSP. Generally, the better your pension benefits, the less you'll be able to tuck away in an RRSP. However, because of the way in which the PA is calculated, you will be able to contribute at least $1,000 to an RRSP. This is explained in more detail in chapter nine. (Errors have been found in the pension adjustments. If your statement doesn't seem reasonable check with your payroll department or call Revenue Canada.)

Tax reform has also changed the contributions you can make to money purchase pension plans and deferred profit sharing plans (DPSPs). The rules are complex but members of DPSPs or money purchase plans can find a full explanation in the RRSP guide available at their district Revenue Canada office.

Although it will be more complicated for people in pension plans, there is new flexibility in the RRSP rules. The 1991 tax year was the first in which you could carry-forward unused RRSP contributions. You'll have seven years to make up a missed contributions. However, your contribution is deductible against the income in the year it's made, not against income in the missed year. Also, because your greatest tax benefit from RRSPs derives from the tax-sheltered growth rather than the deduction, there is still a tremendous advantage to making your contribution every year.

You cannot contribute to your RRSP past age seventy-one and your plan must be collapsed into cash, an annuity or a registered retirement income fund by the end of the year in which you turn seventy-one. However, you can still contribute to a spousal RRSP if your husband or wife is under age seventy-one but you must have earned income. And, for 1992, 1993 and 1994 you can roll $6,000 of a company pension into a spousal RRSP. (Beginning with the 1993 tax year, the government will recognize common-law relationships for spousal contributions. Such relationships are already recognized for survivor benefits under RRSPs, RRIFs and annuities and for tax-free transfers on marriage breakdown.)

Alimony and maintenance payments

You can deduct alimony and maintenance payments if you make these payments periodically after signing a separation agreement or receiving a court order. You can't deduct a lump-sum payment.

Expenses of earning a living

Generally, you can deduct many of the expenses that you incur in your attempts to earn income. These include:

- Moving expenses. You can deduct the cost of hiring movers, storing furniture, staying in a hotel, eating in restaurants, the penalties for paying off your old mortgage early, and some of the costs associated with selling your old home and buying a new one. To deduct any of these expenses, you have to move at least forty kilometres closer to work.
- Child care expenses. You can deduct $5,000 for a child under age seven (or a disabled child under age fourteen), but only $3,000 for children aged seven to fourteen. A child care claim must be backed up with the name, address and social insurance number of the person whom you paid and must be claimed by the parent with the lowest income.
- Investment losses and expenses. You can deduct the costs of borrowing to invest, as well as losses from rental property or tax shelters. But be wary of a tax complication known as CNIL (cumulative net investment losses), which can make life messy for investors intending to claim the $100,000 lifetime capital gains exemption. The CNIL rules were created to stop investors from enjoying a double tax break – a deduction for interest expenses and a claim under the lifetime capital gains exemption. Under CNIL rules, if your investment losses or expenses exceed income from interest or dividends, you'll create a net investment loss for the year. If you realize a taxable capital gain, your ability to use your lifetime exemption will be reduced by your net loss. This net loss accumulates – if you don't "use" it one year, it's carried forward to the next, building a CNIL account. (Investors who would like a full explanation of CNIL and recent changes to

the rules should call their district taxation office and ask for the capital gains tax guide.)
• Fees for investment advice or accounting service. This does not include the cost of having a basic income tax return completed.
• RRSP administration fees. Try to pay your fees directly rather than from the funds in your RRSP. If taken from your plan they are not tax deductible.

In addition, you can deduct safety deposit box fees and annual fees or dues paid to your union or professional association.

Credits where credits are due
Now let's examine the credits you can use to lessen your tax burden.

Medical expenses
You can claim your medical expenses for any twelve-month period ending in the tax year, but only 17 percent of the expenses that exceed either $1,614 or 3 percent of your net income, whichever is less. You can claim fees paid to a private health or dental plan, but not the fees paid to a government plan or those paid by your employer. The list of eligible medical expenses is exhaustive. Those expenses many people miss are dental bills, eyeglasses, contact lenses, wheel chairs and hearing aids. You must submit receipts for medical expenses. Under the most recent tax changes, the disabled can now claim a credit for the cost of an organ transplant and the cost of structural modifications to their home if they will give someone in a wheel chair greater mobility.

Tuition and education expenses
You can claim 17 percent of tuition fees over $100. The education credit is about $10 for each month that you're a full-time student. These credits apply only to post-secondary education or a school attended to upgrade your skills. These credits can be used by a student or by the person on whom he or she is dependent. In Quebec, tuition fees remain a deduction.

Age sixty-five and over
Every taxpayer over sixty-five years of age can claim the age tax credit. In 1992, it will reduce your tax by $591; $440 in Quebec.

Pension income

This credit is 17 percent of the first $1,000 of your qualified pension income to a maximum credit of $170 against your federal tax. In Quebec, you can claim 20 percent of the first $1,000. Qualified pension income includes payments from RRSPs and pension plans, but not lump-sum payments or benefits from the Canada Pension Plan or Old Age Security.

Disability

This $720 credit ($440 in Quebec) can be claimed if you support a relative by blood or marriage with a severe mental or physical disability. This relative must live in Canada.

Charitable donations

The virtues of charitable giving are not ignored by Ottawa. You can claim a credit for as much as 20 percent of your net income for money donated to registered charities. Be aware – the charity has to be registered. You can claim 17 percent of the first $250 you donate and 29 percent of the rest. If your cup runneth over, donations beyond 20 percent of your net income can be claimed over the next five years. You can also:

• Give all your money to the Crown – or its museums, art galleries and agencies – and claim every cent as a credit.

• Donate that old rocker you inherited from Grandma and claim its fair market value. The rules are tricky, though. Whatever you donate must be of authentic cultural or historical significance and you have to give it to a designated institution.

• Make contributions to certain U.S. universities and claim them against Canadian income. Any other U.S. donations must be claimed against U.S. income.

Political contributions

You can reduce your federal tax bill with a contribution to a federal political party. But not every province lets you reduce provincial tax through contributions to a provincial party. The federal tax credit is 75 percent of the first $100, 50 percent of the next $450 and 33.3 percent of any donations beyond $550 to a maximum credit of $500.

Sales tax credits and child tax credits

Sales tax credits and child tax credits can reduce the tax you pay or, if you don't owe any tax, Ottawa will send you the cash. These "refundable" credits are designed to help low-income families. The child tax credit (up to $601 for each child in the family) is reduced by child care expenses and by income you earn above $25,921. This tax credit will be abolished in 1993 when it is replaced by the new child benefit, explained under Tax Strategies for Parents later in this chapter.

The sales tax credit was replaced in 1991 by the goods and services tax credit. This credit (worth as much as $295 to a single person, $397 to a married couple and $102 for a child) is reduced by income over $25,921. It is eliminated once an individual's income reaches $32,005 or a couple's income reaches $33,890. These income thresholds will move with inflation. To claim these credits you must file an income tax return, even if you don't owe Ottawa a cent. In Quebec, the sales tax credit was also abolished. Parents will receive up to $500 on the birth or adoption of the first child, $1,000 in two payments for a second child and $6,000 over four years for each child after that.

Tax strategies no one should ignore

Of course, you should make use of all the credits and deductions that are available to you. But making the best use of tax breaks often requires careful planning. For greater tax savings, consider the following:

Don't ignore your RRSP or pension plan

Ottawa has knocked the power out of almost every strategy for avoiding taxes except one – plans to save for retirement, whether through registered pension plans, RRSPs or DPSPs. RRSP contributions cut your tax bill immediately because they're deducted from your taxable income. Not only will you then have more money to invest, but your investments will grow rapidly because income earned in an RRSP isn't taxed. In Chart I you can see the much more rapid building of wealth when a taxpayer in a 41.3 percent marginal tax bracket invests $1,000 a year at 8 percent inside his RRSP rather than outside.

A hefty tax refund resulting from an RRSP contribution can make your summer a richer playtime, or it could be used to pay down

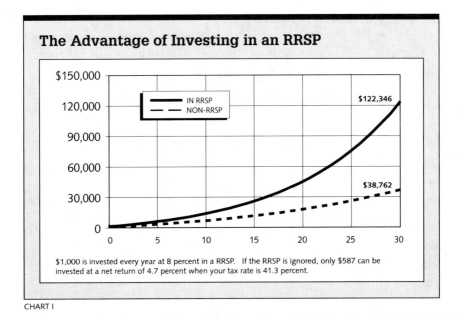

The Advantage of Investing in an RRSP

$1,000 is invested every year at 8 percent in a RRSP.   If the RRSP is ignored, only $587 can be invested at a net return of 4.7 percent when your tax rate is 41.3 percent.

CHART I

your mortgage. If an $8,000 RRSP contribution gave you a $3,500 refund and you had a 10 percent $50,000 mortgage, you could use your refund to eliminate that mortgage in less than nineteen years instead of twenty-five years. If you're already ten years into that mortgage, you could pay it off in twelve years and seven months instead of fifteen years.

It has always been a good strategy to make your RRSP contribution as early as possible. Now that the tax deduction for the first $1,000 of investment income earned during the year has been abolished, it's an even better idea. Since all the interest you earn outside your RRSP will be taxed, you should immediately shift any RRSP savings that might be languishing in a bank account into your plan so they can grow free of tax. In fact, if you have your RRSP contribution deducted at source (or you can give your employer evidence that you have already made your annual RRSP contribution) your monthly tax bite from your pay cheque can be adjusted. You could use the extra cash flow to make non-RRSP investments or to increase your mortgage payments.

Share your debt load with Ottawa

Tax reform has not changed the tax advantage of borrowing to invest. Whether your investment is in a business, the financial markets or a tax shelter, you can still deduct interest costs from taxable income. However, you can't deduct the cost of any personal debts. If you have cash that you intend to invest in stocks and you plan to borrow to buy a car, use the cash for the car and borrow for the investment. Also, you should always repay your personal debts before you repay your investment debts.

The wisdom of borrowing to invest and using cash for personal expenses had given rise to a widespread strategy of debt juggling that was axed by a 1987 Supreme Court of Canada trial known as the Bronfman Trust case. In the past, you could sell your investments, pay down the mortgage on your house, then borrow to buy back your investments. In essence, a mortgage loan that had been non-deductible suddenly became deductible. Now it's very tricky to turn personal debt into investment debt. To be acceptable to Ottawa, your transaction cannot be artificial – in other words, the nature of your investment must have changed.

This doesn't mean you can't make your debt load more tax efficient. If you've decided to juggle your investment portfolio, there is still flexibility. For instance, if you intend to sell your CSBs and invest in real estate, you could use the CSBs to pay down your mortgage on your home and then borrow to buy the real estate.

The deductibility of interest expense for investments, along with the $100,000 lifetime capital gains exemption, had resulted in another widespread tax-avoidance strategy that Ottawa was determined to stop. Investors were deducting the interest on loans taken out to make mutual fund investments – investments whose gains could be sheltered under the lifetime exemption. Ottawa threw a wrench in the strategy, which provided double tax savings, by introducing the CNIL rules which can cause you to lose access to your capital gains exemption – at least temporarily.

Always keep detailed records of your investment transactions. Keep your investment borrowing separate from your personal borrowing and don't use the same bank account or personal line of credit for everyday expenses and investing. Be sure the flow of borrowed money, interest payments and investments can always be traced. Otherwise, you may not be allowed the deductions.

Tax strategies every married couple should consider

Although sound tax planning can save thousands of dollars over a lifetime, you may find some tax strategies run up against the psychological baggage you carry into your relationship. After all, every couple handles money in a way that is tied to their traditional values and sense of financial independence as individuals. You can't ignore emotional comfort, but try not to let your sentiments force you to feed the public treasury more than you must. Married couples – and common-law couples, who will be treated like married couples under the tax system beginning in 1993 – should consider the following:

Sharing your credits and deductions

For the most favourable tax impact, the spouse with the higher income should claim all deductions, since they're worth more to taxpayers in higher tax brackets. Conversely, the spouse with the lower income should claim credits. This strategy will put more money in the hands of the lower-income spouse for investing and can be your first step into the realm of income splitting. This is especially true of your charitable donations and medical expenses. If you donate more than $250 as a family, only one of you should claim the credit since the tax savings on donations over $250 jump to 29 percent. It doesn't matter whose name is on the receipts.

It also makes tax sense for the person with the lowest net income to claim the medical expenses since you can only claim expenses that exceed 3 percent of your net income. You should also claim your spouse's dividends if it will lower his or her net income and increase your married-status tax credit. The tax savings from the credit will more than cover the extra tax you'll pay on the dividends. You might want to treat your political contributions a bit differently. This tax credit is also tiered but your greatest savings are on the first $250. If you contribute more than this amount you should split your political contribution with your spouse. You'll also save more tax if you contribute a bit each year, rather than plough money into a political party just as it gears up for an election.

Income splitting is not dead

Income splitting is a strategy through which the taxes you pay as a family are reduced by switching income from the hands of a family member who is heavily taxed into the hands of someone who will pay little or no tax. It can be a powerful tool, so it has repeatedly been the target of close scrutiny by Ottawa. Today, most income splitting strategies are fraught with tax traps, known as attribution rules. But there are still strategies you can adopt to reduce your taxes.

Let's look at a family where the husband earns $35,000 and the wife earns $20,000. She spends all her salary on the household; he saves his money and handles the investments for the family. It's a traditional division of responsibilities, but it's not smart planning. Nor would it be effective planning for each to pay 50 percent of expenses. The husband should pay all the food, shelter and clothing costs – and even her personal debts, insurance premiums and income taxes. She can then invest as much of her income as possible. Less tax will be paid on the investment income, the investment pool will subsequently grow more quickly and eventually both incomes will be about equal – which will reduce the family tax burden.

Most other income-splitting strategies are not as simple. Under the attribution rules, almost every penny of investment income earned by your spouse or children on money, securities or property you've lent or given them will be taxed in your hands instead of theirs. There are ways around these attribution rules, but you should tread carefully and keep meticulous records. Many income-splitting possibilities have been curtailed or eliminated by Ottawa. Let's examine those that are left.

If you give your husband or wife money to invest, you'll have to pay the tax on any income earned on that gift but you won't have to pay the tax on any income the income earns. Sound confusing? Let's say a woman gives her husband $20,000, which he invests in Canada Savings Bonds at 10 percent. At tax time, she'll have to pay the tax on the $2,000 interest those CSBs earn. However, if he then reinvests the $2,000 interest, anything he earns on that second investment will be taxed in his hands. It's complicated but you really have nothing to lose. If you make the investment yourself, you'll still have to pay tax on the first year's income. By giving the money to your spouse you don't hurt your tax position but your spouse will be building his or her own wealth. It can be very effective, but you must keep track of the funds and who must pay tax on the income. The easiest way is to put the original money in one kind of investment, perhaps Canada Savings Bonds, and invest the income in something different, maybe mutual funds.

You can buy property – perhaps a cottage, antique furniture or a painting – that was inherited by your spouse or brought into the marriage. This puts more cash into your spouse's hands for investment purposes. But be sure you abide by tax rules that stipulate you must pay fair market value for the property and that your spouse must recognize the capital gain or loss for tax purposes.

As a professional or business person, you can pay your spouse a reasonable salary for his or her services. You can lend money to your spouse at the government's prescribed rate and the income earned from the investment made with the borrowed funds will not attribute back to you. Obviously, this will create tax savings only if the income from the investment is greater than the interest paid on the loan. The prescribed rate is the average yield on treasury bills over the previous three months and is usually lower than prevailing market interest rates. Your spouse must pay you the interest on the loan within thirty days of the end of the year.

You can lend your spouse money to earn almost any type of business income and that income will not be attributed back to you. You should note that in the case of a limited partnership your spouse must be actively involved in the business activities of a partnership or the income will be taxed in your hands.

The wisdom of spousal RRSPs

The spousal RRSP is one of the last income-splitting techniques blessed by Ottawa, although it is often misunderstood and seldom used. Yet by making contributions to a spousal RRSP you can create two equal streams of income in retirement and save thousands of dollars in taxes every year. If a retired couple has an income of $60,000 flowing to one person, the tax bill would be $18,000 – and that person will lose the OAS payment. By splitting that $60,000 into two $30,000 incomes, the taxes could drop to $13,100, for a saving of almost $5,000 – and the couple will receive two OAS payments. This can be done by rearranging your RRSP contributions so some or all of your yearly limit goes into your spouse's RRSP.

Here's how it works. If you're allowed to make an RRSP contribution, you can put it into your own plan or you can put it into a plan registered in the name of your husband or wife. You still claim the tax deduction for the contribution. This isn't an additional RRSP contribution and your spouse doesn't have to be working to enable you to make a spousal contribution. If your spouse also makes a contribution to his or her RRSP, it doesn't affect your contribution or your tax deduction. You can even split your contribution between you and your spouse. At tax time, you claim the deduction for all the contributions you make and your spouse can claim any contributions to his or her own RRSP.

Before deciding to contribute to a spousal plan, take a close look at your expected retirement income. If one person has a good pension plan and an RRSP, yet the other expects little more than a government pension, use a spousal RRSP to balance household income. If you each have only RRSPs, try to make them grow together. Inheritances may or may not be received but if any are reasonably certain be sure to include them in your plans. Your goal is to create two equal streams of income at retirement.

A word of caution, however: if money is taken out of a spousal RRSP within three years of the contribution being made, the contributor – not the person withdrawing the money – will have to pay tax on the withdrawal.

Don't forget your married status credit
If you support your husband or wife, he or she can earn up to $538 and this credit is not affected. The credit is reduced by 17 percent of net income earned beyond this $538 but won't disappear until your spouse earns at least $5,380. Don't lose any more of the credit than necessary; try to reduce the spouse's net income by making every deduction, claiming all the credits and contributing to an RRSP.

Tax strategies for the divorced
Even the finest financial plans can go awry when a marriage breaks down. Family law reforms across the country can make the fiscal breakdown complex and the wrangling bitter. In many provinces your family assets may have to be divided equally, including your pension benefits and RRSPs. Funds can be transferred tax-free from one spouse's RRSP to the other's, but only if there is a written agreement or court order. After a marriage breakdown, the special three-year attribution limit on withdrawals from a spousal RRSP no longer applies.

You should also structure your mutual financial affairs with an eye to the rules of Revenue Canada. You can deduct alimony and maintenance payments only if they're paid periodically and you're abiding by a written agreement or a court order. If you make any payments before signing the agreement or before a court order is obtained, make sure the payments are covered in related documents or you won't be able to deduct them. Ottawa has also decided you can't deduct a lump-sum payment – although this could be a better way to end your marriage because you would avoid the strain that can be created by a never-ending financial link. Don't count on your lawyer for financial advice – talk to an accountant or a financial planner.

Tax strategies for parents

The size of your family dictates what credits you can claim. For 1992, you can deduct $71 for each of your first two dependent children under nineteen and $142 for each other child – but you must subtract 17 percent of the net income a child earns beyond $2,690. The credit will be wiped out if your child earns as little as $3,525. There's also a $269 tax credit for older children if they're disabled ($1,156 in Quebec). This credit is reduced by income in excess of $2,690 and will be eliminated once the child's income hits $4,282.

Try to avoid losing this credit needlessly. As his first pay cheque burns in his pocket, the lessons of tax planning should be fed to your child along with the lessons of financial management. You might be able to keep his income below the threshold by employing the tax avoidance tools any working soul can use. For example, a student can deduct moving expenses if he moves at least 40 kilometres to go to school or to take a summer job. He could also make a contribution to an RRSP to get his income below the $3,525 threshold.

If your child doesn't have enough income to use the tuition and education tax credits, a parent can claim it, up to a maximum of $600. Don't forget the equivalent-to-married tax credit. This credit, worth $914 in 1992 ($255 in Quebec), is most often claimed by single parents. But it can be claimed for any relative by blood, marriage or adoption who depends on you for support.

The child benefit announced in February 1992 will replace the three existing programs for helping parents by consolidating the family allowance, child tax deduction and refundable child tax credit into one monthly payment. (The government also boosted support to families through an increased deduction limit for child care expenses and an increase in the goods and services tax credit.)

These three programs were delivered in three different ways; the family allowance cheque was mailed monthly, the annual child credit reduced your annual income tax burden; and the refundable child tax credit was mailed as a lump-sum payment after your tax return was assessed. The new benefit, scheduled to take effect January 1993, will be a monthly payment, usually to the mother. The payments for the year will be determined by your income in previous years. They will not be taxed, as the family allowance was.

To ensure the benefit meets the needs of families more fairly, the child benefit will be based on family income, not individual income, and the number of children. The annual value of the benefit will be as high as $3,635 for a family with three children and an annual income of $20,000; the benefit will be only $681 for a family with three kids and an income of $75,000. (This higher-income family would not receive any benefit if there are only two children.)

The payment will be calculated by the government; taxpayers will not have to apply for it or make any of the calculations on the tax form now required with family allowances, the child credit and the refundable child tax credit. The first payment, to be made in January 1993, will be based on family incomes reported for the 1991 taxation year. In July 1993, the payment will be based on 1992 tax information. Every year in July, payments will be updated to reflect your income in the previous year and any change in your family, such as the birth of a child or a marriage breakdown. The benefit will also be adjusted for increases in the consumer price index in excess of 3 percent.

You can still income split with your children

Just as you can reduce your family tax burden by income splitting with your spouse, you can cut taxes by sharing your tax burden with your children. At one time, the savings were so impressive that brokerage houses established schemes to make this type of income splitting extremely easy. One brokerage house ran an advertisement aimed at every parent's heart: a photo of two chubby legs with the caption, "Along with the pitter patter of little feet you can hear the jingle jangle of tax-free money." Revenue Canada was not amused, and slowly put an end to most income-splitting strategies.

After 1985, the most popular strategy was lending money to children older than eighteen, since the income earned on the money did not attribute back to the lender. Under tax reform, even this is gone. Now you must give your child the money or lend it at the prescribed rate for the income to be taxed in your child's hands.

However, the attribution rules don't apply to capital gains earned by children or to business income earned by a family member. Just as you can hire your husband or wife to work in your business, you can hire your children. Just pay them a reasonable wage for the work they do and keep detailed records of the hours worked and the duties performed.

Investing in a RESP
The contributions you make to a RESP are not tax deductible, but the money you set aside will grow untaxed. When money is withdrawn to send your son or daughter to a post-secondary institution, the earnings will be taxed in the hands of the child, who may pay little or no tax. Prior to February 1990 the only limit on contributions to RESPs was a maximum total contribution of $31,500 in a plan, all at once if you wanted. Now your contribution in any one year cannot exceed $1,500. These plans should be used with caution, since any earnings could be lost if they aren't used to pay the expenses of higher education.

Tax strategies for low-income earners
The federal income tax system is not used strictly to raise revenues. It's also used to assist poorer Canadians. This is done through refundable tax credits – credits you can claim even if you do not owe tax. So far there are only two: the refundable child tax credit and the refundable goods and services tax credit. For 1992, the refundable child tax credit of up to $601 is provided for each child under age eighteen. An extra $213 for each child under seven years of age was given to families that did not claim child care expenses. This credit will be replaced in 1993 with the child benefit explained above. All of the other credits can only be used to reduce your taxes. In 1992, adults could receive as much as $295 under the GST credit and children as much as $102. Couples could receive as much as $397.

Tax strategies for employees

As an employee, your tax planning opportunities may seem scarce. But don't belittle the lucrative and tax-efficient perks your employer can offer. For one thing, it will always be less expensive to pay the tax on a benefit your employer is willing to give you – group life insurance, health or dental plans, club memberships – than it is to buy it out of your own pocket. This is also true of disability insurance, but there is a serious pitfall: if your employer pays your premiums and you are unfortunate enough to be disabled at some time, your disability benefits will be taxed. If you pay the premiums yourself, the disability benefits will be tax-free. Since disability benefits will never exceed 60 to 70 percent of your usual income – and will often be much less – it's usually a good idea to pay the premiums yourself then every dollar you receive can be used to pay expenses.

In addition to these benefits, there are many company plans that can be tax-effective in building your wealth over your working career:

- Thrift and savings plans,
- Stock purchase plans,
- Stock option plans,
- Interest-free loans.

Under thrift and savings plans, most firms will match whatever you contribute to the company savings plan. Others will match a portion of your savings. It's free money, so get as much as you can.

Under stock purchase plans, your employer lends you money, usually at no interest, to buy shares in the company. An interest-free loan is a taxable benefit, but you can deduct the deemed interest as a cost of borrowing to invest in the shares. It's a tax-effective way to build your wealth since it has no impact on your taxes and your investment won't cost you a dime in interest. But invest in the company only if you have faith in it and believe its shares will go up in value. If the share price drops, you still owe the money you've borrowed. An interest-free loan benefit will also be treated as an investment expense and could increase your CNIL account.

Stock option plans are usually reserved for company executives and managers. You're granted the right to purchase shares at a fixed price in the future. When you buy the shares, the difference between the fair market value and the price you pay is taxed, but you can deduct part of that benefit. You end up with employment income that is only partially taxed.

As greater flexibility creeps into compensation packages, more companies are offering employees interest-free loans. If you can use the money wisely, perhaps to invest, you could save thousands of dollars. Remember, it's always cheaper to pay the tax on the benefit than it is to pay the interest on a loan with after-tax dollars.

Defer your taxes by deferring your bonus
Your room for manoeuvring here is small because your employer must pay your bonus within 180 days of the company's fiscal year-end or it will lose the deduction. But sometimes you only have to delay the bonus by one day. If you receive your bonus on December 31, you will have to pay tax on it four months later. If you delay your bonus until January 1, taxes won't be due until April of the next year, sixteen months later.

Ottawa has brought in a slew of tax rules to make it extremely tricky to defer income or taxes in any palatable way other than through pension plans, DPSPs, RRSPs or sabbaticals. Almost any sort of scheme is likely to be hit by something known as the salary deferral arrangement (SDA) rules, while any promise of a richer pension could run afoul of the retirement compensation arrangement (RCA) rules.

Under the SDA rules, in the year you have a "right" to the bonus, it will be included in your income as a taxable benefit, even if you haven't yet been given the money. Your employer cannot deduct the bonus until it is included in your taxable income. You can get around these rules if the bonus is tied to performance and there is a significant risk you won't earn the bonus. Incentive bonuses have become more prevalent as a management tool, but they aren't overwhelmingly popular among the risk averse as a tax-planning tool.

Under the RCA rules, money put aside for your retirement will be hit by a special 50 percent tax paid by your employer when the money is set aside. The tax will be refunded when the money is finally paid to you and you pay tax at your marginal tax rate, but it sure takes the sparkle out of a retirement plan. Earnings on the money put aside are also taxed at 50 percent. You can avoid the RCA rules if the promise of funds at retirement time is not actually backed by money put aside for you in a special account. But most people would rather have their money in hand than risk the danger of the company retiring before they do.

Car allowances are confusing but still worth while

Under original tax reform proposals, the benefit of having a company car was to be so emasculated that taxpayers and tax experts were outraged. Although Ottawa backtracked, the rules are still tortuously complex and could bump up your tax bill. The rules continue to change constantly but a company car remains an attractive perk: you can use the car for personal reasons and most of your expenses are picked up by your employer. Unless 90 percent of the kilometres driven are for business purposes, you will have to include in your taxable income:

• A standby charge equal to 2 percent of the original cost of the car for every month you use it for personal reasons,

• Two-thirds of the lease payments, if the car is leased, which correspond to the days the car is used for personal reasons,

• The share of the car expenses paid by your employer that relate to your personal use. For example, if you use the car for personal reasons 25 percent of the time, you will be taxed on 25 percent of the operating and maintenance expenses paid by your employer. You do have another option: if your personal use of the car is less than 50 percent, you can claim a flat 50 percent of the standby charge instead of a percentage of actual operating expenses.

If you have a company car, you can significantly reduce the taxable benefit by keeping your personal use of the car to a minimum. You should park the car in your employer's parking lot while you're on vacation, and on weekends if you don't use it, and keep track of the days the car was in the mechanic's garage or parked at the airport while you're away on business. You can exclude these days when calculating your standby charge. Keep in mind that the standby charge will be reduced if you use the car for less than 10 percent of your driving. Keep meticulous records, logging every business trip.

Because the standby charge is based on the original cost of the car, it does not decline over time as the car depreciates. The charge would be reduced if your company sells the car to a leasing company and leases it back for you. (Of course, you might also consider buying the car from the company.)

If you use your own car for business and are given an allowance to cover your expenses, this is not a taxable benefit. If your company doesn't provide car allowances, you may be able to deduct some of your car expenses from your income. You even have a choice: if the car allowance your employer provides is insufficient to cover your expenses, you can declare the car allowance as income and then deduct your full car expenses from your income on your tax return.

Tax strategies for the self-employed

If you're self-employed, you are an accountant's delight. Tax planning for professionals or owners of small businesses is complex, but it is flexible. You should seek professional advice but you'll find your tax planning strategies lie in five main areas:

- Your deductions,
- Choosing a year-end,
- Employing family members,
- Your legal status,
- Estate planning.

The list of deductions you can claim when you run your own business is exhaustive but you must keep accurate records. You're a target for Revenue Canada's auditors, probably because sloppy or overzealous tax avoidance by your peers has caused the taxman untold irritation in the past. Keep every slip of paper that proves either income or expenses and use a separate bank account as well as a separate credit card for your business activities. If you can't pay by cheque or get a receipt, jot down the expense and the date on a slip of paper and keep it among your records. If your office is in your home, it must be a room used strictly for business. Keep within Ottawa's bench-marks when buying or leasing a car and keep a log of your car mileage. Never forget, if you are ever audited by Revenue Canada, you will have to prove every single expense you've claimed or you'll find the visit painfully expensive.

When starting a business, you have two opportunities to reduce your taxes. You have the flexibility to choose a fiscal year-end other than Dec. 31, which could allow you to defer taxes for up to a year, and you can incorporate. The tax and legal ramifications of incorporating have always been complex. As you might expect, tax reform has added new twists and traps. You should talk to an accountant with expertise in advising small businesses.

You can reduce your family tax burden by hiring your spouse or your children and deducting their salaries from your income. Don't be foolhardy: you might pay your bookkeeper wife $20,000 a year to keep your books but Revenue Canada will frown if you pay your nine-year-old daughter $20,000 a year for keeping the office fridge full of ice.

The income you pay your spouse or child will be taxed in his or her hands, possibly at a lower tax rate than you pay. They will also be able to contribute to an RRSP and claim all the deductions and credits any other working person can claim. If the savings cover the expense, a professional can set up a management company owned by family members to hire staff, purchase supplies and manage the business. However, with the implementation of the GST, the value of a management company as a tax-savings tool is now being questioned.

There are various strategies, such as estate freezes, that allow you to reduce taxes that will be paid upon your death or when your company changes hands. Talk to your lawyer or your tax advisor.

Tax strategies for high-income earners

If there are losers in the fallout from tax reform, they are people with high incomes who were aggressive tax planners in the past. Tax planning hasn't died, but tax exotica has been buried. You can use all of the tax planning strategies that any other taxpayer can use – and probably to greater advantage. But looking around for big savings through tax shelters is like walking in a mine field. Ottawa has even created a sweeping general anti-tax-avoidance rule, a weapon of last resort to curtail taxpayers who appear to be avoiding tax by distorting the intention of the Income Tax Act. The anti-avoidance rule is the bogey man in the accountant's closet – he's not sure if it's as ominous as it sounds. But for a while, at least, tax professionals will be a little less likely to move their clients into creative tax strategies.

The tax shelter industry has been slammed by two events. The first was a series of changes in the tax laws. The at-risk rules of 1985 and the curtailment of soft-costs deductibility and depreciation have seriously diminished the tax incentive behind all shelters including films, mining, oil and gas, and real estate syndications.

In the past, an investor could deduct the cash he had invested as well as any money that had been borrowed in his name, even if he wasn't liable for the loan if the project went belly-up. Under the 1985 at-risk rules, your deductions are restricted to money you can actually lose. Real estate investors were also hard hit by the changes to the deductibility of soft costs. Most of the soft costs in an investment are the professional fees – the architects, engineers, lawyers and accountants – not the cost of bricks and mortar. In the old days, you could deduct all of these costs immediately. Under today's tax rules, most are deducted over five years or the life of the property. As bruised as they might be as tax savings, these losses, expenses, credits and deductions will still add to your CNIL account, making it difficult for you to tap your lifetime capital gains exemption. On top of this, you could be exposed to the alternative minimum tax, explained in detail later in this chapter.

The second circumstance causing serious problems for tax shelters has been the insipid performance of the stock market. The returns on many tax-shelter investments have become volatile and unpredictable.

It has become more important than ever to seek tax-shelter advice from a professional who is unencumbered by the lure of a fat commission. You should never forget that the essence of a tax shelter is to entice you into an investment so fraught with risk that you would probably not make it without the tax embellishments. If you don't step gingerly, you may find yourself in an expensive tax trap instead of a lucrative tax shelter.

Another tax tactic once used by high-income earners, forward averaging, also went out with a whimper as tax brackets fell. It was a complex strategy used to smooth the tax burden from year to year for taxpayers whose annual incomes varied radically. Since you had to pay tax at the highest rates on any money you forward-averaged, it was a strategy of last resort. If you have forward-averaged in the past, you have until 1997 to bring that money back into income.

The new tax regime for investors
Whether it comes as a relief or a disappointment, tax breaks will play a diminished role in mapping out your investment strategies. One of the main goals of tax reform was to take the tax distortions out of investing – to let your financial decisions rest on the economics of an investment, not on the tax benefits. Although your decision will be less driven by tax implications, the tax bite cannot be ignored. Besides the quality and risk of investments, your financial

decisions must hinge not on what something earns or costs before tax, but on what it earns or pays after tax. Let's look at the effects of tax rules on the three main areas of investment income:

Interest income. Every penny of interest you earn on money in bank accounts, CSBs, mortgages, bonds and even deferred annuities is added to your income and taxed at your normal rates as if it were salary or wages. Taxes on interest have dropped only because tax rates have dropped. There are no longer any tax breaks under the new tax regime. You're even taxed on the first $1,000 of interest you earn. Under the accrual rules, you must report the interest you've earned on an investment at least every three years. Under Bill C-28 it became necessary to report interest every year on investments acquired on or after January 1, 1990, whether it's been received or not.

Canadian dividends. Because the corporation in which you've invested has already paid taxes on the dividends it pays to you, there is a dividend tax credit you can use to reduce your taxes. To claim this complicated credit, you must "gross-up" – a peculiar phrase meaning "increase" – the dividend you've received by 25 percent and then calculate your federal tax on this increased amount. You then subtract the dividend tax credit of 13.33 percent of the taxable dividend. Finally, you add your provincial tax.

It's confusing and, with today's tax laws, many financial experts aren't even convinced dividends are better financially as a source of income. You may pay less tax on a dividend than on interest, but you will usually have received less in the first place. At the end of the day you're left with the same amount of money in your pocket.

Capital gains and losses. In the sweeping tax reform of 1972, capital gains became taxable for the first time in Canadian history. Nearly thirteen years later, Michael Wilson shocked the financial community when he decided taxpayers could have their first $500,000 of capital gains tax-free. He then set about methodically removing the tax advantages of capital gains. He dropped the exemption to $100,000 for everyone except farmers and small-business owners. He brought in the CNIL to make matters more difficult and increased the taxes on capital gains which you earn beyond the $100,000 lifetime exemption. Finally, in February 1992, the exemption was removed from recreational and investment real estate. The change came into effect immediately. If you sell a property which you owned before the budget came down, the portion of any capital gain eligible for the exemption will be based on the number of months which you owned the property prior to February 28, 1992 divided by the total number of months the property is owned. (As time passes, a smaller and smaller portion of gain can claimed under your exemption.)

Investors will still want to earn the $100,000 in capital gains that can be sheltered under the lifetime exemption, but once this limit is reached, the spread in the tax treatment between capital gains and other investment income narrows dramatically.

Once the $100,000 exemption is exhausted, you must pay tax on three-quarters of any capital gains you earn along with your wages and interest income, at your normal rates. Even though rates have dropped, the fact that they are applied to more of your capital gains means capital gains taxes will jump. Any capital losses you suffer are reduced by the same percentages, but can only be used to reduce your taxable gains, not your taxable income. Losses can be carried back three years or forward indefinitely.

The tax on investments is constantly shifting. Few were surprised when the lifetime capital gains exemption was reduced to $100,000 from $500,000, and there are many who believe it will disappear entirely. If you've been thinking of selling an asset that will trigger a gain, think a little faster. When it comes to the capital gains exemption, take advantage of it while you can. And don't forget the CNIL rules. They can make life messy for investors intending to claim the $100,000 lifetime capital gains exemption. Any investment losses not offset by investment income are dumped in your CNIL account, where they can build year after year. Since CNIL hits only investors trying to claim the exemption, one way to avoid getting caught is to use up your lifetime exemption before you incur any investment expenses or losses. You'll also avoid problems if you build a pool of interest- and dividend-income investments before embarking on an investment strategy that could create losses.

Unfortunately, the CNIL rules have proved to be an expensive trap for investors in tax shelters, since the strategy behind many shelters rested on the tax savings generated by heavy losses and up-front expenses, coupled with rich gains in the future that could be sheltered. These investors have also been hit by the alternative minimum tax.

How menacing is the alternative minimum tax?

During the 1984 federal election, New Democratic Party leader Ed Broadbent taunted his opponents with tales of the tax-avoidance shenanigans of the rich. Tempers flared, and during a debate featuring party leaders, Prime Minister Mulroney promised that "anyone in this country of wealth and substance should pay tax and it should be a handsome tax." The promise wasn't forgotten. In 1985 Canada passed the Alternative Minimum Tax Act to ensure that the wealthy shoulder their share of the tax burden. The alternative minimum tax has been criticized by many financial advisors as an ineffective, unnecessarily complex law that squashed a mosquito of a problem with a ten-ton fly swatter. Others have welcomed the curbs the tax has placed on those who were so determined not to pay tax that they took risks they could not afford.

The act was designed to catch taxpayers who avoided paying taxes by overindulging in tax shelters, receiving most of their incomes as Canadian dividends or rolling their pension incomes into RRSPs. Unfortunately, since most tax-shelter investors run out of nerve before they bump into the alternative minimum tax, it's the unwary who are trapped – farmers selling their farms, the businessman selling his corner grocery store or people who have been fired and given severance allowances which they've tried to protect by rolling the money into their retirement plans.

If you think you might be caught by the minimum tax, you can get the one-page AMT Calculation Sheet from Revenue Canada. It may look daunting, but it simply requires you to add back to your income the deductions for your RRSP or pension plan contributions, capital gains exemption, capital cost allowance deductions for tax shelter investments, and Canadian dividend credits. From this you deduct $40,000. This gives you a new taxable income on which you must pay about 26 percent tax. This is the minimum amount of tax you can pay. As a simple rule of thumb, you may face the minimum tax requirement if you pay less than 17 percent federal tax on your gross income in excess of $40,000.

The minimum tax is not as menacing as it might seem at first blush. But it can create an unpleasant surprise for the owners of small businesses, farmers, aggressive investors and employees who want to roll retiring allowances into their RRSPs. Depending on your tax situation, the minimum tax may well be refunded in future years. Seek the advice of a professional to avoid making a costly mistake.

Tax strategies for the retiring

Many financial experts believe it's unfair that you can no longer roll your pension into your RRSP and consider it deplorable that you can't treat pension benefits as earned income against which you can make RRSP contributions. Still, there are a few tax tactics you can use to reduce your taxes in retirement:

Build healthy RRSPs for both spouses

The tax burden of a retired couple will be less if family income is taxed in the hands of two people rather than one. Throughout your working life you should try to build your husband's or wife's RRSP through a spousal plan so it will match your pension or RRSP in retirement. Even if you're over seventy-one years old – by which time you must wind down your RRSPs – you can make a contribution from your earnings to the RRSP of your spouse if he or she is younger than seventy-one. Although you can no longer roll your pension into your own RRSP, you will be able to continue to roll as much as $6,000 of your pension into a spousal RRSP each year. Although you'll have only until 1994 before this strategy is axed, it's never too late to start. Even if you can't build up your husband's or wife's RRSP until it matches your pension, put in as much as you can afford. Any tax saving is better than none.

Roll your retiring allowance into your RRSP

Taxes on retiring allowances can be brutal, but they can be avoided. Prior to 1989 you could transfer to your RRSP up to $2,000 for each year that you worked for your company and belonged to its pension plan and up to an additional $1,500 for each year you did not belong to its pension plan. Under the new rules, you can roll over only the $2,000. The old limits remain in effect for service before 1989.

Beware of the alternative minimum tax

One of the targets of the minimum tax was taxpayers who were rolling money from retiring allowances or pensions into RRSPs. If you think this might include you, call or write Revenue Canada and ask for their AMT Calculation Sheet. Look it over and call your financial advisor.

Don't forget your grandchildren

In preparing your will, you could reduce your heirs' tax burden by leaving money to your grandchildren rather than your children. The money could be placed in a trust with your children named as trustees, and the income could be used for the care and education of your grandchildren. The income would likely be taxed at a lower rate than if your children inherit the money themselves.

Don't ignore the age and pension credit

If you can't use the age credit, don't ignore it. Your husband or wife can claim any portion of the credit you cannot use. This isn't true of the pension credit for retirees. You must have enough pension income to claim the pension credit or it will be lost. Be sure there is enough money flowing to each of you to claim the credit. If your spouse doesn't have any pension income, you could roll some of your pension into a spousal RRSP (unfortunately, this will only be allowed until 1994) to create an income against which you can claim the credit.

Split your Canada Pension Plan income

If you and your spouse are taxed at different tax rates, you should request separate CPP cheques. This could mean your pension income will be taxed at a lower rate. The QPP cannot be split.

Most common errors can be costly

Having worked hard to reduce your taxes, don't blow it by making what may seem to be minor mistakes. If you fail to file your income tax return by April 30, you'll be fined 5 percent of the tax you owe. Another 1 percent will be tacked on for each month you're late. On top of the penalties, Revenue Canada will charge you interest at a rate that will be the T-bill rate plus 2 percent on the unpaid tax. Needless to say, the penalties for trying to evade tax are the harshest. You'll be forced to pay the tax you owe and a fine that can top $25,000. You could even be sent to jail.

The GST

Even the cynics who regarded the changes to our income tax structure to be mere tax tinkering held their breath as they waited for the second stage – the elimination of the manufacturers' sales tax and the introduction of a value-added tax. They were not disappointed. Despite widespread conviction that the existing tax was unfair and a drain on the economy, the government's decision to replace it with a 7 percent goods and services tax swept the country into a furor.

After months of public hearings, that often dissolved into shouting matches, along with heated debates among economists, consumer activists, labour leaders and politicians, the GST was finally passed by the House of Commons. It then moved into the Senate where the real brawl began. Weeks of arguments, shouting and filibustering by the Liberals – they even read the Senate rule book in both French and English – led to behind-closed-doors negotiations and a quieter war in the Red Chamber.

The GST did come into effect on January 1, 1991 and chaos did not engulf the nation. However, nine months after the tax had been introduced, consumer groups were arguing with the federal government over whether consumers were being gouged by companies taking advantage of the GST to raise prices unfairly. In a report released July 18, 1991 the GST Consumer Information Office, a watchdog created by the federal government, showed that the price of 140 everyday items had generally risen or fallen in line with expectations. On the other hand, a group of volunteers in six provincial consumer associations surveyed the price of a basket of fifty-two items and found that prices went up more often than down, or did not go down as much as Ottawa has predicted.

If you have questions about the GST you can write to the GST Consumer Information Office, P.O. Box 3515, Postal Station C, Ottawa, Ontario, K1Y 4T7 or call 1-613-990-8584.

Tax reform in the 1990s

The GST is modelled on similar value-added taxes that have been adopted over the past decade by other countries. Most European countries, including Britain, have a VAT. Judging by the experience of some of those countries, if astutely implemented, the shift to the GST could eventually be integrated with a system of refundable tax credits that could make it possible for the government to ease the burden of poorer Canadians more effectively than in the past.

Despite the sweeping changes, all of these reforms will not eliminate the crushing national debt. The government insists that tax reform represents a shifting of the tax burden rather than an increase.

In the first three months of 1991, the government collected about $400 million more than anticipated; many companies filed their returns monthly rather than quarterly, giving Ottawa revenues in February and March that it had not expected to receive until April. The optimistic hoped the windfall would be used to pay down the deficit but by the end of the year GST revenues had fallen back in line with expectations, partly due to higher unemployment and a jump in bankruptcies. This reduced spending and, therefore, the GST collected.

Predicting government's future reactions to a mounting debt and a worsening economy would be foolhardy. For the moment, the federal government has stepped back from trying to influence economic decisions through the tax system. Chastened, it seems to have decided the best incentive they can give corporations and individuals to work harder is to lower taxes. Unfortunately, the provincial governements decided the lowering of federal taxes created a perfect chance for them to raise tax rates. As a result, Canadians are paying more tax today, not less. As a taxpayer, the only way to ensure you do not shoulder more than your share of the tax burden is to be constantly aware of the natural evolution of the tax system into which your finances are plugged.

CHAPTER 4

Covering Your Risks

EVEN IF YOU'VE WORKED hard to create sanity out of the chaos in your finances, you may still not be on a sound financial footing if all your financial planning rests on the expectation that you'll live a long life with few unpleasant surprises. Just in case things don't go as planned, you need insurance.

Your insurance should protect you and your family against four very different kinds of financial tragedies: your death, your inability to work, the destruction of your home or the losses you might carelessly cause someone else.

Insuring your life

"I detest life insurance agents. They always argue that I shall one day die, which is not so." Those were the words of Canadian humorist Stephen Leacock, who eventually did die in 1944 when he was seventy-five. Almost fifty years later, life insurance agents are still intimidating, and their admonishments that we could die tonight are irritating. They ask intimate questions to which you don't know the answers and then spew out a confusing series of numbers. You don't have to go through this. The purpose of life insurance is obvious: if you die prematurely, your family will need cash. You have one critical question to answer: how much cash will they need?

How much life insurance do you need?

Don't imagine you're going to die tonight. It's too depressing. Instead, pretend you died last night but you have a month's reprieve to straighten out your financial affairs. Don't be maudlin. Give each child a kiss and a hug and think about money.

What will happen to the people around you? They have to bury you, call your lawyer, phone your aunt in Inuvik. They still have to eat, the kids will still want to go to McDonald's, and your husband or wife will still want to go to the occasional movie and take a stroll on Sunday for ice cream.

You want your family to remain in their own world. But to live in security and dignity they need money. In fact, your family will need two pools of cash. First, they'll need money to bury you and pay your debts. Then, after the funeral is over, they'll need money to create the income you can no longer earn for them.

Determining what they'll need is not as difficult as you think. You don't need to be precise, but you must be realistic. Grab a pencil. You can do this in three easy steps.

Your life insurance needs in three easy steps

STEP ONE
When you die, a pool of cash will be needed to pay your last expenses and ease your family's way. Jot down the amounts you'll need for each of the following items.

1. Dying is expensive. Funerals cost around $5,000. Legal and accounting fees will be at least $2,000. Your family will also have the expense of administering your estate. There will be probate fees on estates over $50,000. Even if you're only modestly well off, this could total $10,000. + $_____

2. Never forget your taxes. Revenue Canada calculates taxes as if you sold your stocks and investment real estate on the day you died. It wants the capital gains tax and the taxes on any income you've earned so far this year. + $_____

3. You should never leave your family in debt. Your bank loans may be insured with creditor's life insurance, but your credit cards aren't. + $_____

4. Your family's home should be safe. They'll need enough money to pay off the mortgage. + $_____

5. Don't let your children's future education suffer. Each one will need $32,000 for university ($8,000 times four years). + $_____

6. Life is going to be tough. Everyone is in shock and will be for some time. They shouldn't have to worry about the bills for groceries or car repairs. Add a cushion of at least three months' salary. + $_____

Your first pool of cash   = $_____

STEP TWO
You should calculate how much of your income your family would be required to replace if you died. Then you can figure out how much cash they must have to invest and create that stream of income.

1. How much money will your family spend each month without you? They won't have to clothe or feed you, but the property taxes and heating bill won't change. Most families would still need about 75% of the money that they spend now. $_____

2. Subtract the social security benefits your family could expect to receive. A widow or widower would receive no more than $358.24 a month from CPP, $392.52 from QPP if he or she is under age 65 ($381.67 if older), and an extra $119 ($29 in Quebec) for each child. $_____

3. Now subtract the take-home pay your husband or wife is earning today. $_____

4. Never forget Revenue Canada. Your family will have to pay taxes so they'll need about 35% more. $_____

5. You'll want this income to keep up with inflation or your family will slowly become poor. Choose the number of years the income must last, usually until your youngest child is 20 or 25 years old, and multiply the monthly income by the appropriate number. These factors assume that your investment earns three percentage points more than the rate of inflation.

Years this income must last	Multiply by:
5	56
10	104
15	145
20	180
25	211

Your second pool of cash $_____

This is the cash your family has to invest to create the stream of income they need. At the end of this time, the money will be gone. If you want your family to live only on the income earned by the investment and leave the capital intact, you will need 30% to 50% more.

Now add the two pools of cash.

Your first pool of cash for your last expenses. $_____

Second pool of cash needed to create income. + $_____

Money your family will need = $_____

STEP THREE
If the amount of cash your family will need upon your death looks onerous, don't panic. You probably already have some investments – perhaps a little money tucked away or some life insurance. Let's look at it.

1. Group life insurance. $_____

2. Personal life insurance. $_____

3. Cash in your bank accounts. $_____

4. Stocks, bonds or real estate that could create income or be sold. (Don't forget to deduct the tax.)Don't include your RRSP, collapsing it will destroy its tax advantages. Besides, your wife or husband will have to retire someday and this money will be needed later. $_____

5. Anything personal that might be sold. Maybe they'll finally clean out your messy garage, but don't count on it. $_____

Total cash your family would have $_____

6. Now subtract the cash your family would have from the amount your family will need. $_____

THIS IS THE AMOUNT OF LIFE INSURANCE YOU NEED TO BUY. $_____

WORKSHEET VII

I need how much insurance?

Takes your breath away, doesn't it? If you're a forty-year-old man earning $50,000 a year and have two young children, it's very likely you need $450,000 in life insurance. At $450,000 you may be worth more dead than alive! But $450,000 will pay your bills and give your family an income of about $30,000 a year for fifteen to twenty years. By then, the money will be gone.

If you cannot, or will not, afford this much insurance you'll have to dim your post-mortem fantasies. Don't begin by cutting back on the money your family needs during the first year after your death. And be sure to cover the mortgage. If life is to be a struggle, the security of a paid-up home will make it a little easier. Don't hope your husband or wife will remarry. Statistically, he might, but widows usually don't. And, don't hope that a woman will be able to walk back into her law practice if she's been home with the kids for ten years. She can't.

If you've tried to protect your family against inflation, you might decide it would be better if your husband or wife earned a little more to bolster the gradually diminishing income. Simply by removing the inflation protection, a $450,000 policy is reduced to $300,000 and your annual premium might drop from $800 to $550.

Shop, shop, shop

If a $450,000 term life insurance policy costs you $800 and a whole life policy for the same amount costs $3,700, which are you going to buy? It almost becomes an irrelevant question, doesn't it? It certainly will be if you die. Your family won't care what kind of policy you bought, they'll need to know how much money there is.

Once you know how much insurance you need, shop by telephone for the cheapest renewable term insurance you can find. It's nearly impossible for most families to afford anything else. Buy it and get on with life. Don't even try to understand the maze of life insurance products.

Term insurance is pure protection. It covers you for a few years and then you must renew it or your family is no longer protected. Since you'll be older each time you renew, and more likely to die, the cost of your insurance will rise. Finally, when you're sixty-five or seventy you can no longer buy term insurance. By then you shouldn't need it. Your children will have grown, you'll have burned your mortgage and the wealth that you've built for your retirement will also protect your spouse if you should die.

Whole life insurance is for people who need to leave behind a large chunk of cash upon their death, even if that death is at a very old age. The cost of the insurance usually remains the same year after year and the protection lasts a lifetime. Every whole life policy is pure insurance tacked on to investments. You're forced to pay $2,000 in the early years instead of $200 so that, as your protection becomes more expensive, the savings you've built up inside the policy will help cover the escalating cost of insurance. If you change your mind and decide you do not want the insurance – as many people do – you can get some of these savings back.

Unfortunately, life insurance as an investment has blurred the need most families have for life insurance as protection. Life insurance companies tempt us with visions of retiring early to sun-drenched beaches to live on the wealth we've built in our insurance policies. But by mixing insurance and savings you water down both and end up with too little protection and a weak investment. You should buy whole life insurance – or any of its hybrids, such as term-to-100 or universal life – only if there is a clear need for a large sum of cash, even after age sixty-five, from a death benefit.

The controversy over whole life and term life is one of the most contentious and emotional in the financial marketplace. As you listen to the arguments, keep one thing in mind: there is tremendous financial pressure on agents to sell whole life insurance. An agent's income is earned in commissions and bonuses based on the annual premiums you pay for your insurance. Most agents will earn between 40 percent and 80 percent of the premium you pay for term insurance in the first year, yet they'll earn 80 percent to 160 percent of the first year's premium on a whole life policy. If you spend $800 for a $450,000 term policy, the agent might earn only $750 over the first five years of the policy. Your $800 premium would buy only $90,000 in whole life insurance, yet he would probably earn closer to $950 in the first two years.

Unless you know you will need life insurance, even when you're very old, shop for term insurance. You can start by calling a broker who subscribes to a computerized price-comparison service. One such service provides up-to-date prices of 300 policies sold by sixty life insurance companies, including a few of the companies that only sell through their own agents. You'll be given full comparisons

Shopping for Term Insurance

Policy	Premiums Today	Premiums in 5 Years	Premiums in 10 Years	Conversion Options
1.				
2.				
3.				
4.				

WORKSHEET VIII

of the six least expensive policies with prices for the next thirty years. You'll also be given a quick price summary of all the other products checked. Be sure to look at the future prices you're given; there can be surprising differences. The cheapest policy today could skyrocket in price in five years to make it the most expensive policy over time.

Ensure that each policy can be renewed without proof of good health and that price quotes for the future are guaranteed. Avoid policies that have two renewal prices – one for the healthy and a second for the unhealthy person you might become. Each policy should also be convertible to a range of permanent policies, including term-to-100 and universal life. It's not likely, but the option doesn't cost anything and you might need to choose another type of plan in the future.

Shopping for term insurance

Not only is term insurance cheap, it's easy to compare policies. Be sure to look at your renewal rates over the entire time you will need the protection and the kinds of permanent insurance to which you can convert each term policy.

Insurance agents argue that buying insurance isn't this simple, insisting that people need to cultivate financial relationships with experts. They argue that people don't calculate their needs carefully and don't re-evaluate their policies frequently enough. To a certain extent, their argument has merit. Having adequate insurance to protect your family in the event of your death is critical; if you're not going to take the time to realistically assess your needs, call a broker.

Some people do need whole life insurance

Life does not always unravel as we expect. Any one of your children could became disabled and require costly care for many years after you die. It would be extremely difficult for you to build enough wealth to live comfortably in retirement and still leave enough to pay for that child's care after your death. Or you might decide to have children late in life. A fifty-year-old man with a thirty-year-old wife eager to have children will very likely need life insurance into his mid-seventies, if not longer. He's going to be buying diapers and strollers when other men are saving to retire.

There are other reasons why you might need permanent insurance:

• to pay estate taxes. If your wealth is tied up in real estate, stocks and valuable art, Revenue Canada will want to collect taxes on your capital gains as soon as you die. If you do not want those taxes paid from your estate, they can be paid with cash from life insurance.

• to make up for the deficiencies of a poor pension. At retirement you will likely be faced with the choice of a pension income that is guaranteed only for your lifetime or a lower income that will continue for as long as either you or your spouse lives. You may be tempted to take the higher income and buy life insurance with the extra cash. Your pension will disappear if you die, but your mate will have the death benefit to live on. At best this is patching, not planning. It's a strategy that only works at all if put in place when you're young (and your financial efforts more effective if concentrated on building your wealth). If you wait until you're sixty years old, the cost of the insurance will be too expensive for it to work at all. There is also a danger that you will grow tired of paying insurance premiums, cancel the coverage and leave your partner destitute if you were to die.

• to create an estate. If you want to spend every penny you've worked so hard to make but still leave each of your kids an inheritance, you can only do it with insurance.

• to protect a family business. If your family business has been a resounding success, your estate may be hit with a tax bill that it can't pay without leaving the company broke. There is a $500,000 lifetime tax exemption to make it easier to pass the family firm on to your children, but that may not be enough.

These are needs you usually won't know you have until you're well into middle age. So buy term insurance when you're young, and as you creep up on age fifty take a hard look at your need for permanent insurance. The longer you wait to convert your term policy, the higher the cost. But you can still buy permanent insurance at age fifty for a fair price.

There is another reason to buy whole life insurance, but it's a poor one: forcing yourself to save. If you see life insurance as sacred, won't allow the policy to lapse after a few years and cannot save any other way, perhaps a whole life policy might help mend your tattered financial affairs. Ignore one spurious argument for permanent insurance: you will die one day, so life insurance is definitely a permanent need. Only rarely should anyone need life insurance in old age. And don't allow an agent to convince you that your life insurance policy is an investment tax shelter. Ottawa severely restricted the tax benefits in 1982 when it began taxing investment returns from policies that did not fall within strict bench marks. Still unhappy with the money being shovelled into life plans, Revenue Canada brought in a 15 percent investment tax on all life policies in 1987. There is still a tax advantage to permanent insurance policies, but it lies in building a pool of money that can be used to pay for pure insurance, not in creating a cash surrender value. Collapse your policy and the cash value will be taxed again.

Meandering through the whole life maze

If you are wealthy enough to worry about estate taxes, are you sure you shouldn't just pat yourself on the back? No? Then you'll have to get into the scrum and spend enough time to find your way through the maze of insurance policies. Don't choose your insurance carelessly – the financial penalty for collapsing a permanent policy early can be painful.

Keep these things in mind as you shop:

• You probably need only a small amount of permanent insurance. It takes far less cash to pay estate taxes than it does to create an estate large enough to protect a young family.

• You should be interested only in how much money you have to take out of your pocket to pay for the policy year after year. The cash surrender value that accumulates in a whole life insurance policy is of little interest, since you have to collapse the policy to get at the money. If you do this, your family will no longer be protected. You can borrow the savings in the policy, but if you die, the insurance company will take the money you owe from the death benefit your family probably needs. Don't be duped into believing you can have both the insurance and the savings.

• Some policies are vulnerable to changes in interest rates. If interest rates fall, will your premiums jump or your protection shrink? Could you afford to pay more to keep the insurance you need?

• All permanent policies are really the same – pure protection along with a pool of savings that will help pay your escalating cost of protection. Traditional whole life insurance has spawned two hybrids: universal life and term-to-100.

The real difference among life insurance policies lies in the way you pay for your protection. It's much like choosing a mortgage after you've picked the house your family needs. Do you want to pay over a few years or many years? Do you want flexibility in making those payments? Are you willing to take risks or do you want everything guaranteed?

The simplest, and least expensive, permanent insurance is term-to-100. It's really a stripped-down whole life policy that has only enough savings in it to keep premiums constant until you're 100 years old. Nearly 50 percent of the policies do build cash values, but as far as the life insurance industry is concerned, term-to-100 is only term insurance because it doesn't last forever.

Because most of these policies are not cluttered with dividends and complicated cash values, they are reasonably easy to compare. Here are a few questions you should ask your broker:

• Will your annual premium remain constant until age 100, or can it increase every few years?

• Will the policy have any cash value in the future? Some policies have a cash value in as little as sixteen years; others only on your sixty-fifth birthday. Unless the person you're trying to protect is frail and could die before you, you have little interest in these savings.

• When can you stop paying and take a paid-up policy?

Term-to-100 is perfect for paying estate taxes or creating an inheritance. If you're one of those rare individuals with a fully paid-for house, a fat RRSP, a plump stock portfolio and buckets of cash, you could try to tackle the intricacies of universal life.

Universal life is whole life insurance that separates the pure insurance from the savings and lets you manipulate each. You can also decide, within limits, how much to pay in premiums each year. You can pay less in years when you're short of money or send in a few extra dollars when you're flush with cash. You can pour so much money into the cash reserve that in as little as six years that reserve could pay your insurance costs for the rest of your life. You can control the way the savings are invested by choosing a short-term interest account tied to prevailing interest rates, a guaranteed interest deposit, or even an equity mutual fund. You can also control insurance coverage, increasing or decreasing the death benefit – although you'll usually be required to provide medical records when trying to increase the benefit.

A word of warning: freedom can be dangerous. You have to shop for universal life with painstaking care. Ask every one of these questions:

• What are the penalties for cashing in the policy? Most universal life policies carry heavy sales commissions and start-up fees – as much as 55 percent of the first year's premium. Could you lose all of this money? Are there stiff surrender charges?

• Is the cost of the pure insurance fair? It's often very expensive and not all policies offer future price guarantees. Many of the policies with renewal guarantees require medical evidence of good health. This could make your future insurance costs expensive.

• Are annual administration charges guaranteed not to rise?

• The return on your investment will not be guaranteed, but how does the insurance company arrive at that return? Can this formula change?

• Is the broker using a reasonable rate of return on the savings in your policy to calculate future costs? These savings should be invested conservatively and are unlikely to earn more than 9 percent a year.

• What will happen to your insurance or to your premiums if the rate of return drops? Because the return on your investments will not be steady, your pure insurance and your costs can go up and down like a jack-in-the-box. These policies should be monitored.

Universal life hit the marketplace with a crash in 1982, but no one heard it except the insurance industry. Canadian consumers yawned. The idea is good, but most insurance companies emptied their plates of all the risks in an insurance policy and dumped them in your lap. Avoid universal life plans that do not guarantee the quoted costs of your pure insurance, administration fees and the way your investment return is calculated. Life insurance should eliminate financial risks, not create more. Since few policies will offer all three guarantees, you end up with a narrow range of choice.

Finally, there is traditional whole life. Don't buy it unless you will pay no more for it than you would for term-to-100 insurance. Unfortunately, comparing the prices of whole life policies is tricky because the policies are so complicated. It's easier if you break them down into two categories.

The first category consists of "participating" policies. The insurance company charges you more than it actually expects your protection to cost, and at the end of the year that extra premium is returned to you as a dividend. The word "dividend" has a nice ring to it, but an insurance dividend is not the same as an investment dividend. It is the return of an overcharge. The second category consists of non-participating policies. These don't pay dividends.

In the past, participating policies have been less expensive over time, but history may be a poor guide to the future. The 15 percent investment tax on life policies brought warnings from life insurers that dividends paid on whole life insurance would be cut by 20 percent to 40 percent or death benefits reduced by 10 percent to 20 percent. Since this tax is being levied on old and new policies, you should take a look at any you now have.

You should be aware, too, that both participating and non-participating policies unfold in different ways:

• You can agree to pay for a certain number of years, say, twenty years, until the policy is fully paid. You don't have to pay premiums beyond that point, but the full death benefit, or part of it (if you paid a reduced premium), will still be paid upon your death.

• You can agree to pay the premiums for the rest of your life and the full death benefit will be paid when you die.

• You can agree to pay the premiums until a certain age, perhaps age eighty-five, and the policy will endow – meaning the company will pay you the full death benefit, even if you are still alive.

"But I want something back."

"Life insurance is a rip-off," you say. "I've been paying for years and I've never been given a cent back." So you're angry that you're not dead?

Buying insurance may be distasteful. It's expensive and it would be nice to get money back from years of pumping hard cash into something we think we don't really need. We all like money-back guarantees, but if you spend the extra insurance dollars in creating "living values" in a whole life policy, is that money well spent?

If you really want to spend the time pondering the question, realize that this is an investment, not an insurance, question. Will your investment return be greater through a whole life policy or buying term insurance and investing the rest elsewhere? Your mortgage should be paid and your RRSPs should be very fat before you even start pondering the issue. But as an example, if you buy term insurance and sign up for a CSB payroll deduction plan where you work – a form of forced savings – your return will be about the same as that of the best universal life policy. Of course, the investments will be yours to control.

Should you switch life insurance policies?

You should switch policies if it is to your benefit. Life insurance is not sacred. Just be sure the new policy is in place before you cancel the old.

With whole life, you've already lost the money you paid through outrageous commissions. Now you want to know if you're likely to lose more money by keeping the policy in place. There are two milestones you have to look at – 1982 and the mid-1960s. Whole life policies bought before 1982 may be good, if very cautious, tax shelters because any earnings in these policies will not be taxed by Revenue Canada. If you bought your policy before the mid-1960s, the terms of that policy may allow you to borrow from it at 5 percent or 6 percent – an advantage over today's much higher interest rates.

Should you insure your children?

Insuring your children's lives doesn't make a lot of sense. You would miss a child emotionally, but not financially. You don't even need insurance to bury a child. A funeral is expensive but, to be frank, you'll no longer have the expense of caring for the child. Neither is whole life insurance a good way to save for a child's education.

Should you insure a homemaker?

The death of a parent who stays at home to care for young children can cause unexpected financial difficulties. The working parent will have to pay for babysitting or day care. More hired help will be needed to take care of housecleaning or gardening and the family will probably eat more meals in restaurants. You may be able to absorb these extra costs, especially if your children are older. If you cannot, you'll have to decide whether you want these costs paid for by an insurance death benefit.

Which riders do you need?

Insurance policies are available with a number of riders, which you may or may not need. Let's examine them:

The accidental death benefit: This is the ultimate lottery. If you die in an accident, the death benefit paid to your family is doubled. This rider is inexpensive because it's not likely to pay. Fewer than one in sixteen deaths is caused by an accident, so buy enough insurance to cover your family's needs and forget about how you might die.

Guaranteed insurability: This allows you to buy more insurance in the future without medical evidence of good health. It's expensive, amounting to as much as half of the cost of buying the insurance itself. If you think you'll need more insurance in the future and don't want to risk not being able to get it, buy it now.

Guaranteed renewable and convertible riders: These are inexpensive safeguards. You'll want to be able to renew your insurance for a reasonable price. You'll also want the option of converting to a permanent policy.

Waiver of premium: This is a miniature disability-income insurance policy that will pay your life insurance premiums if you're unable to do any kind of work for which you're remotely suited. Take it, but be sure you also have a good disability policy.

Insurance companies and AIDS

Acquired immune deficiency syndrome has made disability and life insurers extremely cautious. Almost all life insurance companies now demand blood tests from those buying any type of policy of more than $100,000. One disability insurance company requires blood tests if you apply for a policy that will pay more than $3,500 a month. These blood tests may also result in the early detection of another seventeen diseases, including diabetes. This may mean you won't get insurance, but you could find out about a disease early enough to prolong your life.

In the end . . .

You probably won't die young. But until you've built enough wealth to be sure your family will not suffer financially if you die prematurely, buying enough life insurance is a critically important part of your financial plan. It can also be complicated and emotion-laden, so don't multiply your costs and confusion by muddling your protection and investment strategies.

American consumer activist Ralph Nader has called the life insurance industry a smug sacred cow feeding the public a steady line of sacred bull. Too many Canadians have fallen for its spurious arguments for whole life policies. In 1990, 81 percent of all new life insurance policies bought by individuals were some sort of whole life insurance. The average death benefit paid on a policy was $15,250. The average life insurance policy in force was $74,800. Could your family stay in their own world with so little money?

If you're not sure you need whole life insurance, you probably don't. If you're confused, don't buy it. First, get enough term insurance. Then, if you're still unsure, spend the time necessary to understand your needs and the insurance products that are available.

Disability insurance

If you owned the goose with the golden eggs, which would you insure first: the goose or the eggs? Well, you're the goose – and your car, your home and all the toys and comforts you buy for yourself and your family are the eggs. Which have you insured?

Becoming disabled may seem inconceivable, but we live in a tough world. Last year, disability insurance companies in Canada paid $2 billion to people suffering from a litany of health problems – among them stress, heart disease, cancer, back pain, injuries from accidents, strokes, arthritis and cancer. Even the Epstein-Barr virus, a recently identified illness that strikes people in their 30s and 40s with fatigue, depression, nausea and aching muscles, is cause for disability payments.

If you think disability will never be your problem, consider the harsh realities:

• There are three accidents every day in Canada that leave people confined to wheelchairs for life. These people are usually hurt in auto accidents, sports accidents, by diving into shallow water or by simply falling.

• Every year, 50,000 Canadians suffer a stroke. Only 10 percent will be fit to return to work and 45 percent will never work or walk again.

• Eight out of ten people suffer back pain at some time in their lives. Of those back pain sufferers, 5 percent, or one million Canadians, will find their pain chronically disabling.

• One in three Canadians will be disabled for more than three months during their working lives. Only one in fifteen will die during their working lives.

• Half of all people who lose their homes blame illness or injury for their financial troubles.

• There are 1.9 million disabled Canadians. Most became disabled after they became adults.

Not surprisingly, disability insurance is expensive. If you want to receive $3,000 a month in disability income, your policy could cost $3,000 a year in premiums. You may already have some protection under a group disability plan at work, through unemployment insurance, workers' compensation and the Canada or Quebec Pension Plan. But this insurance is seldom enough.

Workers' compensation will protect you only if you're injured on the job, usually by accident. It's very difficult to tie an illness to your workplace. To collect CPP disability benefits, you must suffer from a disability that is likely to lead to your death or be unable to work at any paying job. Even if you're unfortunate enough to collect, payments are never generous. Under most group plans, your disability income will be no more than two-thirds of your current income – to a maximum of perhaps $3,000 a month. You'll hit this ceiling if you're earning $54,000 a year. If your employer pays your insurance premiums, your disability income will be taxed. Since this income is intentionally low to encourage you to return to work, paying taxes on the meagre bit of money you will receive could make life unbearable. Whenever you can, pay your disability premiums yourself.

If you set out to buy your own disability insurance, as too few people do, it will seem complex and difficult to compare policies. But as confusing as they might appear, all disability policies are structured the same way.

Disability insurance questions you should ask

Before buying any policy, there are four questions you should ask:

Are there any guarantees? You want a policy that the insurance company cannot cancel or change in any way. This guarantees your coverage and freezes your premiums at their original level for as long as you keep the insurance. Be sure your policy will cover you for every disability, whether it's caused by injury or sickness. Avoid policies that protect you for life if you're disabled in an accident, but only for a few years if you're ill. Only 7 percent of disabilities are caused by injuries.

How seriously disabled must you be to collect? Will you be paid if you cannot work in your own job or only if you are unable to work at all? Often you will be covered for only two years if you can't work in your own occupation. After that, you'll have to accept any kind of work you're capable of doing. The definition of disability is critical, and there are only two types: own-occupation and any-occupation. You should also know whether you must be bedridden, forced to stay at home or kept under the care of a physician to prove you're disabled.

Will you be paid if you can work only part time? If you wrench your back or can't stand the stress at work, you may be able to work only two or three days a week. Your policy should kick in once you lose 25 percent of your income. Many policies will insist that you be fully disabled before you receive a partial disability benefit. This protects you if you're recovering, but if you have arthritis or your doctor just tells you to slow down you may never collect.

Can you work without losing some of your benefit? Some policies will deduct any money you earn from your disability income. You could end up feeling confined to your home and unwilling to work at all for fear of losing your disability income. Under the best policies you can work at a job outside of your occupation without losing a cent.

Custom-tailor your disability policy

The level of protection is not the only choice you must make when it comes to disability insurance. Consider the following:

When do you want your disability income to start? Most benefits will start between thirty days and two years after you've become disabled. Obviously, a policy that doesn't kick in for six months is cheaper than one that starts paying the moment you injure your back on the squash court. You can cut the cost of your policy in half by choosing to wait ninety days for your benefit rather than only thirty days. On the other hand, waiting 120 days will save you only another 5 percent. The insurance companies know that even heart attack victims are usually back at work within three months.

How long do you want your disability income to last? Once your disability income starts flowing, it can last for two years, for five years, to age sixty-five or for your lifetime. If your disability does last ninety days, there's a 70 percent chance you'll be back at work within two years and a 90 percent chance you'll be back within five years. Because insurance companies are aware of this, a benefit that will last until you're sixty-five is only a bit more expensive than a benefit that will end after five years. Even though you're not likely to be disabled for life, the consequences of not having the protection would be horrendous. It's worth the small cost.

Will your disability income keep pace with the cost of living? If you're disabled for life, inflation can slowly destroy your disability income. If you're forty-five years old now, a $3,000-a-month disability income today would be a pittance in twenty years. You should increase your insurance coverage each year as your income rises, just to be sure your first disability cheque will be enough. To ensure your disability income will keep pace with inflation after you're disabled, buy a policy that will pay a benefit that will increase with the cost of living. Protecting yourself from inflation is expensive – it can increase your premium by 50 percent – but you will be shielded from poverty.

Even if your disability income rises with inflation, your insurance coverage may suddenly fall back to its original amount when you return to work. Your policy should allow you to buy more protection. If you're only working part time, your partial benefit should also grow with the cost of living.

How much disability insurance should you buy?

Unlike life insurance, the amount of disability insurance you can buy is limited. Insurance companies will not allow you to receive more money through disability than you can earn by working. They don't want life to be so cosy that you won't return to work. Most people, especially if they're single or the family breadwinner, should buy as much coverage as the insurance company will sell – 60 percent of income. If you're disabled, money will still be tight. Your disability income will just feed and clothe your family. You may even have to dip into money you've saved.

If both you and your spouse are working, you could split the insurance. Each of you could buy enough protection to be sure you can still live comfortably with only one person working.

Unfortunately, there are people the insurance companies will not insure – including authors, artists and stunt men. And many labourers can't buy insurance that will pay a disability income for more than five years.

Shopping for disability insurance

Using Worksheet IX as an example, you can design your own list to compare the policies of different companies or to compare the costs of juggling the features of a policy. If you decide to buy a policy from one company, you can look at the differences in price as you change each feature.

Shopping for Disability Insurance

Questions to Ask Your Broker	First Policy	Second Policy	Your Group Plan
Can the policy be cancelled or changed by the insurance company?			
Is the policy guaranteed renewable until you're 65?			
Does the policy protect you if you're unable to work in your own occupation or specialty?			
Are you protected from a disability whether it caused by an accident or by sickness? You do not want a policy that only protects you if disabled in an accident.			
How many days after you are disabled will your benefit start?			
For how many years will you receive a disability income?			
Will your benefit keep pace with inflation?			
Will you receive a partial benefit if you can only work part time?			
How much will the policy cost?			

WORKSHEET IX

Even the best policy may not be enough

A disability could cause financial disruptions that will not be remedied by your disability income alone. You may be responsible for deferred taxes and business loans. And there won't be enough money to put aside for your children's future education or your retirement. Several insurance companies have brought in new disability insurance policies and riders to fill these gaps. You can buy policies that will provide money to pay interest on business or professional loans, to pay deferred taxes and to replace your pension or

RRSP contribution. If disabled, you can receive as much as 20 percent of your current income, up to a maximum of $1,000 a month. The money will be placed in a trust where you can manage it for investment purposes, but you will not receive the funds until you're sixty-five.

Insuring the roof over your head

Homeowner's insurance is a snap to buy. It's almost impossible not to have enough, and many of the policies are actually written in lucid English and French, not legal gobbledygook. They're also easy to compare, since there are only two ways your insurance policy can protect you. You're either insured against nothing but the perils named in the policy (a named-perils policy) or you're insured against everything but the exclusions listed in the policy (an all-risk policy).

From these, the insurance industry has created three types of homeowner's insurance packages. The standard, or basic, policy insures your home and its contents only against the perils listed in the policy. A broad policy, which costs 15 percent more, protects your home against all perils but will protect your contents only against those perils listed. A comprehensive policy, which costs 15 percent to 20 percent more than a broad policy, protects both your home and its contents against all risks.

Policies within each category don't vary much from company to company. But it is the little differences that could be very expensive in the future. To be sure you're protected:

• Examine the perils that are covered in a named-perils policy. You'll always be insured against damage from fire and wind, and usually against damage from civil riots. But some policies do not insure you against damage caused by smoke from your fireplace or theft. You'll be insured against an aircraft falling on your house, but not always against smashing into the garage with your own car.

• Look at the risks not covered by all-risk insurance. Damage to your camera will be excluded by one policy, but not by another. You might not be protected against sewer backup or damage to your home from snow melting on your roof. Watch for the perils you're likely to face. If you live on a flood plain, make sure your policy doesn't exclude floods.

• Check the coverage on your furs, jewellery, silverware, stamp and coin collections and software for your home computers. Insurance companies will usually pay no more than $2,000 for furs and jewellery, $5,000 to $10,000 for silverware, $200 for collections and $5,000 for software but every policy is different.

Most homeowner's insurance is sold as a package that covers your home, your belongings and any other buildings on your property. It also provides liability coverage and provisions for enough money to live in a hotel if your home becomes uninhabitable. If you don't like this type of package you can custom-tailor your insurance, but it will cost more for less protection.

Why buy a deluxe policy?

Buying the best brings peace of mind. With a deluxe policy, you're covered for any loss unless it's explicitly excluded in the policy. The onus is on the insurance company to prove that you're not covered. There are a few other perks included with a deluxe policy:

• protection against accidental damage – paint spilled on your Persian carpet or a Royal Doulton figurine broken by a curious child.

• protection against "mysterious disappearances". If a ring or a camera is missing and there's no evidence of theft, you won't have to argue with the insurance company.

• coverage on furs, jewellery and silverware is higher. If the coverage on your broad policy is not high enough, you must have your valuables appraised and listed individually in the policy. This can be expensive.

• you're more likely to be insured against sewer backup in a deluxe policy, but might have to pay extra for such coverage by a middle-of-the-road policy.

• avid camera buffs won't have to buy riders to protect their equipment against mysterious disappearance or damage.

If you're buying a comprehensive policy, look at the new single-limit policies. These provide one blanket amount of insurance rather than separating the insurance into one amount on your home and another on your belongings. You have the same amount of protection, but if you suffer a loss you can decide how to split the insurance between your building and its contents.

How much insurance should you buy?

It's very difficult not to have enough insurance. Since 1984, insurance brokers have been using the home evaluation calculator – a simple guide to the cost of rebuilding your home with bricks and mortar at today's prices – to determine the amount of insurance you require. This guide is updated every six months to keep pace with rising construction costs, but for coverage to be accurate you must answer your broker's questions carefully. Go outside and measure your home's ground floor from the back to the front and from one side to the other. Do you have marble tiles in your bathroom, oak-mantel fireplaces, wool carpets or a sauna? The insurance company is not interested in the real estate value of your home – if it burns to the ground, you will still have your land. But it needs to know your home's value for rebuilding purposes.

To be certain, your policy should include a guaranteed replacement extension. If your house is insured for $100,000 and it burns to the ground, the company will pay to rebuild it even if it costs $125,000. Most companies now include this guarantee in all their policies, but a few will charge an extra $3 or $4. Some companies will not guarantee homes more than thirty years old, others will charge 15 percent extra.

Buying enough insurance on the contents of your home is not as easy. Every policy will insure contents for at least 60 percent to 70 percent of the value of the home. But if you buy designer clothes and expensive china, this won't be enough. Ask your broker for an inventory form and list everything you own, along with its replacement cost.

It's a snap

Once you've decided whether you want the basic, broad or comprehensive policy, there are only a few things you must do:

• Shop for the best price. You could save 30 percent on your annual premium. A broker can help, but you'll have to call the companies that sell insurance only through their own agents. A broker will also know which companies handle claims quickly and which are slow or quarrelsome. He'll know which companies in this slightly unsteady industry are financially stable. You should choose your broker carefully. If you run into trouble over a loss, he'll be on your side of the battle.

• Increase your liability insurance from the $250,000 minimum. Many brokers are now automatically increasing all of their clients' liability insurance to $1 million. If you don't want the extra coverage, you'll have to refuse in writing. At a cost of about $10 to $20, it's worth it. Your chance of being sued for $1 million is small, but it could happen.

• Don't buy insurance that will pay only the market value of your lost possessions. How would you and the insurance company agree on the value of a three-year-old suit or a ten-year-old couch? Most companies now write replacement-cost protection into every policy, but with others it's an extra $10 to $15.

• If you take your computer or camera out of the house, be sure they're covered. They can be easily dropped or snatched.

• Choose a $500 deductible instead of $250. The deductible is the amount of loss you will have to absorb before the insurance kicks in. Every company is different, but you can save 15 percent to 20 percent – enough to buy the comprehensive policy instead of the broad policy.

• Your business computer may not be covered by your homeowner's policy, especially if you transport it between your home and office. Check with your broker.

• Take photographs of each room in your home, as well as the interiors of cabinets and cupboards. Put the photos in your safety-deposit box.

• Have your antiques and memorabilia professionally appraised and insured separately. Your Chippendale chairs and 1950s comic books are not insured, even under a deluxe policy. Keep the appraisal in your safety-deposit box.

Ignoring insurance can be costly for tenants

Your landlord's insurance doesn't protect you, it only protects him. Start a kitchen fire and you'll have to pay the bills for his stove, your furniture and your neighbours' clothing – anything damaged by your flames and smoke. If a thief breaks into your apartment and smashes the windows or scuffs the walls, get out your wallet.

A tenant's insurance package will insure you against both liability claims and damage to or theft of your belongings. Unlike a homeowner, you don't have a bench mark to help value your contents. You'll have to take inventory and value everything yourself.

Don't irritate your insurer with small claims

Insurance brokers often advise their customers not to make small claims. Insurance companies expect to pay when there's a catastrophe, but a rash of tiny claims can make your insurer irritable and suspicious. It may cancel your insurance and you could find it exceedingly difficult to get the protection you really need – fire insurance on your home. Don't treat your insurance as a maintenance contract, but as protection against economic disaster.

There's also a small financial incentive not to file small claims. Your premium will not rise because of a claim, but most companies will reward you with a discount of up to 15 percent if you have not made a claim in five years.

Buying auto insurance

Purchasing auto insurance is even easier than buying coverage for your home. Whether your policy is simply printed on a sheet of paper or bound and embossed in gold, every word in every policy is identical. In every province, whether you buy your insurance from the government or from private insurers, policies are all written by provincial statute. You are left only to decide the risks you're willing to bear and to choose among the extras. Automobile insurance carries four kinds of protection:

1. Liability insurance to protect you if you injure someone or damage someone's car or property in an accident. You cannot legally drive a car without it. Few people carry less than $1 million worth of liability coverage.

2. An accident benefit that will pay any medical expenses not covered by your provincial health plan, cover funeral expenses if you die in a car accident, provide a small disability income if you can't work and provide protection against an uninsured driver. These are written into the policy and coverage cannot be changed.

3. Protection against damage to your car. Most people buy collision insurance with a $250 deductible and comprehensive insurance with a $50 deductible. If you're in an accident, you'll have to pay the first $250 to repair your car. But under your comprehensive insurance, if your windshield is broken by vandals or by a stone thrown up from the road, you'll pay only the first $50. But if you have an old clunker that's not worth $100, forget about the collision insurance. If the cost of repairing the car's damage exceeds the value of the car listed in the Red Book, the insurance company

will refuse to have it fixed. They'll give you the book value and have it towed to the dump. On the other hand, if you own a Porsche or a Jaguar, your insurer may insist on a $1,000 deductible. Vandals love these cars, and they're so expensive to repair your insurance company knows it will cost $1,000 just to park in the mechanic's bay. Drive carefully.

4. Finally, if you can't use your car, the insurance on your vehicle will insure the car you must borrow or rent. This protection applies only if your car has been destroyed, damaged, lost or stolen.

Beyond these basics, you have as many as fifty statutory endorsements you can choose to add to your policy. A few are arcane, such as protection on fire-fighting equipment mounted on a moving vehicle. Among those you're more likely to choose are:

• a loss-of-use extension. This will pay rental fees for the car you rent after yours has been damaged or stolen. Avoid policies with a daily maximum. It won't be enough.

• a rental-car extension. When you rent a car, perhaps while on vacation, most rental companies will force you to pay the first $2,000 in damage unless you buy the collision damage waiver, often $10 a day. Instead, you can buy an extension to your own automobile policy that will apply your car's insurance to the rental car, making the waiver unnecessary. Be careful: you could still run into problems. If you drive an old clunker that you don't insure against collision, you won't have collision insurance on the car you've rented. Rental-car extension is only valid in Canada and the United States.

• a waiver of depreciation on a new car. If you wreck your new car within thirty months, the insurance company will pay you the car's original value, not its depreciated value.

• a family benefit extension. This is your protection against an underinsured driver. If a driver injures you or a member of your family and can't pay the court settlement, your insurance will.

With each accident claim, your insurance premium will rise. Always discuss with your broker the repercussions of reporting an accident to your insurance company. If making a claim will boost your premiums by $100 a year for the next six years, you might be better off not reporting a $400 fender bender, even if you have a $250 deductible. The extra $150 out of your pocket to repair the damage yourself isn't worth the extra $600 you'll have to pay in premiums.

Don't leave home without it

Anyone who has ever stepped out his front door has at least one story of travel woe. Getting sick in Amsterdam or Albuquerque is not like getting sick at home. It can be astronomically expensive and your provincial health insurance will not cover all of your costs. In the United States, the daily cost of hospital care is usually $1,000 to $1,400 a day or more; Ontario's provincial medical care plan (OHIP) will pay only $400 a day. Even simple stories of lost bags or a sprained ankle are tales of trips gone awry and, sometimes, empty pocketbooks. Medical care outside Canada can cost two to three times as much as your provincial medical plan will pay.

Travel insurance can cover a number of possible problems: financial losses caused by accidents, illness or death; lost or damaged baggage; and the cancellation, delay or interruption of your trip. You can buy complete coverage in one package or you can purchase each kind of travel insurance separately. There's really not much difference between company policies and, since travel agents tend to offer only one plan, it's difficult to shop for the best price. You must buy the trip cancellation insurance when you buy your ticket, but don't buy the rest of the package if you don't need it. If you work for a large company, your medical care while travelling is probably covered by your employee benefits plan. If it isn't, purchase coverage yourself. But be sure to look carefully at the medical restrictions in the policy. Your property insurance policy may insure you against damaged baggage or thieves in your hotel room. Check before buying more coverage.

Umbrella insurance

If you're wealthy, you may want to buy an umbrella policy – a personal liability policy that boosts your insurance to as high as $6 million. Most liability claims are covered by your homeowner's or automobile policy, but we live in a legal environment that is moving toward higher and higher settlements. If you hit a swimmer with your yacht but can't pay the liability settlement, the courts could seize your house, summer home, Mercedes and the yacht. If you're wealthy, you're vulnerable. Protect yourself. Umbrella policies cost around $75 for an extra $1 million in insurance.

CHAPTER 5

When The Best-Laid Plans Go Awry

AS UNPLEASANT AS THE prospect may seem, many of the emotional upheavals in our lives can have serious financial consequences. If you're fired, widowed or divorced you'll have to juggle financial matters when you're under psychological strain. When even the best-laid plans go awry, you should move slowly and thoughtfully. And even if you do not usually turn to others, you would be wise to travel through a crisis in your life with the help of a trusted financial advisor.

You're fired! Now what?

Despite the initial shock, a lost job is not a lost life. Indeed, pink slips are not all that unusual. Since the downturn in the economy in April 1990, hundreds of thousands of jobs have been lost as companies across Canada cut staff in the face of tough competition and reluctant consumers. There are now 444,000 fewer permanent jobs in the Canadian economy – many of which will never exist again. Keeping your head as the axe falls isn't easy, but staying calm will help your financial health and your ability to get on with life. You will survive. Getting fired may even be your chance to make radical and profitable changes.

Just don't panic. Don't sign any papers until you've recovered your composure and can negotiate without anger or bitterness. In most cases, you'll be offered a compensation package that could include a severance payment of as little as two weeks' pay or as much as two years' salary or more. If you think you've been wrongfully dismissed or your compensation package is woefully inadequate, speak to a lawyer. Under tax rules introduced in April 1989, you can deduct legal expenses for actions as far back as 1986 taken to gain a severance payment or pension benefit.

You can receive your severance pay in two ways: as a retiring allowance of one or more payments or as a continuation of your salary after you've left the employer. If you receive a retiring allowance, the payments will be taxable. You can defer at least some of that tax by transferring payments to an RRSP. Prior to 1989, you were able to transfer to your RRSP up to $2,000 of a retiring allowance for every calendar year or part of a year you were with your employer and a member of a pension plan; you could transfer an additional $1,500 for every year in which there had been no vesting of employee contributions in a registered pension plan or DPSP. These limits were replaced in 1989 by a single limit of $2,000 a year but the old rules apply to service prior to 1989.

If you choose to receive your retiring allowance as a stream of income you cannot shelter any of it in an RRSP. However, if paid an income you will be considered on payroll and will also receive employee benefits. The advantage of these benefits has to be weighed against the disadvantage of not being able to shelter the severance in an RRSP. If you are let go later in the year, you might consider receiving the severance allowance as two lump sums in two different years, perhaps some in October and the rest in January.

All the money contributed to your pension plan can be moved into your RRSP or to your new employer's pension plan. You might consider spreading the receipt of any money that can't be sheltered in a pension plan or an RRSP over several years. It could help keep taxes down in the year of your dismissal.

Don't forget that you'll need life, disability and medical insurance. These benefits will probably end the day you leave, but check. Even though your employer might be unwilling to budge on your cash settlement, he or she might be willing to continue your benefits. If not, you'll have to buy insurance yourself. Your family can't afford to be without the protection; the risk to their welfare is too great. Unfortunately, once you're out of work you won't be able to buy disability insurance.

Many companies now provide relocation and career counselling as part of their severance packages. This counselling usually includes psychological testing, career planning, a job search plan, interview training and financial advice. If such assistance is offered, take it. Professional career counsellors can make the task of finding a new job less intimidating. Searching for work can be a full-time job in itself, and without professional encouragement you could be frozen in your tracks by anxiety.

You'll also need to get your personal finances organized. Sit down with your family and draw up a budget covering all of your expenses for the coming year, marking those that could be reduced if necessary. Compare this with your income. You probably have at least some money stashed away in CSBs or other liquid investments to supplement your severance pay. You may even be eligible for unemployment insurance. If you must cash in investments, be sure to start with those that will be least damaging to your long-term financial health; turn to your RRSP only if it's absolutely necessary. Don't alter your lifestyle drastically, but be realistic. If you're an executive, be sure you have money to last at least a year – it may take you that long to find a job.

Losing your job hurts. But if you can keep your head emotionally and financially, you'll be able to recover quickly from the trauma.

Financial life after divorce

"A divorce is like an amputation," Margaret Atwood wrote in her novel *Surfacing*, "you survive, but there's less of you." For the one in three couples whose marriages break down, the split affects not only their emotional well-being but their finances as well. Legally, ending a marriage is quick and easy. It can take as little as a few hundred dollars and a separation agreement that can be written and signed in a few hours. The tough part is determining who gets what – a process that often has severe emotional and financial implications.

The divorce process has changed a great deal in the past two decades. Alimony is out and the concept of splitting the family goods fairly has become more prevalent. While the rules vary from province to province, the underlying principle is that marriage is an economic and financial partnership in which each partner is entitled to an equal share of the property. In some provinces this applies to personal and business assets.

Generally, the only assets not subject to sharing are those acquired before the marriage, those inherited during the marriage and those excluded under a legal contract. Because of the wide scope of most provincial divorce legislation, lawyers and financial advisors now suggest that couples consider drawing up a marriage contract, especially if there is a family or professional business. A marriage contract may seem an unsavoury prospect – a kind of blueprint for divorce before the vows are even spoken. But it can help reduce emotional and financial stress if a marriage falls apart. (Remember, too, changes in the family laws in your province could nullify your contract. If the law changes, you may have to rewrite the contract or resign the original to affirm that the contract still stands.)

As with any decision involving financial security, don't act hastily if your marriage founders. And don't sign anything without professional advice. One of the first steps both husband and wife should take is to learn their legal rights and obligations under a separation or divorce agreement. They should each know their rights to the property of the marriage, regardless of who now owns it or who paid for it.

Sharing the family goods does not necessarily involve an even split. Each spouse should be able to live comfortably after the marriage is over. If one has built a lucrative career while the other has cared for a home and children, doling out a dollar for him and a dollar for her will not leave them in comparable financial positions. The career created by the working spouse over the years is a financial "asset" and should be considered when deciding who gets what. Each spouse should know what it will cost to live alone – to set up and run another household. Realistic budgeting will be critical in determining how marriage assets should be divided. Your individual financial needs will determine whether your family home, usually the most valuable capital asset in a marriage, must be sold.

Your financial needs will be far more complicated if you have children. Who will look after the kids? Will they live with one parent and visit the other, or can you share custody? Who will pay for their clothing, dental work, summer camps and trips? Financial support for children is a critical part of a financial settlement between divorcing parents. Each parent should complete detailed financial statements of income, expenses and personal child care costs. These statements must be accurate because they will have a bearing on all future negotiations and litigation. In determining the money you'll need, don't forget that you will be taxed on any periodic child support or spousal support payments you receive. If you want to make a clean break from your spouse, a lump-sum payment may be the quickest route to independence. But if you're the one making the payment, be aware that it is not tax deductible, while regular maintenance payments are. Make sure the payments you make are part of a formal agreement or court order. If not, they are unlikely to be deductible.

Most couples should live with the provisions of an interim agreement for at least a few months before sealing their fates with a separation agreement. Once in force, a separation agreement is rarely changed by the courts, except when it comes to financial provisions for child support. The jealousy, anger, fear, guilt and desire for revenge that exist when a marriage ends can cause you to take action that you might later regret. Under a legally binding interim agreement, each partner's financial and legal obligations are set out, but only for a short period. After your emotions have settled and you have a better understanding of your financial needs, a formal separation agreement can be signed.

An amicable divorce may be next to impossible, but you should try to settle your affairs without going to court – although each spouse should retain the services of a lawyer. Consider visiting a divorce mediator – someone who will work with both of you to negotiate solutions to your problems. Remember, going to court can be costly and can cause even greater unhappiness.

Coping alone

It's sad but unfortunately true that most married women will be widows. Women live longer than men and tend to marry older men. As a result there were 1,124,700 widows in Canada in 1991, but only 237,100 widowers. Many of these women find themselves not only bereaved and alone, but also confused and frightened. They may know nothing of the family finances they must suddenly manage. The loss of a husband brings many older women face to face with financial responsibilities they may never have had previously, leaving them vulnerable and afraid to act.

Every married couple should sit down and discuss what would happen if one of them died. What would the survivor inherit and what should be done with it? Look at the income that would be received. If neither of you is retired, would there be any income? Would your life insurance provide enough for the survivor to live comfortably? What employer benefits would be left? If you're retired, what would happen to your pension? Have you named a beneficiary for your RRSPs, pension plans and RRIFs? You should know the location of bank accounts, safety-deposit boxes and all your important documents – wills, insurance policies, stock certificates, bonds, deeds and partnership agreements. Take a look at these documents. Make a list of your possessions, investments and debts and a second list of all your financial advisors – your lawyer, accountant, insurance agent, stockbroker and financial planner.

If you someday find yourself in the unfortunate role of grieving widow or widower, give yourself time to cope with your loss before trying to make decisions about long-term financial needs. Don't make immediate or binding changes in your life, such as selling your home. It will be six months to a year before you're thinking clearly, so don't cash bonds or stocks unless you need the money to live on. Put any inheritance or death benefits from insurance into a treasury bill savings account or money market mutual fund until you're emotionally able to make effective decisions about your finances. If you don't have financial and legal advisors, consider using the services of your spouse's lawyer and accountant. They'll be familiar with your partner's financial and legal situations. You can decide later whether you want to make a change.

You will also need to develop a budget, so keep track of how much money you require for living expenses. It will take several months to adjust to your new economic circumstances and to work out a plan. You need to know how much you spend on food, clothing and housing, as well as on other activities such as travel and entertainment. Don't forget to include income tax and medical expenses. When you have a clear idea of your needs, you'll be in a position to decide how much money you require and whether you have enough.

Once you're organized and emotionally settled, consider consulting a professional financial advisor. He or she can help determine how to organize your financial affairs to ensure you have sufficient income to meet your requirements. This is especially important for a widow whose husband handled all the family finances. The advice of family and friends will be well intentioned, but not necessarily sound. On the other hand, the advice of professionals may be tainted by self-interest. Choose carefully and make sure the solution recommended is not just a reflection of the product the advisor sells.

It will take time to recover from the loss of your spouse. It will also take time to develop your own financial strategy. Don't rush.

CHAPTER 6

The Emotional Traumas of Mr. Market

BEFORE YOU BEGIN YOUR trek into the nitty-gritty of investing, you should meet Mr. Market. Mr. Market is the creation of Benjamin Graham, who in 1949 wrote a book called *The Intelligent Investor*. Graham's influence has reached every corner of the financial world, but it found an especially comfortable niche in the mind of Warren Buffett, chairman of Berkshire Hathaway Inc. in Omaha, Nebraska and one of the most consistently successful investors in America.

Graham once told Buffett that he should imagine stock market prices as coming from this fellow named Mr. Market, his partner in private business. Every day, Mr. Market names a price at which he will either buy your share of the business or sell his to you. Even though your business may be stable, Mr. Market's daily price is not. "For sad to say, the poor fellow has incurable emotional problems. At times he feels euphoric and can see only the favourable factors affecting the business. When in that mood, he names a very high price because he fears that you will snap up his interest and rob him of imminent gains. At other times he is depressed and can see nothing but trouble ahead for both the business and the world. On these occasions he will name a very low price, since he is terrified that you will unload your interest on him.

"Mr. Market has another endearing characteristic: he doesn't mind being ignored. If his quotation is uninteresting to you today, he will be back with a new one tomorrow. Under these conditions, the more manic-depressive his behaviour, the better for you.

"But, like Cinderella at the ball, you must heed one warning or everything will turn into pumpkins and mice: Mr. Market is there to serve you, not to guide you. It is his pocketbook, not his wisdom, that you will find useful. If he shows up some day in a particularly foolish mood, you are free to either ignore him or to take advantage of him, but it will be disastrous if you fall under his influence."

It's irreverent, but Buffett's description of the emotional traumas of Mr. Market* captures the fear and greed that colour the investment psyches of most people. It's difficult to do, but investors must insulate themselves from the contagious emotions that swirl about the marketplace. You can become an intelligent investor by sticking to five irrefutable laws of investing:

• Know the investments and their inherent risks.
• Know yourself.
• Create a strategy.
• Be tolerant of your mistakes.
• Muster the discipline to stick to your decisions.

The task of becoming an intelligent investor should not be intimidating. You can build up your wealth and secure your financial comfort with the help of knowledge and common sense. Don't dabble and don't "play" the stock market. It will demean the effort you've put into earning your money and the risks you're taking as you try to make your money work for you. Investing isn't a game – it's your road to financial independence.

The guaranteed, perfectly safe 33 percent annual return

The first step in your investment strategy is failure-proof. It's also absolutely risk-free. And it's simple – all you have to do is pay off your debts.

There isn't an investment that can beat paying off your personal debts. Here's why: you have to pay your debts with money you have left after you've paid your income taxes. If you're in a 45 percent tax bracket and borrow money at 18 percent on a credit card, paying off that debt has the same impact on your finances as earning 33 percent on an investment. But it's almost impossible to earn the kind of risk-free "return" you get from paying off your loan without taking risks. Furthermore, if your savings are earning interest, you're paying a hefty chunk of it to the taxman.

Why would you pay 33 percent a year to borrow money at the same time that you lend it to someone else – say a bank or a trust company – and end up with only 5 percent in your pocket? Consumer debt is expensive and erodes your ability to build up your wealth. Get rid of it as soon as you can. There's one caveat. Don't wait until your mortgage is paid before establishing an investment portfolio. If you do, you'll have sunk all of your money into your

---

* An excerpt from a recent report to Berkshire Hathaway Inc. shareholders.

home, an investment that can't provide quick cash if the need arises. What's more, you won't gain any investing experience. By the time you're fifty, your mortgage will be paid, the kids will have grown and you'll be at the peak of your earning power. But you'll have no idea how to invest your money.

Instead, you can pay down your mortgage and invest at the same time. At around age fifty, you'll have an explosion of cash and the experience to work with it.

Saving the painless way

You were chided at your mother's knee as a child and cruel reality hasn't softened – you know you have to save some money, at least a bit for a rainy day. Trouble is, saving isn't always easy. Some people save willingly, others have to force themselves.

Either way, set a savings target – at least 10 percent of your take-home pay each month – and put that money away each month. Whether you're a spendthrift or thrifty, you can make saving painless if the money is spirited away before it even hits your pocket. To do this, you can:

- Tell your employer to deduct money from your pay and deposit it in your savings account.
- Join the CSB payroll deduction plan. When you sign up to buy a CSB through work, your employer arranges a loan, buys the CSB for you, then deducts money from your pay cheque over the next twelve months. At the end of the year, your loan is paid and the bond belongs to you. Although you pay interest on the loan, it's tax deductible and you're earning interest on the bonds all year. For as little as $40 every two weeks, you'll have a $1,000 bond in your hands at the end of the year.
- Buy mutual funds through pre-authorized cheques. You can start with $500 to $1,000 and make monthly contributions of as little as $50.

Saving is not spending all your money. Each of us, no matter how financially sophisticated, has to do it. But even the most diligent saver will just be treading water if the money that has been squirrelled away isn't put to work. You have to make your savings work for you – you have to invest them. To do that intelligently you have to know why you buy bonds or stocks or real estate and how these investments are likely to act.

The investment pyramid

The world of investments has become so bewildering that even the experts tend to bury themselves in a corner of the financial market-place. To avoid becoming confused, never forget that there are only two ways to invest your money – you can lend it or you can become an owner. Either way you're taking risks, although you might not be aware of them. Everyone is aware of the risk of losing money, but too many investors ignore the risk of having their purchasing power eroded by inflation.

As a lender, you can invest in debt securities such as GICs, term deposits, CSBs, bonds and mortgages. These investments usually provide a steady stream of income through the interest they pay, which is why they are known as fixed-income securities. Eventually, you get your money back. If you buy bonds you're lending your money to a government or corporation. When buying GICs or term deposits you're lending your money to a bank, credit union or trust company. When you invest in mortgages, you lend money to someone to buy real estate.

As an owner, you're putting your money into equity investments. When you buy shares in a corporation, you become one of the owners of that company. If you buy shares with voting rights you have a say in the management of that company, usually through a vote at the annual meeting – even if your shares are owned within a mutual fund. Of course, you can buy more tangible equity investments like real estate, gold, and antiques. Any increase in the value of your investment is a capital gain, while a drop is a capital loss.

Whether you choose to be an owner or a lender, you need a framework within which you can fit your fixed-income and equity investments. That framework is the investment pyramid, a structure that ranks investments by market risk – in other words, the risk of losing your money. Every investor should start by building a foundation and moving up the pyramid as their investment funds grow and aversion to risk lessens. Let's take a closer look at the parts of the pyramid.

The investment foundation. At the foundation of the pyramid are safe investments that can be quickly turned into cash – deposits in banks and trust companies, CSBs, money market funds, treasury bills and short-term interest-bearing securities. While there is little risk in these securities, there's also little chance of high returns.

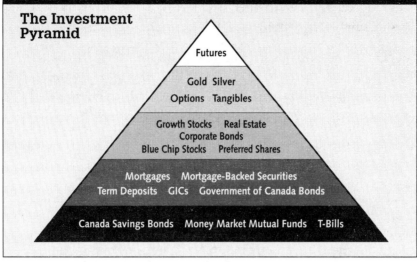

The Investment Pyramid

Futures

Gold Silver
Options Tangibles

Growth Stocks Real Estate
Corporate Bonds
Blue Chip Stocks Preferred Shares

Mortgages Mortgage-Backed Securities
Term Deposits GICs Government of Canada Bonds

Canada Savings Bonds Money Market Mutual Funds T-Bills

CHART II

There are two reasons for holding cash and liquid investments: they provide a cushion that can be used in times of financial crisis and they give you the freedom to move into unexpected investment opportunities.

Fixed-income securities. This is a small step up from the first level. These are still debt instruments – GICs, term deposits, Government of Canada bonds, strip bonds, mortgages, mortgage-backed securities and mutual funds that invest in these securities. Although corporate bonds and debentures are fixed-income securities, they're riskier so they're a little higher up the pyramid.

Most of these securities are as safe as cash, but every bond and mortgage has a price that will fluctuate with changes in interest rates. If rates fall, the value of the security rises. But if rates rise and you must sell, you could lose money because the security will be worth less. The intensity of price swings depends on the term to maturity of the security. The term to maturity is the length of time you must hold on to the bond or mortgage before cashing it in at its full face value. The longer the length of time remaining until the maturity date, the more the investment will react to rate changes. Of course, if you don't plan to sell, this is irrelevant – you'll still be paid the interest you were promised. Preferred shares also provide a fixed income through dividends that react to changing interest rates in much the same manner as bonds.

Stocks. If you buy stocks, you can choose to invest in everything from preferred shares to risky shares in junior oil and mining companies. In the middle are growth shares and blue-chip stocks. When you own a common stock you own a piece of a company's prosperity, and the price of that stock will fluctuate with the fortunes of the company, the health of the economy and the sentiments prevailing in the stock market.

Real estate. This isn't your home, but the real estate you buy as a working investment. You can invest in residential, office, retail or industrial real estate. You can buy a building yourself or you can pool your money with others in partnerships or mutual funds. Real estate can provide both income and capital gains, but it's never an armchair investment. It must be managed, cannot be sold easily and is usually highly leveraged. Real estate is a volatile investment, although it has proven to be one of the best hedges against inflation.

Speculative investments. These constitute the tip of the pyramid, and are for experienced investors only. Gold, coins, art, antiques, wines and rare books are investments you can touch and take pleasure in owning. But prices are erratic and your knowledge must be exhaustive if you want to be an investor rather than a connoisseur. Options and futures are financial tools often used by governments and businesses, but for most individuals they're a complex gamble on the future of the stock market, currencies and commodities. You must be able to make split-second decisions and tolerate financial losses.

The risks of investing

Face it: risk is inherent in every investment you make. Yes, even in CSBs, GICs and your bank savings account. In fact, there are four major risks every investor has to protect against:

Market risk. This is the risk that investors lose sleep over – the chance that the price of an investment will drop after you buy it. The bust in Alberta real estate in 1984, the stock market crash of

Total Rates of Returns on Treasury Bills, Bonds, Mortgages and Stocks

DECEMBER TO DECEMBER

TOTAL RETURN (% CHANGE IN TOTAL RETURN INDICES)

Year	Inflation	91-Day T-Bills	Long Bonds	Residential Mortgages	TSE 300 Stocks
1957	3.21	3.83	7.94	4.14	-20.58
1958	2.67	2.51	1.92	5.82	31.25
1959	1.30	4.62	-5.07	3.67	4.59
1960	1.28	3.31	12.19	6.81	1.78
1961	0.84	2.89	9.16	5.55	32.75
1962	1.26	4.22	5.03	5.49	-7.09
1963	1.65	3.63	4.58	5.50	15.60
1964	2.03	3.79	6.16	5.43	25.43
1965	2.39	3.92	0.05	3.94	6.68
1966	3.50	5.03	-1.05	4.12	-7.07
1967	3.76	4.59	-0.48	4.51	18.09
1968	3.99	6.44	2.14	5.73	22.45
1969	4.53	7.09	-2.86	3.47	-0.81
1970	3.33	6.70	16.39	11.18	-3.57
1971	2.90	3.81	14.84	12.88	8.01
1972	4.70	3.55	8.11	7.79	27.38
1973	7.78	5.11	1.97	5.55	0.27
1974	10.83	7.85	-4.53	3.44	-25.93
1975	10.78	7.41	8.02	10.86	18.48
1976	7.47	9.27	23.64	13.86	11.02
1977	8.00	7.66	9.04	13.47	10.71
1978	8.97	8.34	4.10	5.23	29.72
1979	9.12	11.41	-2.83	3.79	44.77
1980	10.16	14.97	2.18	6.52	30.13
1981	12.35	18.41	-2.09	12.82	-10.25
1982	10.86	15.42	45.82	28.15	5.54
1983	5.73	9.62	9.61	18.69	35.49
1984	4.41	11.59	16.90	11.79	-2.39
1985	3.90	9.88	26.68	14.42	25.07
1986	4.17	9.33	17.21	10.93	8.95
1987	4.40	8.48	1.78	8.74	5.88
1988	4.02	9.41	11.30	8.31	11.08
1989	4.97	12.36	15.17	12.44	21.37
1990	4.82	13.48	4.32	11.20	-14.80
1991	5.61	9.83	25.30	19.31	12.02
Dec/61-Dec/91 (30 yr)	5.75	8.35	8.38	9.52	9.60
Dec/66-Dec/91 (25 yr)	6.46	9.22	9.51	10.46	10.34
Dec/71-Dec/91 (20 yr)	7.15	10.12	10.48	11.22	10.84
Dec/76-Dec/91 (15 yr)	6.77	11.31	11.65	12.23	13.05
Dec/81-Dec/91 (10 yr)	5.27	10.92	16.81	14.26	9.99
Dec/86-Dec/91 (5 yr)	4.76	10.70	11.26	11.93	6.38

The ScotiaMcLeod long-term bond index measures total performance of issues whose term is greater than ten years and which have an average term of 16.5 years. All total return indices, except the TSE 300, are copyright © ScotiaMcLeod Inc., 1992.

TABLE II

October 1987 and the fall in the price of gold in 1981 were all manifestations of market risk.

Interest rate risk. Interest rates have an impact on most investments. The price of bonds generally moves in the opposite direction of interest rates. When rates are rising, bond prices will fall – and the dip can be wrenching if you hold bonds with long maturities. Interest rates also have an impact on stocks and real estate, although it's not as immediate as many investors believe. Rising rates dampen economic growth, but the stock market can continue to climb if the general outlook for the economy and industry remains strong.

Purchasing power risk. In the decade from 1980 to 1990, the increase in the consumer price index averaged 7.9 percent a year. In the same period, CSBs yielded an average 8.9 percent, just a step ahead of inflation. In the ten years from 1981 to 1991, the return from CSBs averaged 9.6 percent while the consumer price index averaged 5.3 percent. But under today's tax laws, this return is fully taxable. Inflation and taxation can have devastating consequences on your ability to build wealth. At the end of the day, if you cannot buy as much as you could have the day before, you've lost money just as surely as if it had fallen out of your pocket. The flip side of the inflation risk is deflation – when the price of tangible goods moves down instead of up, you'll get wealthier by holding long-term bonds.

Business risk. Even if the market for a particular kind of investment is strong, you could lose money if your particular investment was a poor choice. If you don't stick to quality investments, you are deepening the market risks.

You can't eliminate risk, but there are ways of reducing it. You can diversify your investments so you will be protected in different ways. You can stick to quality investments. And you can invest consistently through rising and falling markets.

Finally, temper your expectations with reality. Don't invest in the stock market or real estate if you think you'll need funds within the next couple of years to send your teenagers to college. If you expect overnight miracles, you're bound to be disappointed. To become an intelligent investor you must know how your investments might react over time. The financial world may not unfold exactly as it has for the past thirty years, but hindsight is one of the few guides you have.

One of the best records of historic and recent investment performance is the annual *Investment Returns* report compiled by the economists at investment dealer ScotiaMcLeod Inc.

According to its 1991 report, in the thirty years up to December 1991, the TSE 300 index has risen by an average of 9.60 percent annually, while bonds have returned 8.38 percent. But the investment world is unpredictable. Over the past ten years, bonds have outperformed stocks – 16.81 percent to 9.99 percent. This may be an aberration, forced by an unprecedented federal government monetary policy that took prime interest rates from 12 percent to 18 percent and down again. But it makes decisions difficult. As an investor, should you place your bets on the trend of the past thirty years or the past decade? And despite the emphasis on stocks and bonds, sometimes cash is king. In 1990, investors holding cash in their nervous hands earned a return of 13.48 percent, while the brave souls who stuck to the stock market lost 14.80 percent and those who stayed with bonds earned only 4.32 percent. The year 1991 turned everything around; cash returned 9.83 percent, bonds 25.30 percent and stocks 12.02 percent.

CHAPTER 7

Know Your Investment Soul

WHAT DO YOU WANT YOUR investments to do for you? You can't avoid the question. Fortunately, establishing your goals isn't nearly as complicated as it might seem. You can invest for:

• **Income.** If you want your investments to provide a steady stream of income, your money should be placed in debt securities or stocks that will provide regular payments of interest or dividends.

• **Growth.** If you want to build your wealth and don't need income, you should invest in stocks, real estate or tangibles – investments that will likely rise in value over time.

• **Safety.** Your money is invested for safety if you invest a dollar and you will get a dollar back. Thanks to inflation, it may be worth only ninety-five cents in today's money by the time you get it, but it will still be called a dollar. The only real safety is in cash, GICs, bank and trust company deposits, CSBs and quality bonds or T-bills with short maturities.

• **Liquidity.** This is your ability to sell an investment quickly at a fair price. Stocks and bonds can usually be sold on any business day, but you might take a trouncing if prices are low. Real estate and collectibles can be hard to sell. If you're looking for true liquidity, stick to cash.

Your needs will be slanted toward one of these goals, but in fact most investors need a bit of everything. Even pensioners who must invest for safety have to ensure that their income keeps pace with inflation – and for this they'll need growth. Investors who want to build their wealth will be concerned mostly with growth, but few could stand the risks and volatility of a portfolio containing only equities.

Every investor needs to build a portfolio of investments that will provide the safety, income and growth that he needs financially and feels comfortable with emotionally. To do this you must decide the percentage of funds you want to invest in stocks, bonds and cash – in a ratio known as an asset mix. Popular wisdom says 85 percent of an investor's returns will come from his asset mix, not from the selection of individual securities. It may sound odd, but it makes sense. After all, the most brilliant stock selections will add little kick to your wealth if stocks make up only 10 percent of your portfolio and the bulk of your money is in debt securities that turn out to be dismal performers. Yet even a mediocre stock-picker will enjoy impressive returns if a major chunk of his portfolio is in stocks, almost any stocks, when the market is rising.

The discipline of creating a personal asset mix has become even more appealing since the October 1987 stock market crash as shell-shocked investors take comfort in the strategy as protection against sudden and dramatic downturns. But distortions over the past decade in the relative performance of bonds, stocks and cash has pushed many investors to look for growth in more than one market. Anyone who ignored the bond market because of historically low performance missed the 42 percent return on long-term bonds in 1982. The economic gloom that prevailed in the financial marketplace that year kept most people out of the stock market – and they missed the 35 percent rise in Canadian equities.

In reality, few investors are agile enough to be able to move in and out of the markets quickly enough to catch all the upswings and miss all the crashes. The inability of investors, even professionals, to accurately predict performance, along with the recent divergence from historical rates of returns, has made it foolhardy not to establish a disciplined asset mix.

Your personal investment profile

Knowledge of investments and their inherent risks can lessen the confusion that often hampers financial decisions. But it won't necessarily eliminate your unruly emotions. To create the balanced portfolio that fits your needs, you need to probe your financial and emotional tolerance for risk. In a perfect world, financial and emotional tolerance would dovetail. In reality, you may have to compromise.

How much risk can you afford to take?

The risks in your investment portfolio should reflect your financial well-being. The most obvious evidence of that well-being is your net worth – the difference between what you own and what you owe – your income and your living expenses. If your net worth is ten times your expenses, you can afford to take far more risk than if it is only twice your expenses. Look at your income. If you're barely stretching your money from pay cheque to pay cheque, you're less able to take risks than someone who is able to save great chunks. Don't kid yourself. Even if you're rich, if money flows through your hands like water through a sieve you can't afford to take as many risks as someone of more meagre wealth but a frugal lifestyle. Before you make an investment, ask yourself these questions about your financial health:

- How secure is your job?
- Do you want to be able to convert this investment into cash whenever you like?
- How long do you plan to have this investment?
- How close are you to retirement?
- Do you want to buy a house or send your kids to college in the next few years?
- Do you need income from this investment? How much income?
- Is it important for this investment to grow?
- Would a loss disrupt your lifestyle?
- How much of your income can you save?
- How healthy is your net worth?

Your emotional risk tolerance

Just as there are two extremes of investment goals – income and growth – there are two extremes of investor psychology: the fearless risk-taker and the scared-silly. Probing your emotional tolerance for risk is less scientific than looking at your financial risk tolerance. Let your gut instincts set your threshold of pain after you've studied the various alternatives. You can test your mettle by looking at the returns from stocks and bonds over the past thirty years.

There have been some memorable moments – a 26 percent drop in the stock market in 1974, a 15 percent drop in 1990. The year 1987 was curious – the stock market dropped 31 percent between mid-August and the end of October, but finished the year nearly 6 percent ahead. With this in mind, do a little more probing:

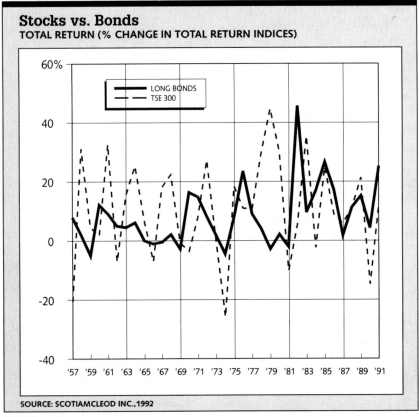

Stocks vs. Bonds
TOTAL RETURN (% CHANGE IN TOTAL RETURN INDICES)

SOURCE: SCOTIAMCLEOD INC.,1992

CHART III

• Would you feel ill if your stock market investments dropped in value by 10 percent or 20 percent or would you screw up your courage and go bargain hunting for cheap stocks?

• Would this investment make you lose sleep?

• Will you have regrets that will keep you muttering to yourself: "If only I'd . . ."?

Most people are acutely unable to predict their reactions to financial risk. Our culture glorifies risk-takers, so people often take too much risk and end up being uncomfortable with their investments. You'll have to go by your gut feel, creating a strategy that seems comfortable, yet matches your needs. You should have a balanced portfolio with equities to provide growth and fixed-income securities to diminish the damage from downturns.

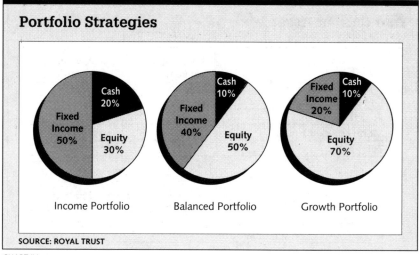

Portfolio Strategies

Income Portfolio   Balanced Portfolio   Growth Portfolio

SOURCE: ROYAL TRUST

CHART IV

One bit of advice for couples who do not share the same investment temperament – create separate portfolios. If you build one
portfolio in an attempt to compromise, you'll both be unhappy.

Never put all your eggs in one basket

Investment gurus have spent decades devising formulas for portfolio strategies. The simplest is one in which you subtract your age
from ninety to calculate the percentage of your portfolio that should
be in equities – a thirty-five-year-old investor would have 65 percent of his portfolio in equities, a seventy-five-year-old would have
only 15 percent of his portfolio in equities.

Although many investors follow this strategy, or a variation of it,
it ignores your investment psyche, lifestyle, responsibilities and
security of income. Financial advisors have recognized the unique
needs of individuals, especially the need among young investors,
for safety of their investments. Royal Trust, for example, has
devised three portfolios – for income, balance or growth – into
which they fit investors after they answer similar questions to those
you've just answered.

These model portfolios can then be juggled for individual clients.
An aggressive investor might go for the growth portfolio and want
more exposure to stocks. The equity portion of his portfolio could
be as high as 80 percent, while fixed-income securities and cash
might account for only 20 percent. An investor looking for income

Your Current Asset Mix

	Dollar Amount in Portfolio	Percentage of Portfolio
Cash		
Canada Savings Bonds		
Treasury bills		
Money market funds		
Total cash		
Fixed income		
G.I.C.s		
Bonds and debentures		
Mortgages		
Mortgage-backed securities		
Preferred shares		
Fixed-income mutual funds		
Total fixed income		
Growth assets		
Equity mutual funds		
Common stocks		
Real estate		
Total growth assets		
VALUE OF YOUR INVESTMENTS		**100%**

WORKSHEET X

and needing more security might have as much as 85 percent in fixed-income investments or cash and only 15 percent in equities. An income portfolio typically fits investors younger than thirty as well as investors close to retirement. A growth portfolio is for investors aged thirty to fifty, and a balanced portfolio for those fifty to sixty.

When you're young, you haven't had time to establish your wealth and your income isn't as secure as it will be once your career is firmly established. You're probably trying to buy a home, you may have a young family and cash is tight. You don't want any more risk. As far as your investment strategy is concerned, the need to build a foundation of CSBs, GICs and debt securities fits neatly with the wisdom of making maximum contributions to your RRSP before you begin to build an investment portfolio outside your re-

Your Desired Asset Mix

	Current % of Portfolio	Desired % of Portfolio
Cash		
Canada Savings Bonds		
Treasury bills		
Money market funds		
Total cash		
Fixed income		
G.I.C.s		
Bonds and debentures		
Mortgages		
Mortgage-backed securities		
Preferred shares		
Fixed-income mutual funds		
Total fixed income		
Growth assets		
Equity mutual funds		
Common stocks		
Real estate		
Total growth assets		
VALUE OF YOUR INVESTMENTS		100%

WORKSHEET XI

tirement plan. If held outside your RRSP, these investments would be hard hit by taxes.

You'll probably be well into your thirties before you have the cash to make hefty investments beyond your RRSP and mortgage – precisely at a time when you have the financial and emotional risk tolerance for a portfolio of equities and real estate. Your aversion to risk will continue to mellow as your wealth and your knowledge grow. As you hit age fifty, you'll have a good core of investments and you will have developed the skills to manage a portfolio. By then, retirement will no longer be a distant dream, so you should begin to take slightly less risk through a balanced portfolio. By the time you're within five years of retirement you should revert back to a more conservative portfolio, since you'll soon need to spend your funds.

Financial experts are split on the impact of a pension on your asset mix. On one side are those who stick to the motto: "If you can achieve your goals without taking any risks, then stick to safety." On the other side are those who believe a good pension gives you the financial room to take risks with your other investments.

This lifecycle strategy of portfolio mix suits most people, although you'll have to refine the formula if your situation differs from the norm. Remember, it's your need for income and safety — more than your age or degree of expertise — that dictates the level of risk you can take. The more risks you have in your life, the less you should have in your investments.

Before devising the portfolio you'd like to have, take a look at the mix of investments you're holding already.

Creating your investment strategy

A portfolio strategy is a melding of fact and emotion. The facts are the historic performance and risks of each investment, along with your financial needs. The emotional side is your risk tolerance. Understand why you're making each investment and how each will react to changes in the economy and financial marketplace. Finally, look at your time horizon.

To devise your portfolio strategy, decide how much of your portfolio you should have in cash as a precaution against unexpected crises and to take advantage of other investment opportunities. Set a minimum level, perhaps 10 percent. If there's a paucity of good investments or the economic outlook is unclear, you might consider raising the percentage slightly. Then establish the minimum level of fixed-income securities you need and the maximum level of growth investments you can tolerate.

Once you've established your desired asset mix, move slowly toward it. If you now hold 100 percent cash, but your mix calls for 60 percent equities, move money into the market over the next six to twelve months. Once your portfolio is established, you'll find your investment decisions come naturally. If the stock market has performed well, you'll have too much of your portfolio in stocks and you'll have to sell — when prices are high — to maintain your proper mix. If stock market performance has been poor, your equities portion will shrink, forcing you to buy — just when prices are low. Sticking to your asset mix creates an automatic discipline that will isolate you from the emotional tug of Mr. Market.

Although you can have a never-changing portfolio that shifts only as your personal circumstances change, professional money managers shuffle their ratio of fixed-income securities to equities within the loose bounds of an established portfolio mix. Carefully monitoring the state of the economy, monetary growth, corporate earnings, interest rates, currency fluctuations and government tax policy, they shift the levels of cash, bonds and stocks to capture the best returns. It's complicated and money managers will usually admit ruefully that they can often be wrong. For that reason, diversification and historical performance remain their guiding principles.

Finally, the technique of hedging your risks through diversification becomes even more complex when real estate and tangibles are stirred into the investment brew. These direct investments – gold, antiques, the little house down the street you rent out – do well during times of inflation. At other times, you'll often find that your stocks and fixed-income securities outperform the tangibles.

CHAPTER 8

To Market, to Market . . .

DESPITE THE WISDOM OF having a well-balanced portfolio, even a perfect investment mix will founder if the individual investments perform poorly. To reduce the risk of loss, you must diversify. Your stocks should embrace many industries and many companies, while your fixed-income securities should consist of investments with varying maturity periods. But you should also look for quality, and there's the rub. Can you select good stocks and buy them at reasonable prices? Can you predict interest rates well enough to pick your own bonds? Even if you have the expertise to look after your portfolio, do you have the time or the inclination? Do you have enough money to buy a variety of stocks and bonds? Do you want to manage your investments or do you want to put them in the hands of an expert?

If you're working with less than $100,000, you should consider mutual funds. A mutual fund pools your money with that of others, putting it to work in a variety of investments under the management of an investment professional. Mutual funds do not invest only in equities. There are funds that invest in bonds, mortgages, real estate and precious metals – and each fund is as individual as the manager who runs it.

If you expect your wealth to grow beyond $100,000, perhaps you should seriously consider creating your own portfolio now. Your mistakes will be less damaging and, as you learn, your investing skills will grow along with your wealth.

You don't have to choose either route over the other. You can invest in a few individual securities and buy mutual funds for diversity. If you've decided to invest half of your portfolio in shares, you could put some of that money into several blue-chip stocks and split the rest among mutual funds. If another 40 percent will be in fixed-income securities, you could buy GICs or term deposits with varied terms, as well as invest in a bond fund and a mortgage fund.

The rest of your funds could be in CSBs, a money market fund and a premium rate savings account.

Financial experts would have you believe the financial markets are a jungle. But don't be railroaded into thinking you can't manage your own investments. You can, if you have the time and the inclination. Just do it judiciously.

Keeping your cash cool

If there's a national investment, it would have to be Canada Savings Bonds. And for good reason: they're easy to cash, they pay a competitive rate of return and they're virtually risk-free. CSBs, first issued in 1946 to replace wartime Victory Bonds, are unlike most other bonds because they can be redeemed any time at face value. You can usually buy CSBs between November first and fifteenth and choose between regular bonds that pay interest each year or CSBs that let interest compound over the life of the bond. (You'll still have to pay the tax on the interest every year even though you don't receive it.)

Treasury bills – another form of debt issued by the federal government – are as safe as CSBs, but they are hardly the place to keep your pin money. In fact, it was not until 1979 that brokers and bankers began to break the $100,000 bills into smaller chunks for individual investors. Even so, most brokerage houses require that you buy at least a $10,000 portion of a T-bill. Banks will sell you a $5,000 share, but fees can knock the wind out of a small bill you intend to hold for only a few months. Technically, T-bills don't pay interest (although Revenue Canada taxes your returns from T-bills as interest). Instead, they're sold at a discount – buyers pay less for the bill than its face value – in maturities of 30 to 364 days. If you wanted to put your money in a ninety-one-day T-bill in late 1992, you would have paid $9,902 for a bill with a face value of $10,000 – which would have provided a 4.25 percent annual rate of return. A $100,000 T-bill would have cost $98,974 for a 4.45 percent annual rate of return.

Money market mutual funds invest in treasury bills, bank certificates of deposit and high-quality commercial paper. Commercial paper refers to loans floated by corporations to raise money they'll need for only a few months. These funds pay attractive interest rates and are often a better deal than ninety-day term deposits or bank T-bill investments. You can usually withdraw your money within twenty-four hours; a few funds offer chequing privileges.

There are also bank and trust company accounts that offer interest rates that track the weekly T-bill rate. To earn this premium rate you must usually have at least $10,000 on deposit. On some of these accounts, you earn no interest at all if your balance falls below the specified minimum.

Keeping your income fixed

One of the most effective ways to manage your fixed-income portfolio is to buy GICs of varying terms that will come due on different dates over a five-year period. To understand this strategy, known as a five-year roll, imagine you have $5,000 to invest in GICs. Instead of investing it all for one term and gambling on interest rates, you split the money into five chunks and invest $1,000 in GICs with terms ranging from one to five years.

Each year, as a certificate matures, you reinvest it in a five-year GIC. This is usually the highest rate but not always – if interest rates are expected to fall, the five-year rate can be the lowest as financial institutions try to discourage you from investing for the long haul. Eventually, all the money will be invested at five-year rates but 20 percent of your investments will mature each year. If you already have money in GICs, consider shifting the mix of maturities until it becomes a five-year roll.

The problem is the paperwork. You can keep track of your staggered GIC investments with a ledger and an accordion file. If you're starting the five-year strategy in 1993, mark file slots with the years 1994 through 1998. Put the GICs in their proper slots, according to the years they mature. If you've adopted the cash management system explained in the budgeting chapter, you could use your three-ring binder and the rear section of the accordion file that holds your paid bills.

As with any other investment, you should shop around before locking your money into GICs or term deposits, especially when others will help you do the shopping for free. Financial planners, stockbrokers and deposit brokers can sift through the rates offered by as many as seventy financial institutions, sometimes unearthing an extra percentage point in interest.

The new look of bonds

Bonds were once considered the investments of widows and orphans – safe and unexciting. But what a difference a decade makes. Every day, billions of dollars in bonds are traded on a frenzied market that jumps to the tune of interest rates. In the past ten years, bond prices have spiralled up and down, creating an environment where aggressive investors must be nimble and nearly omniscient. At the same time, conservative investors can find old-fashioned security in quality bonds that offer regular interest payments.

Investors can choose from a smorgasbord of bonds offered by governments, public utilities and corporations – all rated for quality by the Canadian Bond Rating Service or Dominion Bond Rating Service. For security, investors can't beat Government of Canada bonds, which earn the highest ratings and few investors should look at any bond with less than the top AAA or A++ rating.

Any risk associated with a bond stems from its maturity date and the interest rate, known as the coupon rate, that the issuer has agreed to pay until the bond matures. If you buy a new $1,000 bond that pays 10 percent, you would receive $100 a year in interest. But if interest rates for bonds later rise to 11 percent, and you want to sell your 10 percent bond, investors would not be willing to pay the full $1,000 because they could invest at a higher rate elsewhere. As a result, the price of your bond will drop. If interest rates fall, investors will be willing to pay more than $1,000 for your bond because its interest rate is relatively high. The price of your bond also depends on its quality and the remaining life of the bond. If the bond pays a high rate of interest only for a few months, it won't command nearly as much as a high-interest bond with many years left until maturity.

There are two ways of computing the yield of a bond: current yield and yield to maturity. Current yield is the interest you receive divided by the market value of the bond. The yield to maturity takes into account the interest the bond will pay, the days to maturity and the redemption value of the bond.

Before buying any corporate bond you should know whether it's callable – redeemable by the issuer before maturity. If it is, and interest rates drop, the issuer could force you to redeem your bond early. You'll then be left holding cash at a time of declining rates. Your bond may also be convertible to the company's common stock, making its price even more prone to fluctuation but giving you the privilege to trade the bond for shares that may have appreciated in value. With most bonds, you must decide where to invest the interest you receive each year. But if you buy what's known as a strip bond, you won't have this problem. Strip bonds have evocative names like Cougars and TIGRS but are usually bought for RRSPs and RESPs. A strip bond is a Government of Canada bond that has been "stripped" of its coupons. You can buy the residual bond or the individual coupons, which give you the interest payments. The residual bond is sold at a discount to the face value. For example, in September 1992 a $5,000 bond maturing in 2013 was selling for $788.50 providing a 8.95 percent semi-annual yield. When the bond matures you'll receive the full face value, but in the meantime you're not paid any interest.

Mortgage-backed securities

A newcomer to the fixed-income market is the mortgage-backed security, a pool of residential mortgages issued by banks and trust companies. For as little as $5,000, you can buy a share of that pool. Most MBSs are fully guaranteed by the federal government and offer a yield that has hovered just above that of Government of Canada bonds.

The income you receive from an MBS is a mirror image of your own mortgage. As each homeowner makes his monthly mortgage payment, you get a stream of income that is a blend of principal and interest. Over the five-year term of the investment, you'll get back about 6 percent of your principal – when the security matures, you'll get about $4,700 for every $5,000 you've invested.

But the income from a mortgage-backed security can fluctuate. If interest rates drop, homeowners might pay off their mortgages more quickly, thereby providing more income than you might want. You'll face the problem of reinvesting the extra income at lower rates (although you could use it to dollar-cost average into an equity mutual fund). There is a reasonably strong secondary market for an MBS, but if you should decide to sell before maturity you'll find the price is greatly affected by interest rate fluctuations.

Preferred shares

Preferred shares are stocks that act like bonds. They provide a steady, predictable income by paying a dividend – usually expressed as a fixed rate of return – that seldom changes. Although preferred shares were popular in the late 1970s and early 1980s, when their after-tax dividend yield was often better than that of a comparable bond, preferred shares have lost much of their appeal as a result of changing tax laws. Preferred shares react to interest rates with a vengeance, since they are essentially perpetual bonds. You can protect yourself by buying retractable preferreds, which allow you to redeem your shares on a specified date at a specified price. You can also buy convertible preferreds, which allow you to convert your stock into another type of share – often a company's common stock.

Shopping for stocks

When you buy common stock, your chances for capital gains and income depend on the company's future prosperity. If the company does well, the price of its shares, and perhaps the dividends paid, are likely to rise.

But how can you predict what will happen in the future? You can't, unless you carefully analyse the prospects of the company and its industry. When selecting a stock, look at the investment with the eye of an executive. Does the company have solid management and a healthy balance sheet? What are the prospects for the industry? Is the company an industry leader? Does it have a special market niche? Look at the company's sales, earnings per share and dividend record. Consider some of the ratios used as yardsticks by the brokerage industry – among them the price-to-book-value ratio and the price-to-earnings ratio. These "fundamentals" can be gleaned from a company's annual and quarterly reports, from newspaper articles and through a call to the investor relations department of the company.

One of the richest sources of free information is your broker's research department. Large brokerage houses turn out hundreds of reports a year, ranging from lengthy economic forecasts to one-page synopses of industries and individual stocks. These are written in a manner that allows an investor to pick up a report and get a feel for the industry dynamics affecting a company, where a company fits within its industry and the outlook for a firm. In addition, most brokerage houses produce a series of reports each year on the outlook for the economy and the equity markets.

This type of evaluation is known as fundamental analysis. Another stock evaluation technique is known as technical analysis. Technical analysts spend their time poring over graphs and charts of share prices and trading volumes looking for such phenomena as watersheds, crumbling barriers, megaphone bottoms and saucer tops. These analysts believe the values of stocks rise and fall in a pattern that is largely unrelated to the social or economic conditions of the real world. They can be eerily accurate in retrospect, but as a dependable forecasting tool for the average investor, technical analysis has limited use.

Confused? Don't be. Intelligent investing is 10 percent numbers and 90 percent common sense. Don't underestimate your ability to sense the wisdom or folly of an investment after you've studied the company. To hone your common sense, give yourself time to learn by experience. You should also read a few of the classics of investment advice: *The Battle for Investment Survival* by Gerald Loeb, *The Intelligent Investor* by Benjamin Graham and *My Own Story* by Bernard Baruch, a man who amassed a fortune as a Wall Street broker. There are more recent guides as well: *A Random Walk Down Wall Street* by Burton Malkiel, *Winning On Wall Street* by Martin Zweig and *The Money Masters* by John Train.

You can become a successful investor if you follow a few rules:
• Invest in a diversity of stocks. You don't need many — perhaps as few as ten — but they should be in several different industries that are exposed to different economic and political risks.
• Do your own homework and research. You should have a clear and simple reason for buying a company's stock.
• Don't lose patience. If your reason for buying a stock is sound, and there isn't any cause to change your opinion, give your investment time. If you dash in and out of the market, only your broker will get rich.
• Don't be reluctant to take a loss. If a stock is down, take another look at your reasons for owning it. Decide whether to keep it, sell it or buy more.
• If you haven't the time or the inclination for the work required to choose your own investments, buy mutual funds or hire an investment counsellor.

Putting your money into bricks and mortar

Real estate has a certain allure not found in other investments. Perhaps it's the thrill that lingers from buying Boardwalk or Park Place when you played Monopoly as a child. Maybe it's the satisfaction of being able to touch your investment – to run your hand down the bricks or sit under a tree on your own land.

Real estate isn't a paper certificate like a stock or a bond, it's tangible. But investing in real estate is never simple. Although it's proven to be one of the best hedges against inflation, it's almost never an armchair investment. Before you decide to become a landlord and buy a house or small apartment building, ask yourself whether you're ready to deal with tenants and their late-night phone calls demanding that the toilet be unplugged. Are you willing to screen prospective tenants by checking references and employers? If playing the role of landlord isn't appealing, you might want to purchase a building with the intention of fixing it up and selling it at a profit – just be sure you're prepared to get your hands dirty or pay somebody to do the work.

Whether renting or renovating, ensure your profit by buying at a price that will allow you to make money even if housing prices and rents remain static. Make sure the building will bring in enough money to more than cover your costs, or it could bleed you dry.

The most serious hurdle for individuals who want to invest in real estate is the cost. To eliminate this barrier, since the early 1970s, apartment buildings, shopping plazas, hotels and office towers have all been packaged by real estate middlemen in bite-sized chunks for investors lacking the savvy or funds to do business in the big leagues. Syndicates can take several legal forms, but the most common is a limited partnership. A real estate expert, the syndicator, selects a piece of real estate and sells it to investors in chunks as small as $2,500, but usually closer to $100,000 or $150,000. In theory, investors, as limited partners, put up their money and wait for the profits to roll in. Reality can be painfully different. The history of real estate syndications is littered with corporate and personal bankruptcies. To avoid staggering losses you must be familiar with the nuts and bolts of your investment. Syndications are so complex that even professionals find them difficult to judge. Start by asking these questions:

• What is the track record of the syndicator and the general manager of the property? Are they investing in the syndication too?

• Is the property in a good location? Has it been well maintained or will poor plumbing, wiring and heating cause repair expenses?

• Are you paying a reasonable price for the property?

• Will the rental income cover your maintenance and financing costs?

• Who are the tenants and are they likely to stay?

• What guarantees do you have? Are they solid? The natural risks of real estate investing – such as construction costs, the time it takes to lease a building and the break-even on cash flow – should all be covered by guarantees backed by bank letters of credit.

• Is your risk limited to your original investment or can you be forced to contribute more to cover repairs, vacancies or cash shortages?

• Even if you're not forced to put more money into the property, would you have the cash to put more in if it were needed to keep the investment afloat?

Investors who are unwilling to enter into a complex limited partnership can still get a piece of big-league action through real estate mutual funds. Just as their equity or bond fund cousins invest in a diversity of securities, real estate funds invest in properties across Canada.

Although investors were jaded by the near-demise in 1984 of Real Property Trust, the pioneer of real estate funds, real estate funds performed reasonably well over the three years to the end of 1988. But performance varies dramatically from fund to fund and the problems that plagued investors in Real Property Trust – over-valued properties and an inability to quickly redeem shares – remain. Although real estate values are arrived at by independent appraisers, they're still based on personal judgments of what the properties are worth. Over the past five years two funds suspended redemptions while their portfolios were reappraised. In 1992, a third fund suspended redemptions because of liquidity problems. At the best of times, these funds are less liquid than others. Where most other funds are valued daily or weekly, real estate funds are usually valued monthly or quarterly.

Capital gains from the sale of real estate fund units or shares will continue to be eligible for the $100,000 lifetime capital gains exemption, despite the fact that real estate itself no longer qualifies.

Climbing aboard the mutual fund bandwagon

Mutual funds, also called investment funds, have mined a mother lode of savings in the past decade. By September 1992 Canadians had ploughed close to $70 billion into close to 700 mutual funds in the search for diversification and professional investment management. Just over a decade ago there were only 198 mutual funds managing $5.9 billion. With the proliferation of funds, it may be difficult to find those that meet your needs. Before you hand over your hard-earned cash to a fund, you would be wise to find the answers to these questions:

Who manages the fund? Most funds have teams of analysts who study the economy and search out investments. But the final decision often rests with the fund manager. The performance of many funds depends almost entirely on this person's investment acumen. If he or she leaves the fund, its track record becomes almost irrelevant.

Fund managers do move around, and keeping tabs on who's running a fund is just as important as historic performance. You'll have to ask. Funds don't trumpet the loss of a top-flight manager.

How is the fund invested? Funds fall into six broad categories:

1. Money market funds invest in treasury bills, corporate paper, bankers' acceptances and certificates of deposit.

2. Fixed-income funds invest only in interest-bearing securities. Mortgage funds invest in pools of first mortgages on Canadian residential real estate and occasionally commercial and industrial mortgages. Bond funds invest in bonds and debentures issued by federal, provincial and municipal governments, utilities and private companies. There are also funds that invest in a mix of mortgages and bonds.

3. Equity funds invest almost exclusively in common stocks. Some funds stick to blue-chip stocks to provide investors with stable growth and income, while others seek out young companies in developing industries that offer unusual growth potential. You

can also buy funds that invest in companies around the world or target specific countries, like Korea or Japan.

4. Real estate funds invest in commercial real estate such as office buildings, retirement homes, shopping malls and apartment complexes.

5. Balanced funds invest in stocks, mortgages, bonds and the money market.

6. Specialty funds concentrate on narrow areas of investment. You'll find funds that invest in such industries as oil and gas, mining, food and high technology. There are funds that invest solely in gold and gold mining companies, others that invest only in convertible debentures. There are mutual funds that invest only in companies that meet certain moral criteria and shun the likes of cigarette-makers, distillers, armament manufacturers and companies with reputations as polluters.

How has the fund performed? *Financial Times of Canada* publishes a monthly survey of mutual funds that tracks returns for periods ranging from one month to ten years. A more comprehensive survey is published in the *Financial Times* in January and July tracking the year-over-year performance of funds over the past twelve years. These surveys can be used to select funds you want to examine more closely. Look at how specific funds have performed in years of poor stock market performance as well as in good years.

Table III on the next page looks at the average compound performance of different groups of mutual funds over the past ten years. Although useful as an indication of the performance of different types of funds, it is imperative that you look at the annual and compound performance of the individual mutual fund in which you are tempted to invest.

How volatile is the fund? If you pay attention only to average returns and ignore the volatility of a fund, you may find yourself on a roller coaster ride. Use the *Financial Times* survey to assess variances in funds' performances using two different measures. The variability is a measure of the how different the fund's performance has been from month to month over the past thirty-six months: a high number indicates the fund's performance swings widely, a low number means its performance is steady. The percentile ranking rates funds within their own groups: Canadian equity funds are

Average Performance for Mutual Fund Groups

	Total Assets ($ millions)	Mgm. Expense Ratio	1 Yr. Return	—— Compound return ——			
				2 Yr.	3 Yr.	5 Yr.	10 Yr.
Equity funds							
Canadian	$15,170	$2.02	2.4	2.4	0.7	1.0	1.2
U.S.	52	2.04	11.9	7.7	8.3	4.1	12.8
International	119	2.36	11.7	2.6	4.9	1.0	14.2
Real estate	98	2.30	0.6	1.9	4.8	7.1	5.9
Fixed-income funds							
Bond	8,434	1.62	17.3	14.3	10.6	9.9	13.2
Mortgage	439	1.56	12.2	13.2	12.0	10.6	12.2
Bond and mortgage	82	1.60	15.4	13.9	10.0	9.9	13.3
Money market	157	0.95	7.1	9.1	9.8	9.6	9.7
Balanced funds	8,955	1.93	9.5	8.3	6.1	5.5	12.4

Performance is expressed as a percent change over periods ending June 30, 1992. The management expense ratio expresses the expenses, including management fee, charged by the mutual fund per $100 of assets under management. The total assets in the first column are the assets under management by all of the funds in the survey. The figures in the remaining columns represent the average performance of the funds in each category.

SOURCE: SOUTHAM INFORMATION & TECHNOLOGY GROUP

TABLE III

compared to other Canadian equity funds, bond funds to other bond funds. A fund with a ranking of five would be less volatile than 95 percent of the funds in that group and more volatile than 4 percent.

Is the fund part of a family? If you want to shift your investments as market conditions or your personal situation change, you'll probably find it convenient to buy shares in a mutual fund that is part of a family of funds. For example, AGF Management Ltd. offers fifteen funds, Mackenzie Financial Corp. has twenty-two (most of those within the Industrial family), Royal Trust Co. has eighteen funds and there are eighteen funds within the Guardian Group of Funds. You can often move your money easily among fixed-income, equity, foreign, specialty and money market funds. Some companies don't charge for switching, others charge a flat $15 or $20 or as much as 2 percent of the value of the funds being moved.

Will you have to pay a sales fee? You may have to pay a sales commission when you buy into a fund or when you sell your shares. An up-front fee is known as a front-end load; the selling fee is called a back-end load. Some funds give you an option – you can pay when you buy or later, when you sell. No-load funds don't charge sales commissions. Regardless of the fee structure, performance and investment objectives should be your main criteria when considering a fund. Invest in funds that meet your needs, whether they charge sales fees or not. Also consider your need for ongoing advice. If you want the advice of a broker, be willing to pay for it through commissions. Even so, negotiate if you're buying a front-end load fund. You could save as much as 4 percent or 5 percent.

Every mutual fund charges for management expenses. This charge covers all of the expenses of running the fund – from the straightforward costs of staffing an office and buying paper to the fees charged for managing the portfolio and paying brokerage fees. Sometimes this is charged to the fund and will be reported in the financial statements as the management expense ratio. Other funds charge the management expense fee directly to the investor, sometimes deducting it from distributions, sometimes charging it to the investor's accounts.

How quickly can you sell? Some mutual funds value their assets every day, while others do it weekly, monthly or even quarterly. Be aware that you may have to wait for a valuation date to redeem you shares. Some funds are just slow in completing the paperwork necessary before you get your cash. If you need to be able to get your money quickly, don't invest in a fund that will make you wait.

Time and money

When Benjamin Franklin wrote that money makes money, and the money that money makes makes more money, he captured the essence of a simple concept that can have dazzling results – compound interest. Interest compounds when you leave the income earned on an investment to earn still more interest. Over time, your money mushrooms. Invest $1,000 at 10 percent and after a year you'll have $1,100. But that $1,100 will earn $110 the second year, giving you $1,210. After three years you'll have $1,331, and after ten years you'll have $2,594. The money compounds more quickly with each passing year and after another five years, you'll have $4,177.

You don't have to chip in more money, just let the interest payments stay invested so you can earn interest on the interest, as well as on the original sum.

Compounding works with many investments, not just those that pay interest. With stocks, you can use dividends to buy more shares. Many companies offer dividend reinvestment plans that allow you to purchase shares without having to pay commissions to a broker. Taking advantage of these schemes can dramatically boost your returns – which can easily be seen by comparing two Toronto Stock Exchange performance indices. Typically, share price movements reported on the TSE 300 reflect only the share prices of 300 stocks. But the TSE total returns index records performance of the same stocks with dividends reinvested. In 1991, the TSE 300 rose 7.84 percent while the total return index rose 12.02 percent. On the other hand, in 1990, the TSE composite index fell 17.96 percent but the TSE total return index fell only 14.79 percent.

Buying into good times and bad

Every investor who has ventured beyond the comfort of CSBs has at one time or another been caught up in the emotions of the marketplace. It never fails. Stock prices are half-heartedly emerging from the doldrums, edging up unconvincingly. You wait, along with most investors, until the market seems poised to climb forever, before plunging in – just as prices peak. Prices then begin to tumble endlessly and you sell in exasperation, right at the bottom.

You can isolate yourself from these swings by investing regularly, whether the market is heading up or down. This investment strategy is called dollar-cost averaging. With dollar-cost averaging, you invest a fixed sum of money at regular intervals, usually every month or every three months. By investing a set amount, you'll be able to buy more stocks when prices hit rock bottom and you'll buy fewer stocks when prices are high, resulting in a low average cost for shares. Dollar-cost averaging isolates you from market psychology, economic bafflegab and interest rate guessing. It is one of the most powerful tools for building wealth, and it's easy to use. Almost every mutual fund allows you to dollar-cost average, usually through pre-authorized cheques of as little as $50 a month.

But be warned: dollar-cost averaging works only if you're consistent. It's tough to fight your instinct to sell, instead of buy, when

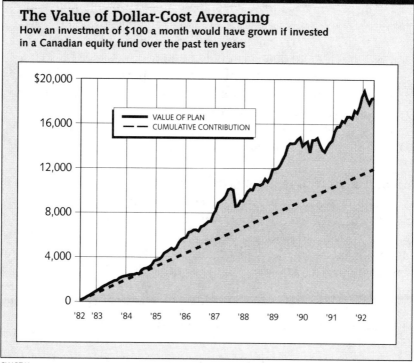

The Value of Dollar-Cost Averaging
How an investment of $100 a month would have grown if invested in a Canadian equity fund over the past ten years

VALUE OF PLAN
CUMULATIVE CONTRIBUTION

CHART V

prices are falling. But if you lose your nerve and stop dollar-cost averaging, you'll defeat the strategy.

Leverage: Risk versus reward

The thrill of leverage is familiar to anyone who has ever sat on a teeter-totter with the heaviest child in the playground perched on the other end. The closer to the edge you sit, and the heavier the other child, the faster and farther you fly upward. When an investor leverages, he borrows money to boost his investment returns. Leveraging can dramatically increase gains from a good investment, but if your investment slips, your losses can be disastrous.

Investors who leverage should be experienced, aggressive and able to sleep well at night despite the risks. If you must leverage, go into it with your eyes open. If you put $5,000 of your own money into an investment and it rises in value by 5 percent, you end up with $5,250. If it falls in value by 5 percent, you will lose $250. If, on the other hand, you take the $5,000, borrow an additional

$95,000, and invest the $100,000 in an investment that rises in value by 5 percent, you end up with $105,000 (less any interest costs for the borrowed money). Once you've paid back the $95,000 you're left with $10,000, a gain of 100 percent instead of 5 percent. But let's flip the coin. If your $100,000 investment declines by 5 percent, you'll be left with only $95,000 – all the money you owe. You'll have lost your entire $5,000. And if your investment drops in value by 10 percent, your loss is $10,000. You would then be $5,000 in the hole with nothing left to dig yourself out.

Measure your investment performance

You cannot possibly know whether your financial plan is succeeding if you don't measure how well, or badly, your investments are faring. Your yield will depend on your portfolio's structure, but there are bench marks you can use. If you invest in bonds, you could compare your returns to those of the ScotiaMcLeod Inc. bond index. If you have a diversified stock portfolio, compare it to the TSE 300 composite index. A portfolio of foreign stocks could be measured against *Financial Times of London* index in Britain or the Nikkei index in Japan.

The only way to measure your performance and keep track of your investments is to keep meticulous records. If you trade individual stocks, buy an alphabetized accordion file or a small file in which you can keep documents relating to each stock. Staple the buy and sell confirmation slips together for each stock and keep a ledger to record dividend payments. Your broker will give you a summary of the dividends from the stocks you've bought through his firm. If you hold on to your stock certificates instead of leaving them with a broker, an annual tally will be sent to you by the companies themselves.

Keys to successful investing

Investing successfully takes knowledge, a strategy, discipline and a tolerance for ups and downs. You must also decide whether you want to be a passive investor or an active investor. If you want to select individual securities and you have the time and inclination to do your homework, consider yourself an active investor. If you choose to be actively involved, it will mean conducting research. You'll have to read the annual and quarterly reports sent to you by the companies in which you hold shares. You'll have to read your broker's research reports and the financial newspapers. You'll have to monitor economic conditions and the forces that drive your investments. These are complex tasks, but don't be intimidated. If you're diligent, you'll find that managing your own investments is emotionally and financially rewarding.

On the other hand, don't feel guilty if you'd rather be a passive investor. You may not have the time or the inclination to manage your own investments, but it remains critical that you adhere to the cardinal rules of intelligent investing. As much as you might want to, you cannot relinquish responsibility for your money. You must know the market, set your investment strategy and take the time to find an investment manager. Whether you're looking for a mutual fund manager or an investment counsellor, the search should be undertaken with care.

No matter what kind of investor you choose to be, it pays to heed these simple rules:

- Know the market and yourself.
- Diversify to reduce your risks.
- Create an investment strategy and stick to it. Realize that your investments will not always be profitable. Always know the worst that can happen so you can act with confidence if an investment begins to sour. Your losses will only be exacerbated by panic.
- Be tolerant of your mistakes; even the most highly respected market experts can be wrong. In the summer of 1987, of 102 market gurus questioned by the American investment journal *Barron's*, only 5 percent predicted there would be a crash. Your aim is to be right more often than wrong, and to never make a mistake from which you can't recover.
- Read the financial press to stay informed of economic conditions, but avoid kneejerk reactions to the day's news.
- Understand how your investments will react to market and economic gyrations.
- Never buy an investment you don't understand and never hesitate to ask questions.
- Keep accurate records.
- Seek the advice of financial experts, but be discerning.

Successful investing is part art, part imprecise science made more difficult by the emotional baggage tied to the pursuit of wealth. The financial marketplace will continue to wind its way through both good times when investors are confident and prices are rising – the bull markets – and through bad times, when investors are pessimistic and prices are falling – the bear markets. Money will continue to be made by people who are patient. It's a marketplace rife with tired clichés but there is one that is especially pungent: "Bears make money and bulls make money but pigs just get slaughtered." There's a second cliché you shouldn't forget: "If an investment has to work out, it won't."

CHAPTER 9

Planning for Financial Independence

THE DREAM OF FINANCIAL independence hooks us all. To some, being financially self-sufficient means having the money and the time to explore the world's natural wonders and drift into its exotic corners. To others, it means fishing all summer long, studying astronomy, restoring an old farmhouse or puttering around the garden all day. Financial independence may mean a relaxing retirement or the freedom to put your entrepreneurial skills to work at your own business without worrying about the financial consequences if your enterprise fails.

Financial independence is your ultimate destination. The day will come when you stop working – you'll either reach the age at which your employer says you must retire or you'll just want to get off the treadmill. You could spend twenty-five to thirty years in retirement, almost a third of your life. To avoid pinching pennies during all that time you need a lifetime strategy of saving and investing.

Don't delay. If you put off your retirement planning you make it much tougher to build enough wealth to be comfortable in your life after work. Not only will you have to save a bigger chunk of your income each year; the range of investment choices suitable for you will dwindle the longer you wait.

How much should you save each year?

Saving for retirement, or financial independence, can take a hefty chunk of your income. Obviously, time is critical. If you begin to save for retirement when you're thirty, you need to save only 18 percent of your income. Wait until you're forty-five and you'll have to save nearly a third of every dollar you earn. The cost of the delay is not just the money not saved, but the compounding growth you'll miss. When you're building wealth, the last few years are the

How Much Money Do You Have to Save Each Year?

To retire at age	You must save this percentage of your income every year if you start at age:						
	20	25	30	35	40	45	50
60	19	22	25	30	38		
65	14	16	18	21	25	31	
70	10	11	13	15	17	20	25

This assumes your salary increases by 2% more than inflation each year and your savings can be invested to earn a return 2% above inflation in a pension or an RRSP. This will build a pool of capital that will provide you with a stream of income equal to half the salary you earn just prior to retirement and will keep pace with inflation after you retire.

SOURCE: FRANK RUSSELL OF CANADA LTD.

TABLE IV

ones that really count – the years when compounding gives you the greatest gains.

Someone thirty-five years old who is planning to retire at age sixty-five would have $122,346 in an RRSP by the time he retires if he begins to save $1,000 a year immediately and invests it at 8 percent. If he delays five years he'll have only $78,954. That's a difference of $43,392 at age sixty-five but only $5,000 difference in the contributions made when he's young.

Inherently, every financial move you make, or fail to make, will have an impact on your retirement. A penny you spend today is a dime you won't have when you're retired. But there are children to raise, homes to buy, mountains to climb. How much can you spend today and how much do you have to save for the future? Roughly, once you hit forty, you should be putting away around 20 percent of your income for retirement. If you're older and have little saved or if you want to retire early, you'd better hustle.

Taking advantage of government help

Perhaps prodded by the spectre of a poor, white-haired nation by the year 2000, the federal government has over the past decade reformed our pension and tax systems. The notion of "old age security" has been buried and responsibility for your future welfare has been dumped in your lap.

You've been given unprecedented freedom and tax breaks to assist in amassing enough wealth to retire comfortably. But it's critical

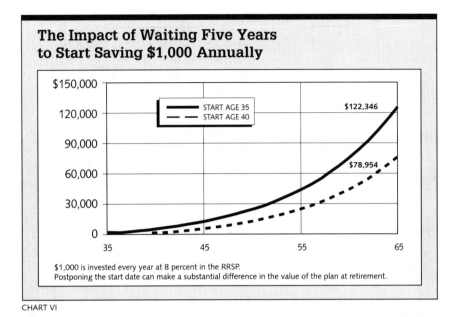

The Impact of Waiting Five Years to Start Saving $1,000 Annually

START AGE 35
START AGE 40

$122,346

$78,954

$1,000 is invested every year at 8 percent in the RRSP.
Postponing the start date can make a substantial difference in the value of the plan at retirement.

CHART VI

that you use this freedom well. If you have a patchwork of RRSP "investments" bought in the fever pitch of February, it's your responsibility to turn them into an organized investment portfolio that will buy the lifestyle you will want during retirement. And if you think pensions are a yawn, wake up. Dust off those benefits brochures and find out just what you can expect from your employer when your career ends.

How does pension reform affect you?

Pension reform has been coming down the track since 1976 with all the speed of a freight train moving slowly through a rail yard, waiting for its cars to be shunted on ten different tracks. The first nine tracks are the laws that govern the quality of pensions – the pension standards acts of the federal government and eight provinces. The last track is the Income Tax Act, federal legislation that governs pension and RRSP contributions.

Your employer isn't required to have a pension plan. But if there is a plan, it must meet certain standards. Except in the two provinces without pension acts, Prince Edward Island and British Columbia, every pension is governed by federal or provincial legislation. (British Columbia passed its first pension benefits act, based closely on Alberta's, in June 1991. Some provisions were effective in 1991 but it will not take full effect until January 1, 1993. Prince Edward Island passed its first pension benefits act in April 1990. The targeted proclamation date is January 1, 1993, with the legislation effective one year later. It is modelled on the Nova Scotia and Ontario legislation.)

The federal Pension Benefits Standards Act covers more than one million Canadians who work for the federal government and any company that is federally regulated – primarily those in the banking, communications and transportation industries. All other employers are covered by the pension acts of the provinces. Although Ottawa and the jurisdictions with reformed pension acts have each introduced their own peculiarities, all pension reforms embrace the same basic principles. Under these reforms:

- You must be allowed to join your employer's pension plan after two years if you earn roughly $9,000 or more each year.
- You will no longer have to wait until you've reached age forty-five and worked ten years for your employer before the plan is vested – the point at which you have the right to your employer's contributions. In Alberta and New Brunswick, for example, pensions must vest after five years of employment. In Nova Scotia and Ontario, and for plans covered by federal legislation, pension benefits are vested after you've been a member of the plan for two years.
- Your employer must pay for at least half of your pension benefit.
- If you change jobs after your benefits are vested, you have far more flexibility than under previous pension laws. You can leave the money in your old employer's plan until retirement, move it into your new employer's plan or transfer it into a special kind of RRSP where the funds are locked in until converted into an annuity at retirement.
- Men and women will receive the same pension benefits, except in Alberta, where women still receive a lower monthly income.
- If your marriage breaks down, your plan must allow you to split your pension credits according to provincial legislation dealing with matrimonial property.
- You can retire as early as age fifty-five and receive a pension, or you can work longer and retire with increased pension benefits.

Although these pension reforms go a long way toward removing some of the inadequacies of the past, many pensions will remain stingy and many people will continue to work for employers who don't offer pension plans. And, of course, many people live in provinces where pension reform has not taken place yet. This is where tax reform steps in.

When and how RRSP rules are changing

Income tax reform affects every working Canadian and when it comes to retirement, it is these reforms that put all of us on a more even footing. If you belong to a stingy pension plan at work you'll have more room to shelter money in an RRSP. If you have a generous pension plan, you'll have less room for RRSP contributions.

Income tax reform has been as painfully slow as pension reform. The latest laws governing contributions to pension plans and RRSPs were drafted in 1984, but implementation was delayed five times in five years. When Bill C-52 received royal assent in June 1990, most of the changes to registered retirement savings plan rules that had been promised for years were passed and came into effect for the 1991 taxation year.

Under the new rules your contribution limit is 18 percent of your earned income to a maximum contribution of $12,500 for 1992 and 1993, $13,500 for 1994 and $14,500 for 1995 and $15,500 for 1996. Thereafter, the limit will rise with wage inflation, as reflected by the average industrial wage. If you don't belong to a pension plan, you can pop the entire contribution limit into an RRSP. Your contribution must be made in the taxation year or within sixty days of year-end to get a deduction for the tax year. If you are a member of a pension plan, your allowable RRSP contributions will be reduced by a "pension adjustment" based on the contribution made to your plan by you and/or your employer during the year and by past service pension adjustments. Your employer will be required to report your pension adjustment on your T4 slip each spring and Revenue Canada will issue individual statements toward the end of each year informing you of your contribution limit for that tax year. (As mentioned in chapter three, there have been errors in the pension adjustments. If your statement doesn't seem right, speak to your payroll department.)

There are a few special circumstances. Taxpayers who leave their jobs and lose their employer's contribution to their pension plan, can contribute 18 percent of their income to an RRSP, up to the maximum, as long as they don't join another pension plan to which an employer will contribute. Employees with paid-up pensions to which deposits are no longer being made by the employer can also contribute up to 18 percent of their income to the maximum.

There's another significant change. Beginning in 1991, your contribution limit is based on your previous year's earnings, rather than income in the current tax year. For the 1990 tax year, your contribution was based on your 1990 earned income; in 1991 your RRSP contribution was based on your 1990 income and your 1992 contribution will be based on your 1991 income. (As a result, you will be able to make an RRSP contribution in your first year of retirement even if you have no earned income. The contribution will be based on your income in the last year at work.)

There are two other significant changes – the carry-forward provision (discussed in chapter three) and the ability to overcontribute to your RRSP by as much as $8,000. You can leave the overcontribution in your RRSP or deduct it in future years. For example, you can make your maximum contribution for 1992 and contribute an extra $8,000. In 1993, if your contribution limit is $12,500 but you only have $4,500, you can deduct the full $12,500 – $4,500 plus the $8,000 contributed in 1992. The advantage of over-contributing is that the investment can grow without the earnings being taxed. However, when it's withdrawn, it will be fully taxed as RRSP income. Since you can't deduct the overcontribution when it's made, you will end up being taxed twice on the same money – once when you earn it and once when you withdraw it from your RRSP.

Over-contributing without penalty is allowed by Revenue Canada to protect you from mistakes. Unless you intend to use an over-contribution as a deduction in the future or can leave it in your RRSP for more than fifteen or twenty years you should use it exactly as the government intended – as a safety cushion.

Questions to ask about your pension

When it comes to your pension, don't leave yourself in the dark. Your company's benefits manager can fill you in on any details you lack. Shuffle through your dusty files. The pension brochure you were given on your first day at work has to be there somewhere. Don't think your future is secure just because you have a pension plan. Some pensions will provide little more than pocket money. Read your pension brochure and then call your benefits manager. Ask the following questions, devised by David Chalmers and Jim

Omelus, financial planners with the James E. Rogers Group in Vancouver:

1. What kind of pension plan do I have?

Pension plans come in two varieties: defined-benefit plans and defined-contribution plans.

Defined benefit plans guarantee a pension that will reflect your earnings and the number of years you've worked for an employer. If there isn't enough money in the fund to cover your promised pension, the employer must make up the shortfall. About 95 percent of pension plan members belong to defined-benefit plans.

Making retirement plans won't be quite as easy if your company provides a money purchase pension plan, also known as a defined-contribution plan. Under this plan you and your employer each invest a percentage of your salary every year. When you retire, the money will be used to buy an annuity. It's difficult to predict what your pension from this plan will be, and it is critical that the money in the plan be invested well. A money purchase plan is much like an RRSP, but unlike your personal retirement savings plan, your pension fund is covered by the Pension Act, not by the Income Tax Act.

2. What formula is used to calculate my benefit from a defined-benefit plan?

Most employers use one of three different formulas:

Flat benefit. These plans pay a flat monthly income that is tied only to your years of work and not to your wages. If the benefit is $25 a month and you've been working for twenty years, you'll get a pension income of $500 a month, whether you've been earning $25 an hour or $5.

Career average benefit. These plans take into account earnings over your career. The formula used for calculating benefits is usually a percentage of your average earnings multiplied by the number of years you've worked for your employer. The most generous pensions will give you 2 percent of your earnings, the more miserly only 1 percent. If you launched your career as a clerk at $23 a week and end your working days as company president at $100,000 a year, your pension income will be reduced by those early years of low pay. If your average earnings were $15,000 over thirty years in a 2 per cent plan, your annual pension would be $9,000 (2 percent of $15,000, multiplied by thirty).

Final average benefit. The benefits formula employed by these plans is based on a percentage of your earnings multiplied by the number of years you've worked for the company. But instead of taking your entire career into account, only your average earnings over a certain number of years are considered – usually the three or five years before you retire. These are the best-paying plans, but you could still suffer a sharp drop in income when you leave work. Suppose you've been working for the same company for the past thirty years and you earn $45,000 in the year before you retire. You've had a couple of good raises in the last few years, so your average over the last five years is closer to $35,000. If you belong to a 2 per cent plan, your pension would be $21,000 (2 percent of $35,000, multiplied by thirty years). That's a 53 percent drop in income.

3. Will my pension keep pace with inflation?
The pensions of civil servants, teachers and university professors often rise with the cost of living, but the enrichment of private pensions is more often at the discretion of your employer.

4. Is my pension integrated with the Canada Pension Plan?
Sometimes your company will reduce your monthly pension by the amount you receive from the CPP. In other cases, you'll receive CPP benefits on top of your full pension.

5. What happens if I retire early?
If you retire early, you will get a lower pension for the rest of your life. After all, you'll have worked for fewer years and contributed less to the plan. In addition, you'll be collecting for a longer period. To calculate your benefit the pension manager uses the same formula he would use to calculate your full pension and then reduces the resulting amount by a certain percentage – often 5 to 10 percent – for each year of early retirement. Therefore, if you retire at age sixty-three you would receive only 80 percent of the pension you would have at sixty-five. If you retire at sixty you would get only 50 percent.

6. What are my retirement income options?

You can usually choose from pensions that will pay only for your lifetime, for the lifetime of both you and your spouse, or for your lifetime(s) with a guarantee for at least ten or fifteen years of payments (even if your death(s) occurs within that guarantee period.) The more guarantees and survivor benefits you choose, the less money you'll receive each month. If you are married and choose an option that leaves less than a 60 percent benefit to your spouse, he or she will have to sign a waiver indicating that the implications of your choice are understood and acceptable.

7. What happens if I quit before I retire? What do I get back?

Under non-vested plans governed by new pension reform legislation, you'll receive your contributions, plus the level of interest you would have received in a non-chequing bank account. You still can't use that money for anything other than retirement but at least you'll have options other than leaving it in your old employer's plan. With non-reform pensions, your contributions will be placed in a locked-in RRSP. If the company's contributions have vested they'll usually be paid to you as a pension upon retirement.

8. When does the pension vest?

While pensions that fall under reformed legislation must be vested within a specified time, there are no vesting standards in those provinces where reforms have not yet come into effect. If you quit before your plan vests, you get back the money you've paid into the plan, perhaps with a little interest. But you lose all the money your employer has contributed.

9. What happens if I die before I retire?

Even under pension reform, rules dealing with death before retirement vary from province to province. The most generous jurisdiction is Ontario, where the full value of your pension benefits will be moved into your spouse's RRSP. Elsewhere, your beneficiary may be left with little more than the money you've put into the plan.

10. What happens if I die after I retire?

Under pension reform, your employer must continue to pay at least 60 percent of your full pension to your husband or wife, unless you and your spouse signed a waiver stipulating that you do not want the survivor's benefit. If your pension is governed by the old rules and you choose a pension for your life only, it will stop upon your death – even if you die the day after you pick up your gold watch.

11. What happens if I become disabled?
Under a defined-benefit plan, your pension should not be affected by a disability. If you have a money purchase plan, determine whether pension contributions will be made to the plan while you're away from work.

12. Must I belong to a pension plan?
No, but there's very little to lose by joining any pension plan governed by reformed rules. Your employer is probably matching your contributions, so you're receiving money you wouldn't other- wise get. Benefits will vest in as little as two years and you can take them with you if you change jobs. On the other hand, under the new RRSP rules, the contribution you will be able to make to your RRSP will be reduced by your pension adjustment.

13. What will the pension adjustment be for my RRSP contribution?
The pension adjustment will be based on the benefits formula in your pension plan. Your employer will report your PA on your T4 slip and Revenue Canada will send a statement, but it's not difficult to calculate the PA yourself. This isn't precise, but it will give you a rough idea of your limit: your PA will be approximately your in- come times the percentage in your pension formula multiplied by nine less $1,000.

If your pension benefit is 2 percent, your PA will be 18 percent of your income minus $1,000 – you'll be able to contribute only $1,000 to your RRSP. If your pension benefit is only 1 percent, your PA will be 9 percent of your income less $1,000. You will be able to contribute another 9 percent of your salary plus $1,000 to an RRSP.

If you're a member of a money purchase pension plan, you'll want to ask all the above questions about vesting, early retirement and portable benefits. You should also ask:

1. How much do I put into the plan and how much does my employer contribute?
Your employer usually matches your contributions, although some will contribute more. There are some plans to which only the employer contributes.

2. How much room does this leave for RRSP contributions?
In money purchase plans, your pension adjustment will be the total amount contributed by you and your employer. Under the new rules, if each of you contributes 5 percent of your earnings to the company plan, you'll be able to put 8 percent (18 percent minus 10 percent) of your earnings into an RRSP.

3. What is the investment return earned by the plan?
Most money purchase pension funds are invested cautiously, sometimes entirely in fixed-income securities. You may not have any control over the plan's investment strategy, but if you feel the return is unacceptably low you should complain to your employer. The investment strategy and expertise of the pension manager play critical roles in determining your retirement income.

Individual pension plans

When proposed government regulations on individual pension plans, or IPPs, were tabled in July 1991, a significant alternative to RRSPs was offered to Canadians. But it may be attractive to only those in high income brackets, such as senior executives and owners of companies, who might use the plan to boost their tax-sheltered savings beyond what is available to them through RRSPs.

Because age and income level are key factors in arriving at the contribution level required to make these plans effective, their suitability is limited to individuals over forty years of age and with incomes of $100,000 or more a year. An IPP is very similar to a defined-benefit pension plan. The benefit received at retirement is specified in the plan when it is first established. (An RRSP is similar to a money-purchase pension plan in that the benefit at retirement will depend on the rate of return generated by your savings and the amount of money contributed.)

An advantage of an IPP is that your contributions can exceed the maximum contributions you would be able to make to an RRSP alone; under the new contribution rules even if you make the maximum contributions to a pension plan you can still make an $1,000 RRSP contribution. The result is an accelerated rate of accumulation. At retirement the funds in the IPP will be used to purchase a life annuity to provide the specified income. Excess funds in the IPP are then taxed and paid at once to the beneficiary. Purchase of an annuity from IPP funds can be deferred by opting to transfer the designated funds to a locked-in RRSP as retirement approaches. As with all RRSPs, this plan must be wound down when the beneficiary reaches age seventy-one.

IPPs are not for everyone; the gains to be had are dependent on age and the higher contributions that are made to the plans. Regulatory requirements include the use of unisex actuarial tables in determining payments and a 3 percent inflation index. The disadvantage of these restrictions are compounded by the high set-up and administrative costs and the comparatively complex nature of these plans. However, these may be outweighed by the uncertain benefits to be generated from an RRSP.

IPPs are offered by several major accounting firms, at least one brokerage house, and by a few financial planning companies and actuaries. Talk to your accountant and look at several plans before opting for this new retirement planning strategy. IPPs have not caught on as expected. The benefits are not that much greater than for an RRSP yet they are more complicated to administer.

Are you going to have enough when you retire?

It's the ultimate financial question. To answer it, you have to know:
- When you would like to retire,
- How much money you will need,
- How much money you will have,
- How you will fill any income gap.

These can be difficult to answer. Although you might like to retire tomorrow, the practical answer will depend on your financial resources. The answer to the second question depends on the lifestyle you would like to enjoy after retirement. Working out how much money you'll have at retirement is more difficult. You have to look at both the income from your pensions and the income that will be produced by the money you've saved and invested already. You'll then have to determine what percentage of your income you would have to save every year until you retire to make up for any shortfall between what you'll have and what you'll need.

It's really not all that difficult, except for one thing – inflation. Most retirement projections involve predicting a rate of inflation between today and the day you retire in order to arrive at an amount of money you should save every year – an endless stream of dollars that never rises or falls. But, this is unrealistic. You probably can't save the same amount every year from now until retirement, nor should you. Your salary will rise as your career progresses, while at the same time your expenses may drop. Saving $1,000 a year might be tough when you're thirty-five years old, paying off a mortgage and raising children. But when the house is paid for and the kids are gone, saving $1,000 or more will be easy. Your savings should mirror your income – as your salary increases with each passing year, so should the money you put aside.

Let's ignore inflation for a moment. Pretend that the cost of living will never rise and you'll never get another raise; you can then work out the percentage of your earnings that you must save each year. Obviously, there will be inflation. But, as your income increases and you continue to save the same percentage of your income every year, obviously the dollars you are putting away each year will also rise. Voilà! An inflation-adjusted retirement plan. It's daunting, but if you're flying blind, the landing could be more painful than the few hours you'll have to spend doing these calculations. Before beginning the worksheet that begins in a few pages, let's look at some of the questions you'll have to answer.

How much money will you need?

Retirement is more than a financial decision. It's also a matter of choosing a lifestyle. Think of the hours you've spent over the past thirty-five or forty years dressing, getting downtown during rush hour, drinking coffee, working and indulging in office gossip. Without a job you'll have forty-five or fifty hours to kill every week. You can't spend it watching the minutes tick past on your gold watch. How are you going to pass the time? Where are you going to live? Are you going to sell your home and move to your cottage in the country?

To work out what it will cost to buy that lifestyle, juggle the money you're spending today to reflect the expenses that will change after you retire. If you're close to retirement, use the detailed budget in chapter twelve. If retirement is a distant dream, you need only look at the income you need today and deduct expenses you won't have to pay during retirement. By the time your work years are over, your mortgage will be paid and you'll no longer be putting money into pension plans and RRSPs. Your life insurance will be paid up and/or no longer needed. The rest of your living expenses will also change, although they won't necessarily drop. You may not eat lunch at work, but the cost of eating at home will jump. You may not have to buy clothes for work, but you may no longer have a company car. The renovations, house repairs or gardening that you've had to put off in the past for lack of time may not be inexpensive. You could find yourself buying more books, going to more movies, travelling more.

How much money will you have?

In retirement, your expenses will have to be met by income produced by your government benefits, pensions, RRSPs and investment portfolio. Let's look first at the income you'll be able to produce with the savings and pensions you have now and then determine how much you should save.

This calculation is not easy, but there are two ways you can make it easier. If you want to be precise or if you want to consider creating an indexed pension, consult the annuity tables available at your local library. Even if you don't plan to buy an annuity, they're a good guide. A short cut is to assume you'll receive a 10 percent return on your capital.

What will you get from the government?

Government benefits are the foundation of your retirement income. They may be the only pensions you'll receive that will keep pace with inflation. You may scoff at the meagre income they provide – together the CPP/QPP and OAS currently provide just over $12,145 a year. But you'd need around $187,000 in cash to buy an indexed annuity that would pay the same income.

Whether these benefits can continue in their present form is a crucial question. Today there are three workers contributing to the system for each retiree, in thirty years there will be only two. With more benefits going out and fewer contributions coming in, there is a good chance that the government benefits of the future may not be as lavish as today's, or that they may be unable to keep pace with inflation. The government has already begun to "claw-back" all or a portion of the OAS from higher-income taxpayers. If you're younger than fifty, you would be wise not to count on receiving OAS at all. It will likely be integrated with the federal Guaranteed Income Supplement to become a safety net for the poor.

CPP/QPP benefits are based on your earnings and the contributions you've made to the plan. The maximum pension you could receive in the fall of 1992 was $636 a month. You can collect CPP/QPP as early as age sixty or delay payments until age seventy. Your benefits will be reduced by 0.5 percent for every month you retire before age sixty-five, and increased if you work longer. OAS is paid to everyone who has lived in Canada for at least ten of his adult years. It doesn't matter whether you've ever been employed. The full OAS pension by the fall of 1992 was $376.11 a month. (To receive the full OAS pension you must have lived in Canada for forty years after age eighteen.)

To determine how all the above sources of income will combine to meet your retirement needs, go through the following calculations. You'll be able to see how your future income will compare with your needs, and whether there will be a gap between your retirement expenses and your income. If there is a gap, you must determine how much capital you'll need to produce enough additional income to make up for the shortfall.

Your retirement savings needs

To determine how much you must save each year, let's look first at how much income you'll need in retirement. Then look at the income you'll be able to create with the savings you have now. Finally, you'll be able to determine the percentage of your income you must save every year to build the retirement nest egg you will need.

How much income will you need?

If you're close to retirement, use the detailed budget in chapter twelve. If not, simply subtract the most obvious expenses you won't have in retirement from your income today.

Expenses you will not have in retirement

Your mortgage	$_____
Contributions to a pension plan	+ $_____
Contributions to an RRSP	+ $_____
Your UIC premiums	+ $_____
Your life insurance premiums	+ $_____
Total	= $_____

How Much Must Be Invested Each Year to Accumulate $1

| Years To Retirement | While You're Saving, Your Capital Will Earn | | | | |
	5%	7%	9%	11%	13%
5	0.1810	0.1739	0.1671	0.1606	0.1543
10	0.0795	0.0724	0.0658	0.0598	0.0543
15	0.0463	0.0398	0.0341	0.0291	0.0247
20	0.0302	0.0244	0.0195	0.0156	0.0124
25	0.0210	0.0158	0.0118	0.0087	0.0064
30	0.0151	0.0106	0.0073	0.0050	0.0034
35	0.0111	0.0072	0.0046	0.0029	0.0018

TABLE V

Your after-tax income today $_____
Expenses you won't have in retirement – $_____
After-tax income you'll need   = $_____
Pre-tax income you'll need   = $_____

How much income will you get from the government?
Don't try to calculate the future value of your CPP/QPP benefits, just look at the benefit you would get in today's dollars. Remember, if you earn more than $50,000 you will have to pay back some, if not all, of your OAS benefit.

Canada or Quebec Pension Plan $_____
Old Age Security   + $_____
                          Total   = $_____   ➡ (A)$_____

How much income will your RRSP produce?
Value of your RRSP now $_____
The return on your RRSPs after inflation.
   If your money is sitting in a bank account at 5% and inflation is running
   at 4%, you're only earning 1%. $_____
Future value of your existing RRSPs. To
   work out the value of your RRSPs at retirement, look at the future value of $1
   in the appendix. $_____

This RRSP nest egg will create a stream of income in retirement. You can assume you'll earn 10% but if you're close to retirement look at the annuity tables in the library. The income from your existing RRSP $________ → (B)$________

How much income will your pension plan provide?

If you're a member of a defined-benefit pension plan, ignore any inflation for the moment. Just take your income this year and plug it into your pension formula, along with the number of years you will have worked for your employer by the time you retire.

Your pension formula $________

Plug in your numbers $________

Your pension in today' dollars $________ → (C) $________

If you're a member of a money purchase pension plan or DPSP, treat it exactly as you did the RRSP savings, but use the investment return earned by the plan less inflation.

Value of funds in plan now $________

Future value of those funds $________

The income they will create $________ → (C) $________

How much income will your investment portfolio provide?

Determining the future value of your investment portfolio is slightly more difficult since you must not forget your tax on the earnings as well as the impact of inflation. If your money is sitting in a savings account at 6 percent, your tax on that is 40 percent and inflation is 3.6 percent, you're earning nothing at all. Don't include your house unless you intend to sell it and the equity to produce income. Assume your rental income and dividend income will not increase.

The value of your investments $________

The future value of these investments $________

Income these investments will create $________

Income from rental property $________

Dividend income $________

Total income from investments = $________ → (D) $________

What income will your savings produce in retirement?

To calculate the amount of income that could be generated by the savings you have now, add together:

Income from government benefits	$_____	**(A)**
Income from RRSPs	+ $_____	**(B)**
Income from employee pension plan	+ $_____	**(C)**
Income from investment portfolio	+ $_____	**(D)**
Total from existing savings	= $_____	
The income you will need	$_____	
The gap in income	= $_____	

Assuming you can earn a 10 percent income on your investments, you will need to create a pool of capital that is approximately ten times the gap in income you've just calculated.

The gap in income $_____ multiplied by 10 = $_____

How are you going to fill the gap?

That gap has to be filled with the money you'll save and invest every year on top of any money you're putting already putting away in an employer pension plan, RRSPs and investments. Table IV tells you how much money you have to set aside each year to have $1 after a certain period of time.

For example, for every $1 you want in fifteen years you have to put away 4 cents if you can earn 5 percent on your money. If your objective is to have $200,000 in fifteen years and you can earn 5 percent, you have to save $9,260 every year, or $200,000 multiplied by 0.0463. Look carefully at the returns you're earning. Some of your savings will be in RRSPs and some will not.

What percentage of your income do these savings represent? Is it 10 percent, 20 percent or 35 percent? It's this percentage of your income — not the dollar amount of the savings — that you must put away every year.

If you can't manage this, there are two strategies you can follow: you could give yourself more time by retiring when you're a bit older, or you could seek a higher return on your investments.

Retiring early can be financially onerous. Instead of working and saving for thirty-five or forty years to live twenty years in retirement, you're trying to work for fewer years and live on your savings for longer. You're trying to build a much deeper pool of wealth in less time. Before you tamper with your dreams, consider investing for a higher return. It may not be nearly as difficult as you think.

Look at the difference bumping up your yield by just 1 percent can make: if you contribute $8,000 to an RRSP each year for twenty years and improve your return from 4.5 percent to 6.75 percent you would have an extra $68,172. It can be done without taking any risks – just move your money from a one-year GICs to five-year GICs.

Improving your return can make an astonishing difference in the money you must save every year. If you save $5,000 a year and earn 7 per cent on that money each year, you'll have built a $204,000 nest egg after twenty years. If you can earn 12 percent, you'll have $360,000. If you only need the $204,000 and can earn 12 percent, you would only have to save $2,800 a year instead of $5,000 and still be able to build the wealth you need for retirement.

You can alter the outcome by giving yourself more time to save – and less time in retirement – or by making your money work harder. But no matter how you do it, there is no doubt that you must employ every tax advantage you can. You're going to need all the help you can get to save for retirement.

RRSPs: The dental floss of your financial world

Oh, c'mon. You know you promised yourself you'd do it – you missed last year and you promised you wouldn't skip it this year. It's a pain, but when you're old and gray, it will make a tremendous difference to your comfort. Ah, the tedium of making contributions to your RRSPs – the dental floss of your financial world.

Although RRSPs are often talked about as if they are a type of investment security in themselves, they're not. An RRSP is an umbrella that can shelter almost any investment you choose. This umbrella protects you from tax by registering an investment as savings for your retirement, hence the name – registered retirement savings plan. In the eyes of Revenue Canada, your maximum annual RRSP contribution is the minimum amount you should be saving to create a comfortable stream of income in retirement.

Don't ignore it. You have nothing to lose. Register an investment as a retirement savings plan and:

- You reduce the taxes you're paying today, thereby giving yourself more money to invest. Put $1,000 in an RRSP and you can deduct it from your income, reducing the taxes you'll have to pay this year. If you're in the 25 percent tax bracket you'll knock $250

The Impact on Your RRSP Nest Egg
of Improving Your Investment Return

After	When you invest $5,000 a year at		
	7%	9%	11%
5 years	$ 36,554	$ 41,721	$ 47,324
10 years	69,082	75,965	83,610
15 years	125,645	146,804	172,027
20 years	204,977	255,801	321,014
30 years	427,304	681,538	995,104

TABLE VI

off your tax bill. Ignore your RRSP and you will have to send Ottawa $250 of your $1,000, leaving you just $750 to invest.
• The savings sheltered by your RRSP grow tax-free until you withdraw them. Wealth grows faster if you don't have to give the taxman half of everything you earn on it. Harbouring money in a RRSP would make sense even if it didn't generate a tax refund.
• You still have access to the money. You can – and should – leave the money sheltered until it's needed for your retirement. But if you're squeezed financially, and your investments allow it, you can collapse an RRSP at any time. Once collapsed, however, the money will be taxed. This isn't a penalty, you're simply paying tax you didn't pay in the year you made the contribution.
• You can be as cautious or as gutsy as you wish. Your RRSP can't hold gold bars, but you can buy mutual funds that invest in gold and gold mining companies. You can't hold warrants in your RRSP, but you can buy options.
• You can buy RRSPs everywhere. Banks, trust companies, insurance companies, stockbrokers, and mutual fund companies all sell investments that are registered as RRSPs. Competition for your savings reaches a fever pitch in January and February.

Your retirement savings investment strategy

In devising your retirement plan, you have to juggle three things: time, the money you can save and the investment return you can earn. Once you've set your time frame for achieving financial independence, you're left to juggle your savings and investment returns. You can see in Table VI the difference a little juggling can make.

Unfortunately, your investment decisions are complicated by the risks in the financial marketplace. Historically, the riskiest investments generate the highest returns over time. But sometimes the financial world is turned on its head. In 1990 you could have earned an ample return on your investments without much risk. Inflation was about 4 percent, while five-year GIC rates were close to 11 percent. That's a real return of 7 percent. At the same time, anyone who expected 11 percent out of the stock market was whistling in the dark.

There is only one certainty: if you just drop your money into an RRSP savings account you're going to have to save like a demon. Don't treat your RRSP merely as a way to reduce your taxes. It may be your only guarantee of a comfortable old age.

What should you do with your RRSP money this year?

Conventional wisdom dictates that you should put your RRSP money into guaranteed investments – bonds, mortgages, GICs, money market funds and savings deposits. If you invest in these instruments outside your RRSP, they will be heavily taxed. An investment that pays dividends or earns capital gains is a better bet for a non-RRSP investment because it won't be as heavily taxed – or perhaps won't be taxed at all. It's a piece of conventional wisdom that's often ignored. If your CSBs are sitting in the bank vault and your common stock mutual fund in your RRSP, join the crowd. Many people find it a comfortable way to hold their securities but it's not very efficient. You should put your fixed-income securities in your RRSP and hold your equity investments unsheltered. The gain can be offset by the capital gains exemption – if you don't have a CNIL account – and grow tax-free.

However, for many Canadians RRSPs constitute their sole means of saving and investing. In this case, you should stitch together a portfolio of both debt and equity investments within your RRSP. This portfolio should hinge on your age, your willingness to take risks and your investment philosophy. And it should be tempered with caution. The debacle of the 1987 stock market crash was a grim reminder that stock prices can fall. But they will rise, and fall, again and again. So will interest rates. Since you'll never be clever enough to predict the future with unfailing accuracy, you need to create a comfortable investment strategy. Don't be confused by the hundreds of investments touted during the midwinter RRSP stampede. They all fall into one slot or another. There are:

• Savings plans: these are simply savings accounts registered as RRSPs. The interest rates on savings plans are too low for these to be considered as investments. You're simply parking your cash.

• Term deposits and GICs: these investments soak up the bulk of RRSP money because interest rates are guaranteed and your capital is safe. They come in terms of thirty days to five years. By staggering maturity dates you can ride the waves of interest rates and reduce your exposure to inflation.

• Mutual funds: the surge in the stock market between 1982 and 1987 made mutual funds one of the hottest RRSP investments for nearly five years, but their appeal wained along with stock prices. However, not all mutual funds invest in the stock market. There are many other types of funds, covered in Chapter Eight, that you can put in your RRSP. Mutual funds give you professional management and diversity, but not all mutual funds can be registered as RRSPs.

• Self-directed plans: these are the RRSPs that let you call the shots. Once you register a self-directed RRSP with your broker, trust company or bank, you can use a wide range of investments to build your wealth – individual stocks, bonds, treasury bills, mortgages and even mutual funds invested in foreign stocks. Just watch that your foreign investments don't exceed the maximum level allowed by Ottawa. In the past, foreign investments were restricted to 10 percent of the value of your RRSP but this limit has risen to 16 percent for 1992. It will rise to 18 percent in 1993 and 20 percent in subsequent years. Not all self-directed RRSPs are risky and time-consuming. You can have a plan that contains only CSBs, T-bills, GICs and government bonds. In fact, at least one investment firm will not charge a fee for such a conservatively invested self-directed plan. You can even hold your mortgage within your RRSP. With mortgage rates at 8.75 percent this can represent a good return but to make it worth while (after paying the setup fees) you must have a mortgage of at least $25,000 to $30,000.

Striking the right balance

There isn't a magic formula for the ultimate retirement potpourri. Some investment advisors believe you shouldn't take any risks with retirement funds. Others believe you must take chances or face the dilemma of not having enough money in your old age.

Your RRSP investment strategy should follow the same rules of investing outlined in chapters six to eight. It should be based on your needs, your tolerance for risk and your own experience.

Remember, you're not stuck with an investment portfolio. Create a framework you feel comfortable with and then shift your investments to match the ebb and flow of the economy, not the ups and downs of your emotions. Don't let sudden shifts in the economy scare you into dropping your entire strategy for a race back to safety. And watch your investments. Set your target every year and assess your performance. If you're not earning the after-inflation return you need, make the changes that will ensure your ability to retire in comfort and security.

What difference does it make?

Other than sheer complacency, the greatest RRSP sin most Canadians commit is waiting until the last possible day to plunk their money into RRSPs. You must make your contribution for a given tax year within sixty days of the end of that year. But don't wait. Putting $5,000 into your RRSP at the beginning of January instead of fourteen months later will give you $25,170 more (if it's invested at 8 percent) after twenty years of RRSP contributions.

Although tax reform makes determining exactly how much you'll be allowed to contribute a little tricky, there are bench marks – last year's contribution, for one. Under new RRSP rules you'll even be allowed to make up for missed contributions. But beware. If you can't save a dollar today, you're not likely to have two dollars tomorrow to make up for lost time. Even if you can, the RRSP contribution is only deductible from the previous year's income; it does not carry back to the year of the missed contribution. This may not be as tax-effective as contributing every year. Finally, if you delay your contribution you are reducing the benefits of tax-free compounding over time – this is of far greater significance than the original tax deduction itself and should not be ignored.

The only good reason for not putting money into your RRSP is because your cash is going into a better investment. Other than paying down your credit cards or your mortgage, there aren't many of those around.

Poverty is not having enough

On the lawns of Parliament Hill, the petite white-haired woman stood before Prime Minister Brian Mulroney. "You lied to us," she said. "You lied to us." It was June 1984, only a few months after the Tories had swept into power, and the thousands of elderly Canadians marching on the Hill were angry. Mulroney had threatened to curb the inflation protection in their old age benefits. The anger was over only a couple of hundred dollars a year, but it provided a striking vision of the graying of Canada.

The elderly may have become a political force, but they're poor. In June 1991, there were 3.1 million Canadians over age sixty-five. The average income for the men living on their own was $19,193, the average income for the women on their own was $16,108. Almost 67 percent of all unattached individuals over age sixty-five had incomes of less than $15,000. Most of these people worked during a time when the pension system in Canada was just being built, yet even today only 49.9 per cent of all men and 37.8 percent of all women who have jobs belong to pension plans. Close to 40 percent of all Canadians over age sixty-five have incomes so low that they qualify for the Guaranteed Income Supplement. Too many Canadians drift into poverty with inadequate savings, unwatched investments and misguided faith in pensions that will disintegrate under the pressures of inflation.

When today's yuppies want to slip their feet into designer orthopedic sneakers and hustle into sports spas for the elderly or pack their bags into the trunks of their aging BMWs to leave slushy winters for the warmth of Florida, they're going to need money. Today's middle aged have plush, expensive lifestyles that most will want to keep in the future. You may not end up rummaging thorough garbage bins, but remember: poverty isn't being broke. Poverty is not having enough.

CHAPTER 10

The Roof Over Your Head

FEW CANADIANS CAN RESIST the lure of profit. Even homeowners are not immune. Relentlessly rising prices that succumb to dramatic collapses only to rise again have turned real estate into a national obsession. We've become convinced not only that everyone should buy a house, but also that we should be striving for ever more expensive houses to build our personal wealth. It's an inflation-fed psychology that has obscured the earthier desire just to live in a place of one's own.

Life is not a business. Real estate is a powerful investment, but the decision to buy a house should be a reflection of your lifestyle – not just a financial transaction. Children, pets and privacy all argue for home ownership, but work that keeps you moving every few years and an aversion to shovelling snow and cutting grass argue against it. A home has to be good for you emotionally, as well as financially, or you'll find it a time-consuming burden. If you want to own a house and can afford to, buy it. If you don't want one, there are plenty of investments that will do nearly as well, if not better, and involve far less work.

Most people believe a house is the best investment they'll make. And, over a lifetime, they're probably right. But your home is more an investment in security than anything else: it ensures affordable shelter for your family. In old age, when money may be tight, your shelter will cost you little more than upkeep and taxes. On the other hand, as a renter you would be exposed to the vagaries of inflation and landlords. Since every penny you make on your home is yours to keep, it is also the best of all tax shelters. You are not taxed on any profits stemming from the sale of your principal residence.

A home may be cosier than a wafer of gold, but as an investment it's just as volatile. Real estate prices do not rise sedately year after year. In Vancouver, house prices climbed by 40 percent in 1980 and another 48 percent in 1981 as money from Hong Kong moved into the city, which was already the centre of the West Coast's booming resource economy. In 1982, the economy died and house prices dropped 29 percent. In Calgary and Edmonton, the collapse in oil prices brought on the collapse of the real estate market. House prices dropped 17 percent between July and December of 1984 and fell erratically for another three years. Even if the economy remains strong, there can be wrenching falls. When mortgage rates jumped by one percentage point in the spring of 1988, the price of Toronto houses dropped 15 percent as speculators dumped their houses and fled the market.

These may have been aberrations, but such irregularities recur endlessly across the country. The decline of nickel markets in 1979 drove families out of their homes in the northern Manitoba community of Thompson. When the people of Saskatchewan became convinced potash would fertilize the world, the price of houses in Esterhazy skipped up – only to fall later.

American humorist Will Rogers once said: "Buy land. They're not making any more of it." Rogers was witty, but he was wrong. Politicians make more land all the time with the stroke of a pen. This farm becomes a housing development, that park becomes a condominium. Sometimes the hand wielding the pen is inept. In 1972 house prices rose in Winnipeg as the city stumbled through the melding of its many municipalities into Unicity. In the confusion, the supply of land for housing dried up.

Over time, owning your own home is a good investment. But day-to-day political and economic change can create havoc in the housing market. If you're forced to sell when prices are down, your home could be the most expensive mistake you ever make.

Take your time buying a house. Don't rush off house-hungry and end up tripping over your bank book in your haste to put down roots. Before you even begin looking at houses, decide how much you can spend. Once you've decided what you can afford, talk to a few lenders. Talk to your lawyer and a home inspector. Understand all the costs – legal fees, land transfer taxes, survey and appraisal fees among them – so you're not caught short just as you're about to take possession of your house.

How much house can you afford to buy

Buying that cosy place of your own comes down to two cold questions: how much down and how much a month?

How Much House Will the Bank Let You Buy

Annual Family Income	Monthly Mortgage and Property Tax Payments*	Total Price of Home You can Afford when Mortgage Rates Are:		
		6%	8%	10%
$20,000	$ 500	$ 78,150	$ 65,500	$ 55,900
30,000	750	130,250	109,200	93,150
40,000	1,000	182,350	152,900	130,400
50,000	1,250	234,450	196,550	167,700
60,000	1,500	286,550	240,200	204,950
70,000	1,750	338,650	283,900	242,200
80,000	2,000	390,750	327,550	279,500
90,000	2,250	442,850	371,250	316,750
100,000	2,500	494,950	414,900	354,000

This chart is a simple guide to the house you can afford if you follow the financial services industry's rules of thumb. It assumes you're spending 30% of your family income on your monthly mortgage principal and interest payments and property taxes, have a 25% down payment and a mortgage amortized over 25 years.

*Property taxes vary widely across Canada. This chart assumes they're $125 a month.

SOURCE: BANK OF MONTREAL

TABLE VII

Typically, you're expected to cover at least 25 percent of the purchase price with your own money – although you can get away with as little as 10 percent – and the mortgage will cover the rest. But most banks, credit unions, trust companies and life insurance companies don't like your mortgage payments and heating costs to take up more than 32 percent of your gross family income. If you spend more, you may be stretching yourself.

But this is only a rule of thumb. Your banker may decide to lend far less than 32 percent, or he might be persuaded to lend more. He may even be willing to lend more than you can afford or need. A steelworker with four children who is returning to work after a shut-down may find that spending 32 percent of his income on shelter is a burden, while a young professional, childless couple could afford to spend far more. You must consider your spending habits. How much of your income are you able or willing to pour into bricks and mortar? Are you willing to cut back on vacations, clothes and restaurant meals? A family that takes pleasure in the quiet of their home may want to spend more on housing than a family that likes to be out of the house playing tennis, skiing, going to the theatre or travelling.

Once you decide how much you can afford each month for mortgage payments, you can calculate the mortgage loan that's best for you. If interest rates are high, you can't afford to buy as expensive a house as when mortgage costs are low. Add the mortgage you can afford to your down payment and you'll know the price you can pay for a house.

When putting aside money for a down payment, leave enough on hand to pay for a lawyer, property insurance and closing fees. In Ontario and British Columbia this could come to 2 percent of the cost of your house, in other provinces it could be 1 to 1.25 percent. If you're selling your house and intend to buy another, don't forget that your real estate agent will take 5 or 6 percent of the selling price in commission. (In Quebec, the sales commission will be 8 percent.) You'll also need money to move and to pay for immediate repairs and decorating expenses in your new house.

Once you've set your target price, lower it by 5 percent. Everyone goes over budget when buying a house. It's so easy to discover a house that's just a little more expensive than you can afford. If you fall in love with it, it's difficult to walk away. Emotions can run high when you're house hunting, so protect yourself by being cautious now.

Finding the ideal mortgage

Buying a home will saddle you with debt that will make you wince. There's only one consolation: you're not alone. At the end of March 1992 Canadians owed $268.1 billion in mortgage debt. Five years earlier, that figure was a much lower $138.2 billion. But the traditional home mortgage is no longer a static, twenty-five-year indenture. It has become the weapon in a heated war among financial institutions for a multi-billion-dollar jackpot.

The battle for mortgage business began in 1983 as Canadians emerged from the last recession not only hungry for houses, but nervous. In their rush to lend to house buyers, lenders launched one mortgage scheme after another to promote greater flexibility and potential savings. You now have the options of paying down your mortgage faster and when you like, applying an existing mortgage to a new house or even blending your old mortgage with a new mortgage if you need funds for a renovation or a bigger home. But before you get caught up in the features of a mortgage, there are a few decisions you must make. At every institution you will have to choose from mortgages that are:

• Open or closed: an open mortgage lets you pay off as much of your debt as you want, at any time, without penalty. It can be impossible, or at least very expensive, to get out of a closed mortgage before it matures. An open mortgage is more expensive, usually by 1 percent or 2 percent, but you can pay it off at any time.

• Fixed or variable: you can opt for a fixed interest rate or you can allow it to rise and fall with market trends. The floating rate is usually tied to the weekly auction of Government of Canada treasury bills. The choice is between security and possible savings if mortgage rates drop.

• Short term or long term: you can choose the term of your mortgage. Six months to five years is the norm, although there are seven- and ten-year mortgages available. Longer-term borrowing is usually more expensive, but don't gamble on short terms if you can't afford an increase in payments. In this case, go for at least three years. For example, you could face a choice between a one-year mortgage at 6.5 percent annual interest and a five-year mortgage at 8.75 percent. On a $50,000 mortgage the one-year will cost and extra $70.90 a month (and you will have paid off a little more of your mortgage) but that's the price you pay for nailing down mortgage costs.

Consider the bells and whistles

In addition to the traditional choices, most lenders offer all the recent innovations. In your search for a mortgage, be sure to keep the future in mind. Even if you don't need the most generous mortgage scheme today, you might in a few years. Besides, why not have the most innovative mortgage on your block? It won't cost you more. Consider these bells and whistles:

• Annual payments against principal: the most important concession from a lender is the right to pay off at least some of your mortgage each year. Many lenders allow one annual payment of up to 15 percent of your mortgage principal, sometimes only on the anniversary date of your mortgage but often at any time during the year.

Your Mortgage Shopping List

Mortgage Features	What Features Are Important to You	Lender #1	Lender #2	Lender #3
Interest rate				
Annual payment of principal				
Frequency of payments				
Right to increase your payments				
Portability				
Early renewal				
Assumability				

WORKSHEET XII

• Increases in regular payments: as you become more comfortable with your mortgage or your income rises, some lenders allow you to boost your regular payments, usually by 10 percent or 15 percent.

• Frequency of payments: depending on the frequency of your pay cheque, you may want to make mortgage payments every week, every second week, twice a month or every month. This flexibility makes it easier to budget; you can also save money over time.

• Portability: when you sell one house and buy another, you can take your mortgage – with the same term, rate and amount – and apply it against the new house. If your mortgage isn't portable, never sign for longer than you're likely to stay in the house. If the buyer doesn't want your mortgage and you can't take it with you, you'll have to pay a heavy penalty.

• Assumability: this feature allows the buyer of your house to take over your mortgage. Most lenders allow this, but in some cases you'll still be responsible for the mortgage. Make sure the responsibility doesn't end up back in your lap if the person who buys your house can't make his payments.

• Early renewal: this feature allows you to renew your mortgage at any time during the last year of your term if you spot an upward trend in interest rates.

• Pre-approval: before you begin looking for a house you can walk into your lender's office, discuss your finances and walk out with a certificate guaranteeing you a maximum amount of money at an agreed-upon interest rate that is good for as long as nine months. By having a pre-approved mortgage, you have the power of money behind you when you make an offer on a house. You also know exactly how much you can spend.

Mortgage shopping

Your shopping should start with interest rates, but it should never stop there. Mortgage rates vary little from lender to lender, but there may be a difference of half a percentage point or so. On a $100,000 mortgage that half point could save you $400 a year or more. But even this saving is unimportant against the potential loss of thousands of dollars if you don't have the flexibility to pay off your mortgage quickly, move it to a new house or renew early. To compare mortgages offered by various lenders, you can use the mortgage shopping list in Worksheet XII.

Financial institutions may have just about exhausted new mortgage strategies. But every year there are slight changes to entice you from one lender to another. It has become quite inexpensive to change lenders, so there is little reason not to switch to the most innovative lender. But no matter how clever your mortgage, get rid of it as fast as you can.

Burning the mortgage

It's expensive to use someone else's money, even to buy a house. If you borrow $50,000 at 8 percent you'll pay $64,481 in interest alone if you take the full twenty-five years to pay off that debt. So heavy are the interest charges that after five years of paying $4,579.32 a year you would still owe $47,750. After ten years, your mortgage would still be $37,183.53.

Why pay $164,481 for a $100,000 house with a $50,000 mortgage? Get rid of your mortgage. For the price of three packs of cigarettes a week, that $50,000 mortgage could be paid off in less than fifteen years instead of twenty-five. The interest paid would drop from $64,481 to $35,000, a saving of almost $30,000.

The banks and trust companies make it so easy to save money. You have the freedom to tailor your mortgage to fit your finances

Paying Down an 8 Percent $50,000 Mortgage

Amortization Period in Years	Feature	Monthly Payment	Total Interest Paid	Time to Pay off Mortgage
25		$381.61	$64,481	25 years
20		$414.18	$49,401	20 years
15		$474.08	$35,331	15 years
25	Repay 10% of original loan ($5,000) each year on the anniversary date. (Final payment is $4,176)	$381.61	$16,231	7 years
25	Increase monthly payment by 10% each year	First is $381.61 Last is $989.78	$28,642	11 years 6 months
25	Accelerated weekly payment based on 25% of monthly payment	$95.40/week or an average $413.40 each month	$49,064	19 years 51 weeks
25	Weekly payment based on monthly payment multiplied by 12 and divided by 52	$88.06/week or an average $381.59 each month	$63,603	24 years 44 weeks

SOURCE: BANK OF MONTREAL

TABLE VIII

and psychology. If you know you can afford $100 or $200 extra each month to pay down your mortgage you can either commit yourself to higher payments or save your money over the year and make one annual payment.

Which of all the mortgage schemes has the greatest impact on your debt? The fastest way to pay off a mortgage, and to save the most money, is to make the full 10 percent yearly principal payment on each anniversary date. On a $50,000 mortgage at 8 percent, you would save $48,250 with a 10 percent annual payment. But it's tough to come up with that kind of money. For most families, increasing the monthly payment by 10 percent each year is more comfortable.

The key to paying off a mortgage quickly is to increase the amount of cash you're giving the lender. Simply increasing the frequency of mortgage payments to match your payday has little effect. Most weekly mortgage payments are based on the regular monthly payment divided by four – which, over a year, is the same as making 13 monthly payments. On a $50,000 mortgage at 8 percent, weekly payments would be $95.40 instead of monthly payments of $381.61. You'd be paying $31.79 more a month yet still pay off the mortgage five years faster.

Working out the right mortgage paydown

You should structure your mortgage so you can pay it off quickly and painlessly. As you meander through the maze of mortgage plans, remember you have to increase the amount of money you pay each month, not just the frequency.

While the financial marketplace and homeowners have become enthralled by new mortgage plans, you've always had the option of paying off your loan in less than the traditional twenty-five years just by reducing your amortization when you sign your mortgage papers or when you renew. If you're forty years old now and you want your home paid for by the time you're fifty, amortize your mortgage over ten years. Set your time frame and tell your banker what you want to do.

The RRSP homeownership plan

In the February 1992 budget, the government announced that each Canadian could withdraw up to $20,000 from an RRSP to purchase a home. The money has to be repaid within fifteen years in equal annual instalments (or more) with the first repayment due on December 31, 1994. If a payment is missed, it must be reported on that year's tax return as income. The program is aimed at stimulating housing construction and resales, and will be in effect for only one year. To take advantage of the plan, the RRSP funds must be weithdrawn by March 1, 1993. Buyers have until September 30, 1993 to close their house deal. All types of homes are eligible for the plan, including townhouses, condominiums, mobile homes and cooperative housing.

There are two sacred financial cows in Canada – building an RRSP and buying a home. This seems to pit one against the other and you will have to weigh the advantage of owning a home against the erosion of your retirement savings. Anyone over forty years of age should seek the advice of a financial counsellor. There might be a better way. However, if you're disciplined, and repay your RRSP "loan" as quickly as possible, you are not likely to compromise the integrity of your long-term savings program.

Don't forget the leaky roof

As any homeowner can tell you, houses eat money. The cost of owning a house is not simply that of mortgage payments. You have to heat your home, insure your property and keep the house in good repair.

It costs roughly 1 percent of the value of a house every year just to keep it in good shape. This covers day-to-day chores and major expenses – a new roof, a new furnace or chimney repairs. Many of these costs roll around only every ten to twenty-five years, but some are more frequent. For instance, you should paint the exterior of your house every three to five years. If you wait until the paint is chipped and cracked, the new paint won't adhere properly.

Failing to carry out some of the maintenance chores can cost you more in the long run. Before your read further, go down to your basement and change the filter on your furnace. A filthy filter can reduce your heating system's efficiency by 10 percent to 25 percent, which can cost you hundreds of dollars each year. Changing the filter shouldn't take more than ten minutes, yet few people can be bothered to take the time. Your heating system and central air conditioner should both be serviced professionally once a year.

Before you buy a house, ask to see the heating and utility bills for the past two years. And hire a home inspector to examine the house so you won't be surprised by carpenter ants or a rotting porch when you move in.

Home inspection has matured as an industry since its beginnings in the late 1970s. A thorough inspector doesn't simply tell you what's wrong with the house and estimate the cost of immediate repairs. He'll explain the life cycles of your home's structure as well as its electrical, heating and plumbing systems. You'll be told how to maintain the house, when the roof, chimney or furnace might need replacing and the types of equipment and materials you can choose to keep your home in good repair.

As a nation, we don't take good care of our homes. Even though Canadians now spend more on renovations than on building new houses, Canada Mortgage and Housing Corp. says a third of our houses could do with some fixing. And not just little things. Close to 10 percent of houses are in need of repairs that would cost an average of $7,000. Nearly 18 percent of houses have water leaks, often in more than one place. Houses need painting, roofs need to be replaced, windows need to be caulked and our garages are a disgrace. Not caring for your house can lead to more expensive repairs in the future and undermine its value.

Your home as an investment

If buying a home is a good investment, then why not sink every penny you have into the grandest house you can afford? Hang modesty, go for prestige.

Why not? Because it contradicts the principles of sound investment strategy. If you're going to treat your home as an investment, you should act like an investor. Don't put all your eggs in one basket. Your home is only one of five elements that make up a full retirement savings plan – the others are the Canada or Quebec Pension Plan, a company pension, an RRSP and an investment portfolio. There is another piece of investment wisdom you shouldn't ignore when considering a house purchase: always look at the downside. Historically, real estate prices keep pace with inflation. But history also teaches us that real estate prices can drop, and stay low for long periods. House prices in Toronto didn't move back up to 1929 peak levels until 1954, twenty-five years later. What would happen to your retirement security if your entire wealth was tied up in your home and Canada sank into a long, deep recession?

There is a more immediate danger in spending your last penny on your house: it leaves you without breathing space if you're faced with a financial squeeze. You can't sell the driveway or your son's bedroom for some quick cash. You can always turn to your personal line of credit or a home equity loan, but remember the banks are never terribly keen on lending money to people who really need it, and they can cancel your line of credit at any time.

Finally, moving frequently is expensive. Real estate commissions, closing costs and land transfer taxes can eat up 8 percent of any profit you might make each time you sell a house. There are also the soft costs of moving – the anxious moments of selling your house and buying another, of moving your children away from their friends and schools and of leaving your own friends behind. If the investment value of your home is important to you, consider these guidelines:

Know the city. The adage is overused, but it's still valid: when it comes to investing in real estate, there are only three criteria – location, location and location. Any neighbourhood you move into should have good schools, amenities, shopping and social services. If you study a city carefully you can pick the neighbourhoods that are likely to become more desirable.

Resist the temptation to buy the most expensive house on the street. The value of your home will be tugged down by the value of the houses around you. It's much wiser to own a modest home in a more desirable neighbourhood, especially if you intend to renovate.

Renovate. If you've been modest, you can work a greater profit out of your home by renovating rather than selling and trading up. Keep your renovations within the stature of the houses around you, so you don't create a mansion among bungalows. Remain traditional in the changes you make – a practical kitchen, a comfortable bathroom. And forget the swimming pool; it'll add little, if any, value to your house.

Know your market. A house does not have an absolute price, but a price range. Real estate brokers talk about the wholesale and retail price of a house – the lowest price the owner will accept and the highest price they can get out of an anxious buyer. Look carefully at the prices that houses are fetching until you have a feel for the market.

Don't spout superlatives about a house as you wander through. Be sedate or a little unsure, even if you like it. You'll have more bargaining power.

If you're aggressive, buy when interest rates are thrashing around.
An abrupt increase can flush out the speculators and dampen afford-
ability. This can force prices down, although if the psychology of
the marketplace doesn't change, interest rates will have little impact
on house prices.

One of the best time to have bought a house in recent years
would have been in 1982, when interest rates were 20 percent and
house prices were way down. The mortgage would have been
murder, but interest rates would have dropped back to 12 percent in
less than a year.

Families who just want a home shouldn't try to outguess the
market. Interest rates and house prices go up and down all the time.
If you need a house, buy it and ignore the swirl around you. Even if
house prices soften, you'll have affordable shelter.

Become a landlord. If you're convinced you should invest in real
estate, instead of buying a posh house for your family you could
buy a less extravagant house to live in and a rental house. You
might even be able to stretch yourself over two or three rental
houses or a small apartment block, since you'll not only have the
flow of rent from your tenants to help cover your costs, but you'll
also get a tax deduction for the capital cost allowance, repair costs
and the interest on your mortgage. Although, you don't have the
same tax advantages when you sell rental real estate as you do
when you sell your own home, it is taxed more lightly than interest
income – even without the capital gains exemption.

A nation of homeowners

Canada is a nation of homeowners. David Greenspan, a Toronto
lawyer and author of *Down to Earth*, an exhaustive study of housing
and land prices, believes it's because working people realize a home
is security.

A few years ago he wrote in *The Globe and Mail*: "All that stands
between many retired working-class people and destitution is an
owned home. Free of mortgage, a home is the best guarantee of old-
age security. Working people who end their working lives as
tenants will become poor. Those who are homeowners will likely
remain unpoor. I say this not because of any ideological belief in
magical and redemptive powers of owning property, but because
pragmatically, home ownership is the best way to cushion the in-

herent insecurity of old age. Shelter costs only the minimal cash for upkeep, taxes and utilities.''

A home may be a lifestyle, not a financial decision. But without the security of owning a home, you must be even more meticulous in saving and investing. If you're not, you may not be able to build the wealth you'll need in your old age.

CHAPTER 11

Investing in Your Child's Future

EDUCATION MAY BE THE BEST investment you can make in your child's future. Not only will it enrich your child's life, it will enhance society. Education creates a people able to manage the complexities of a world increasingly dependent upon knowledge and technology.

But who is going to pay for this education? As governments fight to control rising expenses and staggering deficits, the political territory surrounding education has become a mine field. The years of free-spending and explosive growth in education in the late 1960s and early 1970s have given way to bickering between federal and provincial governments over money. During the past decade, spending on colleges and universities has barely managed to keep pace with inflation, while in the same period enrollment has jumped by 30 percent. As a result, governments spend 20 percent less on each student today than was spent in 1978.

The penny-pinching has left universities with crowded classrooms, buildings they cannot afford to repair and obsolete equipment. The problems have not gone unnoticed, but many have gone unresolved. In a 1986 convocation speech to the University of British Columbia, Brian Dickson, chief justice of the Supreme Court of Canada, called the underfinancing of Canada's university system "tragic" and implored governments to save the higher education system before it begins producing second-class teachers and students "and ultimately a second-class nation."

Allowing significant increases in tuition as a remedy to the problems would require a philosophical about-face by governments, since it would become much more difficult for less affluent Canadians to attend universities. But the public purse is empty and universities are not likely to sit idly as they become more impoverished with each generation of students. Who's going to pay for your child's education? Chances are, you will.

Life after the baby bonus

Children walking onto campus for their first semester this fall will need around $7,000 just to pay tuition and room and board for the year. Since they'll probably be in university for four years, the price tag on a bachelor's degree could easily climb to $32,000. A law degree or an MBA runs closer to $45,000. That's the price today; tomorrow it will be higher. Of course, one child's school expenses can be quite different from another's. The cost of tuition and residence at Dalhousie University is around $7,317 a year, almost $2,000 more than the cost of a year at the University of British Columbia. Also, your costs will be dramatically lower if your child lives at home while going to school.

As a caring parent, you might feel compelled to start building an education fund. If your child is now an infant, you'll have to save almost $800 a year (and invest it at 7 percent) to accumulate $32,000 by the time he's ready to go to university – of course, the cost of university will be much higher by then. If your child is already ten years old, you'll have to save at least $2,300 a year. It's a great deal of money for any family to put aside.

Parents with children of any age are probably better off saving for their children's education by paying down the mortgage on their house. There are two good reasons for this:

• If you invest your own money in GICs or CSBs, you could lose as much as half of all you earn to Revenue Canada.

• At the same time, you're probably paying 3 percent more on your mortgage than you can earn on a GIC – a debt you cannot deduct from income to lower taxes.

By the time your children have finished high school, your mortgage could be paid. All the money that was flowing into your house can then flow into their education. You'll be at the peak of your earning power, so providing for education shouldn't be too much of a burden; even if it is a squeeze, you can always borrow against your home. It takes the right psychological bent to borrow against your home after you've worked so hard to burn the mortgage but you'll be farther ahead in the end.

If you don't have a mortgage or feel more comfortable creating a fund that you know will be used only to pay for your children's education you'll want to do it in a way that attracts the least tax. In the past families would deposit their family allowance cheque into a savings account in trust for their child. Although the cheque itself was considered income to the parent, the earnings on the savings were considered to be the child's. Since most children do not have enough income to have to pay tax, the money was able to grow tax-free. The last family allowance cheque will be mailed in December 1992, replaced the by new child benefit. The benefits are designed to improve the financial well-being of low-income families and many will not be able to put any of the money aside. If you can, the earnings will be treated in the same way as the earnings on the family allowance were treated – they will be taxed in your child's hands, not yours. You can invest it in Canada Savings Bonds or GICs and not face a heavy tax bill. You might even choose a money market or bond and mortgage mutual fund.

If you are not investing the child benefit, you'll want to invest in the stock market. Your returns will be capital gains and either sheltered by your lifetime exemption or taxed at capital gains rates. You could choose any growth mutual fund – including those that invest internationally. Most fund companies have plans that require a small initial investment and, through pre-authorized chequing plans, allow you to invest as little as $50 a month. By starting early, you can ride out the gyrations of a growth mutual fund. You should unwind any stock market investments when your child is a few years away from university so his future won't evaporate in a market collapse.

Another option is registered education savings plans.

The gamble of registered education savings plans

RESPs, registered education savings plans, are widely advertised – dumpling-faced babies peer from the covers of brochures on bank counters across the country – enticing you to invest in plans that will pay for your children's education. The two largest RESPs are the Canadian Scholarship Trust and University Scholarships of Canada. Under these plans, parents of children less than ten years old pay between $9.75 to $58 a month until the plan matures, usually when the child is eighteen. In return, their children receive "scholarships" when they go to college, university or technical school.

You can't deduct a contribution to a RESP from your income to reduce your tax in the same way you can deduct an RRSP contribution. But the money earned by your contribution grows tax-free. If you join the CST, you'll be given back the money you've deposited with the expectation that you'll use it to pay for your child's first year of college education. If your child gets past that first year, he'll receive a scholarship in his second, third and fourth years of study. In 1991, those scholarships were just over $2,125 – enough to cover tuition and some books.

If your child does not continue his education after high school, you get back only the money you put into the plan and lose all of the growth. The fund is like a tontine – you gamble that your child will make it and someone else's child will not. In fact, 30 percent of parents drop out of the plan before it matures and 40 percent of the children don't go on to post-secondary education, at least not within the time restrictions of the plan. Not only must your child complete one year of school before he receives a scholarship, but also he must collect all three scholarships before he's twenty-three years old. That's very little breathing room for any student who would like to take more than one year off between high school and university.

You have complete control of your funds with the RESPs offered by mutual fund managers, life insurance companies and a few trust companies. With these plans you can invest as much as $31,500, but only $1,500 a year, for each child and control your own investments. If you're investing within an RESP, you don't have to worry about taxes. With mutual fund RESPs you can buy into bond or mortgage funds if you're cautious, or equity funds if you're willing to take more risk for more growth. At brokerage firms you could invest in stocks, bonds, mutual funds, CSBs, mortgages and even stripped bonds, but several of the firms which once offered RESPs no longer do so.

These self-directed RESPs are very flexible. The money can be used by any student, even by the contributor, to pursue education at a qualifying secondary institution. You can open one plan for all your children and draw on the income as each child continues his studies. The fees for RESPs are very low (at Royal Trust there aren't any fees at all) but there is one major drawback to these plans. The money you earn in the plan must be used for education at a qualified institution or it will be lost. In fact, when you open the plan you must designate the school that will receive the earnings if they're not used for education. If you intend to invest in equity mutual funds for your child's education, there is little reason to risk the loss of your earnings in an RESP when you can simply invest in the fund without the tax-shelter.

Avoid life insurance as an education plan

Life insurance is never a good way to save for your child's education. It obscures the purpose of life insurance – providing cash at death – and doesn't even work well financially. In the past, many life insurance agents suggested that parents buy an insurance policy with their family allowance cheques, or at least match them. But simple comparisons of life insurance and RESPs indicate that this isn't good advice.

You could buy a $26,390 London Life policy on your newborn son's life for a monthly premium of $32.38. When he's nineteen, the cash value in the policy will have reached $13,410. If he's now five years old, you could buy $23,610 worth of life insurance, but you'd have only $7,073 in cash value when he's ready to go to university. If you bought a policy on your daughter's life with the same premium, you'd have less insurance and a lower cash value.

But how much would you have if you put that money into a RESP? If you contributed to the RESP offered by Sun Life Assurance Co., your money could be invested in the firm's diversified fund, which buys a mix of bonds and stocks. The Sun Life investment team has averaged close to a 14 percent annual return over the past decade with its funds, and if they continued generating similar returns over the next nineteen years your child would have $42,428 in his RESP. If your child is now five years old, the RESP would grow to $19,193 over the next fourteen years.

The returns from the RESP and the insurance policy are both sensitive to swings in the financial markets, and the income from either would be taxable in your child's hands when it is withdrawn, although as a student he may have little, if any, taxable income. But at least with the RESP you're not buying life insurance on your child at the same time as you're trying to save for his future education.

Your child's contribution

Of course, you can also encourage your child to put the money he earns toward his future education. He's not thinking about college as he tosses papers on the neighbours' lawns at dawn, but he might be daydreaming about that new bike he wants so desperately. So make him a deal: if he saves his money for education, you'll buy him the bike. Your child is unlikely to have enough income to pay tax so the money will grow more quickly.

This may not be enough but when your children finally go to college or university, and your children might have to work to pay some of their own school expenses. This is a personal decision you have to make as a parent, but many university students can earn between $3,000 and $5,000 during the summer and save around $2,000 – enough to pay tuition and buy books. There is also a psychological benefit to having a child pick up an expense such as the tuition: sharing the cost can make the education more meaningful. Of course, your children can also apply for grants, scholarships, bursaries and student loans.

Oh Lord, won't you buy me a Mercedes-Benz

Money has taken on a greater importance for today's youth. The persistent trend away from the spiritual toward the financial has been traced by a twenty-two-year study conducted by the American Council on Education and the Higher Education Research Institute at the University of California at Los Angeles. In the fall of 1987, just over 75 percent of U.S. college freshmen felt that being "very well off financially" was essential. Fewer students than ever emphasize developing a meaningful philosophy of life.

For parents, there may be a hidden benefit here. Teenagers who are tired of studying can be difficult to manoeuvre, so if your moral authority has worn a little thin, you might find the lure of mega-salaries in the future to be very persuasive. A good education is not a guarantee of riches and success, but the disenchantment with degrees and diplomas that had its roots in the 1960s is undeserved. In 1990, Canadians with high school educations were earning almost half the income of university graduates – an average of $22,952 instead of $39,716. That's if they were working at all. In 1991, unemployment among those who had not gone beyond high school was running at 10.3 percent, yet only 4.9 percent of university grads were unemployed. Aside from the intellectual satisfaction of knowledge and skilled work, it's hard to buy a Mercedes-Benz on the wages of an unskilled, perhaps unemployed, labourer.

CHAPTER 12

Financial Planning in Retirement

"Don't retire. Wait until you're dead."
  – Steel baron Sir James Dunn to financier Lord Beaverbrook

"Retirement should be a beginning, not an end."
  – A recent advertisement

THE FUTILITY OF DUNN'S admonition is obvious. But sadly, the promise of retirement as a new "beginning" has been tarnished. People would like to think of retirement as a time to enjoy the fruits of their labours, but all too often it becomes a time of financial hardship. People who retired ten years ago with pensions that didn't keep pace with the cost of living have lost 50 percent of their incomes to inflation. Despite an inflation rate of 1.6 percent by late 1992, it's been a tough decade. Over the past twenty years, inflation has averaged 7.15 percent. At that rate, a dollar is worth about fifty cents of today's money in ten years and about twenty-three cents in twenty years. Could you be comfortable with less than half the purchasing power you thought you would have at retirement?

What will your retirement lifestyle cost?
The financial decisions you make when you retire will have a lasting impact on the rest of your life. If you act rashly, you could create barriers to your financial security instead of bridges. By the time you're a few years from retirement, your spending habits will be firmly established and unlikely to change. But when your career ends, there will be some changes, probably in the money you spend on leisure activities and hobbies.

If you haven't examined your spending lately, you'll need to do it now. Without knowing what you spend today, you won't be able to

Your Retirement Expenses

Where Your Money Goes	Now	In Retirement
Expenses that probably won't change:		
Mortgage or rent		
Property taxes		
Heat and electricity		
Telephone		
Property insurance		
Gifts		
Expenses that probably will change:		
Groceries		
Restaurants		
Clothing		
Laundry and dry cleaning		
Travelling to work		
Entertainment		
Hobbies		
Magazines and books		
Pocket money		
CPP and UI premiums		
Life insurance premiums		
Company pension contributions		
RRSP or DPSP contributions		
Medical insurance		
Disability insurance		
Car insurance		
Dental bills		
Recreation		
Travel		
Others		
Monthly living expenses		
TOTAL ANNUAL EXPENSES		

Do you have enough money to meet these expenses? Not just this year but in 10 or 15 years? If inflation chews away at the purchasing power of your retirement income by even 5% a year, in 10 years you'll need 60% more income than you need today. Will your nest egg be able to earn that income?

If you believe inflation will be	Multiply your expenses by
4%	1.48
5%	1.63
6%	1.79
7%	1.97
8%	2.16

Your annual expenses in 10 years will be $_____ x _____ = $_____

WORKSHEET XIII

Your Retirement Income

Source of Income	First Year of Retirement	Tenth Year of Retirement
Old Age Security		
Canada or Quebec Pension Plan		
Private pension		
Deferred profit sharing plan		
Investment income: Rent from real estate		
Dividends from preferred shares		
Interest from bonds		
Interest from savings deposits		
Income from collapsed RRSP		
Earnings from part-time work		
Total income		
Income taxes		
FINAL INCOME		

WORKSHEET XIV

determine what you'll spend in retirement. In juggling your budget for retirement, you'll have to make a few changes. You won't spend money on lunches at work, but you'll spend more on eating at home. You won't have to buy fancy suits or drive to work every day, but you might spend more time in Florida. Your mortgage will be paid, you'll need only one car, and the kids will be gone. You'll no longer have to pay into the Canada Pension Plan, unemployment insurance or the company pension. Your life insurance should either be paid up or no longer needed. But you will have to pay provincial medical insurance premiums and dental bills.

Will you have enough money?

Your income in retirement will likely come from government benefits, your private savings and an employer pension, if you have one. The two major sources of government income are Canada or Quebec Pension Plan benefits and Old Age Security. For a sixty-five-year-old, CPP/QPP paid a maximum of $636 a month in the fall of 1992 but you can choose to retire early and collect less or wait until you're seventy and collect more. The full OAS pension was $376.11 a month.

If you're a member of an employer pension plan, you will have received a statement detailing the benefits to which you are entitled. But you should be aware that these benefits may be reduced by the money you receive from the CPP/QPP and by OAS payments. If your plan provides what is known as an "integrated benefit", your payments will include CPP/QPP and OAS. Be sure to ask – it could pay $10,000 less each year than you expect.

Your government benefits may seem meagre, but at least they're designed to keep pace with the cost of living, for the moment. On the other hand, unless you're a teacher or a civil servant, your private pension plan probably won't. Many employers have made ad hoc pension increases to their retired employees in the past but you can't count on it in the future. You could be uncomfortably disappointed. Except for increases in rent from real estate, there's a good chance that the income from your investments won't rise either.

If you find you're going to just squeak through in your first years of retirement, perhaps you should consider retiring into a second career. If you can't plough some of your investment returns back into your nest egg for at least ten years, your income won't be able to keep pace with inflation. If you're just able to make it in year ten, you'll probably be fine – but you'll likely chew into your savings unless you cut down on spending.

Inflation is a threat, but you can cope with it. If you keep your fingers out of the cookie jar, there are ways to combat the rising cost of living. You can begin collecting CPP/QPP benefits when you're sixty, but they'll be almost 30 percent less than you'll receive if you begin collecting CPP/QPP at sixty-five. You could even wait until you're seventy before tapping your CPP/QPP. You can also dip into your RRSP earlier than age seventy-one, when you must collapse your plan.

Finally, your home is your last financial refuge. If cash becomes tight, you can sell your home, buy a smaller place and use the remaining cash to create extra income. Don't sell your home and move into a rented home without considering the impact on both your finances and your security very carefully.

Looking into the future is difficult, but it's important to do so, especially if you're tempted to retire early. The more time you spend in retirement, the more insidious the effects of inflation.

Today's inflation rate may hover around 1.6 percent, but that's low compared to the twenty-year average. If you seek professional guidance, be sure the inflation predictions are realistic.

Choosing your pension option

The most critical financial decision you make during your working life may also be your last: choosing your pension option. Whether your employer has a defined-benefit plan or a money-purchase plan, you'll have to choose from options that will spin off streams of income for the rest of your life. For the highest income, you can choose a life-only option, under which you'll receive a monthly cheque for as long as you live. If you're married, consider a joint-and-last-survivor pension. It provides smaller payments, but your spouse will continue to receive a pension after you die. You can choose to have anywhere from 50 percent to 100 percent of the pension continue after your death.

Both life-only or joint and last survivor pensions can be bought with five-, ten- or fifteen-year guarantees – if your pension doesn't have any guarantees, payments will stop as soon as you die, even if it's only months after leaving work. The guarantees will ensure that the money you've saved over the years will not be lost: if you die within the guarantee period, the value of the remaining pension payments will be paid to your estate or your heirs.

Only you can decide which option is best. If your husband or wife would still be financially comfortable if your pension died with you, the life-only option may make the most sense. But the pervasive poverty of elderly women has driven pension legislators to take steps to protect women. In Ontario, a married person can't choose a life-only pension unless his or her spouse signs a waiver making it clear this type of pension is acceptable. It is usual to provide 60 percent to a spouse upon death of the first spouse.

If you belong to a money purchase pension, you must buy a life annuity with your pension money, although you aren't restricted to purchasing it from the firm that manages your employer's pension fund.

Collapsing your RRSP

A second critical decision you must make is in winding down your RRSP. You must collapse your plan before December 31 of the year in which you turn seventy-one. You have three choices:
- Take your money and run – an expensive choice. If you cash in your RRSP, the money will be seen as income by Revenue Canada and will be heavily taxed.
- Buy an annuity. You hand your money over to a financial institution, usually a life insurance company, which pays you an income for your life or a period you choose.
- Buy a registered retirement income fund, or RRIF. A RRIF is a tax shelter which can hold most of the same investments as an RRSP. Your wealth continues to grow untaxed, but you must withdraw a minimum amount each year. (The RRIF rules are changing. Previously, you had to withdraw all of the money from a RRIF by the time you reached ninety years of age. The February 1992 budget proposed a "lifetime" RRIF which will become effective in January 1993.)

Make your decision carefully. Once your RRSP is collapsed it can't be resurrected. Annuities free you from making any investment decisions in the future, guarantee you a fixed monthly income and ensure that you won't outlive your money. But once you buy an annuity you lose all control over your savings and you can be left vulnerable to inflation. RRIFs demand ongoing management and investment decisions, which you may not want.

You should consider choosing an annuity if:
- You have no other retirement pension, your retirement fund is small and you need a secure income until your death,
- You belong to a family with a history of longevity and you are concerned about running out of money.

A RRIF is a good choice if:
- You have a good pension that will pay for life,
- You don't need the income from your RRSP early in your retirement,
- You need inflation protection.

You don't have to decide between one or the other, you can have a combination of RRIFs and annuities. An annuity will give you a secure income and a RRIF will provide flexibility and protection against inflation. A RRIF can even be used to purchase an annuity, allowing you to wait for interest rates to rise.

Shopping for RRIFs and annuities

Whether you pick a RRIF or an annuity, you'll have to shop around. A difference of even a quarter of a percentage point in the return on your investment means thousands of dollars over your retirement years. Yet spreads of one or two points are not difficult to find. Although you don't have to collapse your RRSP until age seventy-one, it isn't necessarily a good idea to wait that long. In the two or three years before you plan to collapse your RRSP you should keep an eye on interest rates and try to catch an upswing.

With an annuity, the income you'll receive depends not only on interest rates, but also on your age and expected life span. The older you are when you buy an annuity, the higher your income. And because women tend to live longer than men, they receive smaller monthly payments for the same annuity investment. There are five basic types of annuities:

• An annuity certain for ten, fifteen or twenty years.

• A term-certain-to-age-ninety annuity which will pay a stream of income until age ninety.

• A life annuity that will pay until you die.

• A joint-and-last-survivor annuity provides income for the lifetimes of two people, usually a husband and wife. You can choose to have the full income continue after the first death or it can be reduced by 25, 33.3, 40 or 50 percent.

• An indexed annuity provides a stream of income that rises by 6 percent a year.

Payments from any type of life annuity can be guaranteed for up to twenty-five years. If you die within the guarantee period, the balance of the money is paid to your beneficiaries.

But guarantees have a price, and when buying annuities, that price is in the lower monthly payments. Therefore, the highest income will be from a life annuity without guarantees, and the lowest from a joint and last survivor annuity with a twenty-five-year guarantee.

Within a RRIF you can hold the same investments which can be held in an RRSP – GICs, term deposits and mutual funds. You can also invest in stocks, bonds, mortgages and other instruments through a self-administered RRIF. You can have as many RRIFs as you want, and if circumstances change, you can convert a RRIF into an annuity. If you invest in a RRIF, you must withdraw a minimum amount each year – a minimum that is changing in 1993 with the new "lifetime" RRIF. Under the old rules the minimum is based on the value of your RRIF divided by the number of years until you turn ninety. If you're seventy-one years old, you would be required to withdraw 1/19, since it is nineteen years from seventy-one to ninety. At seventy-two you would have to take out 1/18, and so on. You can also base the RRIF on the age of your spouse if he or she is younger than you.

Under the new rules the minimum withdrawals will be determined as a percentage of RRIF assets. These minimum payments are higher in the early years than under the old rules, but lower after age seventy-eight. Once your reach age ninety-four, you must withdraw 20 percent of the declining balance each year. If you start your RRIF withdrawals prior to age seventy-one, the current minimums (based on your age) will apply until you reach age seventy-one. If you already have a RRIF, the existing minimum withdrawal requirements will apply to age seventy-seven. At age seventy-eight, the new rules take over and the lower minimums will take effect. You can have as many RRIFs as you like, but you cannot withdraw less than the minimum from each.

Investing in retirement

Do you want to sleep well or do you want to eat well? It's a harsh question, but retirement is a time when the threat of financial loss can be very frightening. If your fortunes decline, you won't have time to recover. Investing wisely is a balancing act for the retired. If you put your money into investments that will grow, you risk losing it. On the other hand, much of the return from fixed-income securities will be eroded by inflation.

Every investment decision must be tempered by your need for emotional security. But no matter what you do, you can make your investments more effective by being mindful of tax implications and by watching for lazy money. Huge sums sitting in the bank waiting for emergencies are lost opportunities. By all means keep some cash on hand, but don't be afraid to put at least a little of your money in equity investments. If you retire at age sixty or sixty-five, some of your nest egg will remain untouched for at least ten years, enough time to ride out any stock market ups and downs. However, the bulk of your investments should be kept in a portfolio of fixed-income securities. To provide flexibility and diversity, your portfolio should be spread over securities of staggered maturities. A popular strategy with GICs is the five-year roll described in chapter eight.

Man does not live by bread alone

Retirement can be financially and emotionally difficult. Failing to prepare for the psychological impact of retirement can be as disastrous as not planning financially. You'll need more than enough money if you're to save yourself from idleness, boredom and loneliness. If you have always wanted to build a sailboat, become a serious nature photographer or breed the perfect Siamese cat, start in a small way today before you leave work. Once you retire, you'll have forty hours a week to fill with hobbies, travel, community service, educational studies or a second career. Don't quit work just to find that the time on your hands is like a dead weight.

CHAPTER 13

Having the Last Word

IF YOU DIED TONIGHT, COULD your wife get money out of the bank tomorrow? Would your husband get your life insurance or would he have to wait for a few months until it passed through your estate? Would your RRSP be collapsed and 50 percent taken to pay taxes that could be avoided?

Who would get your home and new car? Would it belong to your wife? Your husband? Are you sure?

If you die without a will, the government will carve up and hand out everything you leave behind – probably in a way you hadn't intended. Even if, by chance, your possessions and your money end up where you want them to, dying without a will is inevitably a more expensive way to go. More taxes will be paid, it will cost more to settle your estate and you could leave your family bickering in the wake of your death.

Parents, especially, can leave their families dangerously exposed. Too many people believe their husband or wife will inherit their entire estate if they die. They won't, no matter where they live in Canada. In Newfoundland the widow of a man with two children will get only a third of his estate. Even if she's destitute, the rest will be shared by the children or entrusted to a government administrator who will sell everything and manage the money with extreme caution until the children turn eighteen. Even if you don't have children, your husband or wife may not inherit all of your estate. In Quebec, your brothers, sisters and parents would also get a share.

When you write a will, you decide what you want done with the things you own after you die. A will can be a few words scrawled on a bit of paper or an exhaustive legal treatise. But only through a will can you be sure a handicapped child will be cared for as you would like. And it's the only way you can pass along your family's summer place to your grandchildren or your jazz records to a friend.

You can draw up your own will, but it must be written entirely in your handwriting. One of Canada's most famous wills was written in 1932, scratched on the fender of a tractor by an Alberta farmer pinned beneath. It read: "In case I die in this mess, I leave all to the wife." He signed his name and he did die. The courts found the will valid. Unfortunately, these holograph wills are often confusing and sometimes impossible to execute. You can even buy a fill-in-the-blanks will in a bookstore for a few dollars. But unless you're struck by panic as you board an airplane, get professional help. A lawyer will tie up the loose ends and prod you to think of the unexpected. He'll make sure the will is properly drafted, signed and witnessed, and your assets properly protected.

A will is only the cornerstone of your plan

Estate planning is more than writing a will. It's also making sure your family doesn't suffer financial grief along with emotional grief when you die. Proper planning can mean something as simple as changing the names on your bank accounts; if they're in your name only, it could cause your spouse unnecessary hardship until your estate is settled. Keep at least some money, perhaps the funds you've set aside for emergencies, in a joint account. (Some banks will even freeze a joint account upon the death of one of the holders. Some financial planners believe you should always have some money in your own name.) The title to a home should usually be in both spouses' names, so when one dies the other takes title immediately. If you're not married, but have purchased a home with someone, you may want your home registered as tenancies in common rather than as joint tenancies. This allows you to will your share of the house to someone else.

Estate planning can also involve gifts to your children or friends while you're alive. You don't have to wait until you die to give your heirs their inheritance. You should also make sure you have adequate life insurance. If you want the death benefit from insurance to go directly to your spouse, make sure he or she is the named beneficiary. If the benefit passes through your estate first, the process will not only take time, but the money could be claimed by creditors. It will also be nibbled at by probate and administration fees.

Estate planning is time consuming

Wills are cheap. You can have a lawyer draft one for $75 to $200. Estate planning isn't expensive, but it is time consuming. You've got to think about how you want your estate shared by your family and friends, imagine what your children's lives would be like without you and, if your children are young, choose a guardian to raise them if both you and your spouse die. (The courts will be guided by your choice but can choose someone else if they believe it is in the best interests of your child.)

The more time you spend thinking before you walk into a lawyer's office, the less expensive your estate plan will be. Ponder two possible events – sickness and death. Consider how you want the people and things you care about to be looked after if:

- You die,
- You and your spouse die at the same time,
- You lose your mental capabilities and can no longer manage your financial affairs.

Before you go to the lawyer:

- List everything you own, including your home, cottage, farm, investments, pensions and savings. Take a good guess at the value.
- List everything you owe, including the mortgage on your home and bank loans. Don't forget taxes owing.
- Check the beneficiary of your insurance and RRSP. Is it your spouse or your estate? Don't guess. If you're wrong, it could cost your estate or heirs thousands of dollars. Go and look.
- Check the titles to your real estate. Are your home and summer cottage owned by both you and your spouse?

There are some difficult questions to think about as well:

- Who will inherit your wealth and belongings?
- Do you have any special possessions such as jewels, art, antiques and photographs that you would like to leave to your children or friends?
- Do you want to leave money to charity?
- Who should inherit your wealth if you and your spouse die? Most wills contain a survivor clause, such as: "I leave everything to my wife if she survives me by thirty days. If she does not, I leave my estate to . . . . ''

• If you have young children, who will raise them if they're orphaned? Be sure to name a guardian if a family squabble seems likely. You can name a guardian for your young children, but it is legally effective for only ninety days. If the court disagrees with your choice, it will name someone else.

• If you have older children with unstable marriages, do you want to be sure their inheritance doesn't find its way into the hands of a son-in-law or daughter-in-law? Unfortunately, you should keep in mind that a marriage that is stable today might not be tomorrow.

• The most difficult parts of estates to settle are farms, cottages, family businesses and partnerships or shares in a private company. How should these be handled? Should they be passed on to heirs or sold? If they are sold, how will the profits be shared?

• Who should look after your financial affairs if you lose the mental ability to do so yourself?

• Do you want to be buried or cremated? Do you want any special funeral arrangements?

• Who will inherit your property if your heirs die before you? Your will might say: "I leave my diamond ring to my sister Christine." But if Christine dies before you, your ring would go to her heirs. Is this what you want, or should your will say: "I leave my diamond ring to my sister Christine, and if she dies before I die, it shall go to my sister Gayle."?

• Who will be your executor, the person who must carry out the instructions you've given in your will?

Your executor has to fulfill your final desires

Choose your executor carefully. You want someone who is financially astute, yet sympathetic to your family's needs and desires. Most people name their husband or wife. Your executor will have to:

• Find your will and carry out all of the instructions in it. Be sure he or she knows where it is,

• Call your lawyer,

• Call your heirs, bankers, brokers and insurance agent,

• Arrange your funeral,

• Prepare a statement of your assets and liabilities,

• File your final tax return,

• Sell securities and property or do whatever else is necessary to carry out your wishes,

• Pay your debts, funeral expenses and taxes,
• Distribute your estate and legacies.

Being an executor is not usually difficult, but it may be quite a burden for your spouse at the time of your death. You can make it easier by ensuring that your financial statements and documents are up-to-date and easy to find. You can also name a co-executor – perhaps an adult child, brother, friend or your lawyer. You can even name different people to do specific jobs. You should at least encourage your executor to turn to an accountant to prepare your final tax return. Your executor is entitled to be paid, although only a professional executor expects the usual 5 percent of your estate's value for his work. Rather than pay your executor a fee, which would be taxable, you can leave him or her a bequest in the will, which would not be taxed.

Your voice from the grave

Once you're gone, your executor can't ask you to explain any details of your will that he doesn't understand. Be sure he's aware of your wishes and concerns before you die, and be sure your will is clear. To remove any doubts, you can leave a memorandum. This is an informal letter you can attach to your will. It can be your last thoughts or your instructions on how to handle certain investments. You can also include the names of lawyers, accountants or investment advisors you would like your executor to turn to for advice.

Unlike your will, your memo is not a legal document and is not legally binding – it simply offers guidance. You can also change it any time. A will cannot be changed by crossing out words or removing pages. Any change, no matter how small, means drafting an entirely new will or preparing a legal supplement known as a codicil.

Easing family feuds

After your death, family arguments could break out. One child may insist you always wanted him to have a prized family heirloom. There may be fights over paintings or antique furniture or jewellery. You can stick names on the backs of chairs, but you can express your wishes more effectively in a memorandum to your will. You should also keep track of any gifts or loans you make to your children that are really part of a child's inheritance. If it's a painting or piece of jewellery you give away, but keep in your possession until you die, make sure everyone is aware of the change in ownership.

You can also explain your intentions, especially if you've disinherited a child or divided your estate in a way your family might find odd. An explanation in writing can help soothe any bitterness or frustration a child might feel. It could also keep the arguments over your will out of a courtroom.

Who will care for the children?

If you and your spouse were to die, leaving young children, how would they be cared for, not just physically but financially as well? You should talk about their welfare with the brother, sister or friend who would raise your children for you. This isn't easy, but you can take steps to ensure money will not create unnecessary difficulties.

When choosing the people who will care for your children, try to avoid creating conflicts of interest. Your children's inheritance will be held in a trust and managed for them by a trustee, a task often assigned to the guardian. Stuffing your brood into your brother's home with his children may crowd everyone, yet he may be reluctant to dip into your children's money to buy the home the much larger family might need. Sometimes naming two people to care for your kids, one as guardian and the other as trustee, can ease your children's financial care.

Give your trustee the power to provide for unexpected expenses. Most wills allow the trustee to designate funds for the children's food and clothing. He should also be able to make things easier for the guardian, perhaps by giving him an interest-free loan to buy a bigger home or cottage. If your brilliant daughter should attend the London School of Economics or your son suffers a serious illness, make sure they can get the money they need.

Unless you make your wishes clear, each child will inherit his share of your estate on his eighteenth birthday. If you've left the money from the sale of your home, life insurance and your RRSP, your children will have a small fortune. Could they handle it? Instead, the money could be given to them over time – a bit when they turn eighteen, some when they're twenty-one and the rest when they reach twenty-five. Or the trustee can use the money to meet each child's needs, unequally if necessary, until the youngest finishes university. Whatever is left could then be divided among the children.

A marriage contract can be part of your estate plan

As long as you're sane, you have the right to decide what will happen to your wealth and belongings upon your death. But there are some strings attached: you have to leave your husband or wife at least a share of your estate. Laws differ from province to province, but under the Family Law Act passed in Ontario in 1986, your spouse is entitled to inherit half of everything you acquired *during* your marriage, regardless of what you've stated in your will. You don't have to share anything you owned before you were married or any gifts or inheritances received during the marriage. But you do have to share any income or growth resulting from these holdings. If you owned a $1,000 CSB when you married and it's worth $1,500 when you die, you'll have to hand over $250 to your spouse. If the value of the business your Dad left has jumped from $10,000 to $500,000, your spouse gets $245,000.

Although Ontario's law is the most comprehensive in Canada, in every province you must leave your husband or wife a legal share of your estate. If you don't, your will can be rejected and a legal share demanded – known as the "right of election against the will." This can be avoided if you and your husband or wife have a marriage contract.

Such a contract is used to protect special assets in the event of marriage breakdown, but it can also be used to help ensure those assets go where you want them to upon your death.

A contract can be especially useful if you're marrying for the second time. For example, you can specify in your will that you want to leave your estate in trust, giving your husband or wife the income but ensuring that the estate itself will eventually pass to your children from your first marriage. Without a marriage contract in which your spouse agrees not to take his or her legal entitlement, the instructions in your will could be invalid.

If your son or daughter has an unstable marriage, there is a danger your estate could become the spoils of a sour relationship. You can protect your children's inheritance by making it clear in your will that any income or growth stemming from the portion of your estate you give your child, plus the inheritance itself, belongs only to your child. Some parents insist that their children sign marriage contracts to protect inheritances, but this can be potentially damaging to a young relationship. None of this applies if the assets you leave behind go into a matrimonial home – if you leave your child money and she uses it as a down payment on a family home, that inheritance might be split if her marriage breaks down since the matrimonial home is treated differently from other assets acquired during a marriage.

Keep in mind, too, that marriage contracts can be emotionally disturbing. They imply that marriage is a financial partnership instead of an affair of the heart. Don't let the bread-and-butter wrangling disrupt your passion. Talk openly with your partner and get the legal work done quickly. It will make the process less painful.

Keeping your estate out of Revenue Canada's hands

The ghoulish death duties that once ate into even the tiniest estates have been axed, but there are still taxes to be paid when you die. Fortunately, taking steps to avoid these taxes is not always complicated.

Revenue Canada can get its share of your estate in two ways. The first bite will come in the form of a whopping tax bill. Without a proper estate plan in place before you die, you'll be taxed as if you've just sold all of your capital goods – including your cottage, common stocks and the rental house you own across town. Tax-favoured investment plans, like your RRSP or pension, could be collapsed and taxed as income. And you'll still have to pay any income taxes you would have normally paid.

The second bite comes in the form of taxes your heirs may ultimately pay because of their inheritance.

Fortunately, there are ways to reduce the tax burden of dying, even if your estate is small. If you're married, your estate and your husband or wife do enjoy some tax protection.

When you die, your RRSP can be rolled into your spouse's RRSP without triggering taxes. To be sure it doesn't go through your estate first, your spouse should be named beneficiary on every plan and in your will. In Quebec, the beneficiary must be named in your will for the designation to be valid. Your RRSP will be added to your spouse's RRSP, or a new plan will be opened. The funds could also be used to buy a RRIF or an annuity.

If your spouse inherits the RRSP through a will, your estate will have to pay probate fees of $5 on every $1,000 in the plan and possibly administration fees of 5 percent. The money will eventually move into his or her RRSP, but your estate will have to pay tax on any income earned by the plan in the meantime. Your spouse should also be the beneficiary of your RRIFs, annuities and pension plans.

If you're single, widowed or divorced at the time of your death, you can name a dependent child or grandchild as beneficiaries of your RRIF or RRSP but the rules are complex. The entire proceeds can be transferred as a lump sum, and it will be taxable in his or her hands, or it can be used to purchase an annuity. If an annuity is purchased, the child will pay tax on the income as it's received. However, the term of the annuity cannot be greater than eighteen years minus the child's age. If the child is dependent because of a physical or mental disability, the RRSP or RRIF can be rolled into an RRSP, RRIF or annuity for the child.

Once you've died, your widow or widower has sixty days to make your final RRSP contribution to a spousal plan. Some banks and trust companies find an RRSP contribution for someone who's dead disconcerting and won't allow it; if your financial institution is reluctant, you can search out an institution that will accept such a contribution.

Anything you leave to your spouse will not be taxed but some of those taxes, particularly taxes on capital gains, aren't forgotten, they're simply deferred. They'll have to be paid eventually, either when your spouse sells the assets or dies. However, you cannot pass on any tax advantages, such as the lifetime capital gains exemption.

You're entitled to earn $100,000 in capital gains tax-free over your lifetime. If you don't use it, you lose it when you die. Instead of rolling your investments over to your wife, you should trigger the taxes by telling your executor to include any capital gains that would fall within your exemption in your final tax return. Your spouse still inherits your property, but she won't inherit your share of taxes along with it. Tax laws change swiftly, so you should also instruct your executor to make any elections under the Income Tax Act that will reduce the taxes your estate might have to pay.

There can also be tax advantages to not giving your heirs their share of your estate immediately, but in creating a trust instead. You could leave $100,000 to your rich doctor son, on which he could earn $10,000 and end up paying Revenue Canada $5,000 in income tax; or you could create a sprinkling trust. With a sprinkling trust, the money would be kept in a trust and the income paid to your son's wife or children and taxed at their personal rates, which could mean they wouldn't be taxed at all. You could create a generation-skipping trust – one that holds your estate for your grandchildren instead of your children. These are not complex strategies, but you'll have to find someone willing to look after the trust, keep accounts and file income tax returns. Creating a trust may not be expensive and could reduce your family's taxes, but it can be a nuisance.

Be leery of jumping into any creative tax planning. Your estate plan is supposed to make life easier for your family, not more complex. You might understand your tax strategies, but can your family cope with them after you're gone? Remember too, Ottawa is increasingly shrewish about tax avoidance. If it disapproves of your strategy, your estate or heirs could get hit with more tax than you expect.

Tying up loose ends

It's not a pleasant thought, but before you die you could go a little dotty. Illness or senility could prevent you from dealing with your affairs properly, yet you may live for many years beyond that point. If you become mentally incompetent and haven't made a contingency plan, a court will appoint a committee to manage your financial affairs under a regime that could be rigid and conservative.

To avoid this, consider giving your husband or wife, adult off-spring or trusted friend power of attorney. This can give them the right to do anything you can do with your money. Power of attorney can also be very specific, delegating the right to carry out only certain tasks. Granting power of attorney is not only for the old. You could lose your mental agility through an accident or illness at any age. Assigning power of attorney will make it easier and less costly for your husband or wife to handle your financial affairs as they should be handled.

The adult children of aging parents might also give some thought to protecting their parents as well. Ask your parents if they've given someone power of attorney or you could end up with a financial mess in your lap.

One thing the person holding your power of attorney cannot do is give away your wealth. If you're elderly or anticipate a serious illness, you can create a living trust. You can place assets – perhaps a portfolio of securities or a private business – in a trust in which you share management with a friend or adult son or daughter. If you lose your ability to manage your affairs, your co-trustee can take over for you, giving your heirs their inheritance before you die if that is your wish.

Should your will be a secret?

Whether you want to keep the terms of your will a secret is up to you. There may be good reasons for being secretive, but sparing your family the pain of discussing your death isn't one of them. It can be difficult to know what sentiments your will might provoke among heirs, but if you're planning any complicated tax strategies, be sure they agree. Your family might rather pay the tax, have their inheritance and be done with it. Certainly, your will should never be a surprise to your executor.

Finally . . .

If you don't have a will, go to the telephone now and make an appointment with your lawyer to draw one up. At the same time, make power-of-attorney arrangements.

When it's ready, read your will carefully. It should be clear and precise. The language might seem arcane, but you should be able to understand it. Once your will is drawn up, sign one copy and leave it with your lawyer. Don't ask one of your beneficiaries to be a witness. The will may still be valid, but he could lose his legacy. Don't put your will in your safety-deposit box – the bank might seal the box upon your death and it could take time to retrieve it.

You should review your will every time there is a major change in your personal or financial affairs. A new marriage automatically invalidates any will you have, but separation and divorce do not. You should also re-examine your will if you move to a different province to make sure it conforms to the laws of your new jurisdiction.

There are no death or inheritance taxes in Canada, but there are in the United States and Great Britain. If you own property or have heirs who live outside Canada, you should give careful thought to the taxes they might have to be pay.

You can leave burial or funeral instructions in your will, but be sure your family knows before you die what you want. They may not find your will and your instructions to scatter your ashes over the South Pacific until it's too late.

CHAPTER 14

Just Remember This . . .

DON'T SPEND MORE THAN you earn. Save at least 10 percent of your income. Borrow only to build your wealth. Pay off your credit card balances in full every month. Always contribute the most you possibly can to your RRSP. Keep tidy financial records. Don't put all your eggs in one basket. Don't take financial advice blindly.

It's simple but it works. The difficulty in managing your money doesn't lie in understanding the intricacies of today's financial marketplace, it lies in knowing what you want and in honing the good money habits you were taught in your childhood – thrift and patience.

Undoubtedly, creating a personal plan does demand financial knowledge. But for that plan to be effective, you also have to have a keen understanding of yourself and your own financial life. Begin by asking yourself a few questions, using your answers as triggers. Jot down the action you should take or changes you should make in your finances. You won't be able to do everything at once, so distinguish between those things that should be done right away and those that you can get to over the next few months.

Your personal action plan

Must do immediately   Will do as soon as possible

_____

_____

_____

_____

_____

_____

_____

_____

Your financial fitness questionnaire

Are you pleased with the way you handle your money? _____

What aspects of your finances make you feel uneasy? _____

_____

Does money ever cause you to worry or create tension
within your family? _____

Why? _____

What can you do to reduce this tension? _____

_____

Do you have financial habits that erode your ability
to build your wealth? _____

What are these habits and how can you get rid of them? _____

_____

Do you have enough money set aside as an emergency cushion?_____

Or do you have too much money sitting in savings accounts, CSBs
or T-bills earning too low a return to keep you ahead of inflation
and taxes? _____

What do you want your money to do for you? _____

_____

Do you have a savings plan for the big expenses that loom in your
future – a home, a car, a vacation or retirement? _____

Do you have a plan to pay off any personal debts?_____

How much of your income do you save every year? _____

Protecting yourself and your family

Do you have enough life insurance on yourself and your
husband or wife? _____

Is it the proper kind of insurance? _____

Has your personal situation changed since you last reviewed your
insurance coverage?_____

Do you have disability insurance? _____

Have you looked at the new disability insurance products that will
cover your RRSP contributions if you're disabled? _____

Do you have adequate property insurance, including $1 million of
liability coverage for your car and home?_____

Your investment strategy

Have your past experiences with investing been good or bad? _____

Why were they good? _____

What did you do to make sure they turned out well?_____

Why were they bad? _____

Was it your fault or the fault of the investment? _____
Does your bad experience stem from taking too much risk, follow-
ing poor advice or just following the crowd? _____
What have you learned from your experiences? _____

How have these experiences shaped your investment strategy
today? _____

Do you understand your investments?_____
Do you have an investment strategy? _____
Are your investments diversified? _____
How have your investments performed over the past year? _____

_____

_____

_____

Reducing your taxes
Do you think about income taxes only at tax time? _____
While you were completing your return last year did you think of
ways to reduce your taxes this year? _____
Have you done anything about it?_____
Do you make your RRSP contribution at the last minute?_____
As a couple, are you building the retirement savings plans of both
husband and wife so you can pay as little tax as possible in retire-
ment?_____

Are you claiming every tax deduction and credit you can? _____
Are your tax shelters costing you more than they're
saving in tax? _____
Are they a good investment? _____
Are you investing to take advantage of every tax break? _____
If you have investment loans, are you aware of how the cumulative
net investment loss (CNIL) rules will reduce your ability to claim
your lifetime capital gains exemption? _____

_____

Where do you turn for good advice?

It's difficult to weave your way through today's complex financial environment and once in a while you'll need someone to help you through the maze. Unfortunately, choosing a financial advisor can be as vexing as the problems you want solved. But be sure you take the time to choose carefully. The cost of bad advice is not merely the fee or commission you pay – sloppy financial advice could cost thousands of dollars in poor investments and lost opportunities.

One place to start is with a financial planner. A financial planner is like a fiscal navigator whose job is to put you on the right path to managing your money, protecting your family and yourself with adequate insurance, paying the least tax and creating an investment strategy. It's an appealing service, but it can be expensive and choosing a planner can be tricky. As a nascent profession, financial planning is unregulated and it has already been tainted by scams and fraud.

If you're tempted to use the services of a planner, start by examining the membership list of the Canadian Association of Financial Planners. Your accountant, lawyer or banker might recommend other names as well, but make sure you ask for the reasons behind their recommendations. Once you've pruned the list, interview at least three planners personally. When you visit a planner, be prepared to reveal your problems. Make sure you find the answers to the following questions:

• What education and experience does he have? The elite of the profession are registered financial planners. To become an RFP, a planner must pass a six-hour exam, meet certain educational standards, have at least two years' experience in the field and abide by the CAFP's code of ethics.

• What professional associations is he affiliated with?

• Can he tap the expertise of specialists in tax, pensions and investments while devising your plan?

• Is he affiliated with financial institutions, such as trust companies or investment firms?

• Can you see a sample financial plan?

• Can he provide references?

• How is he paid?

While there are a few planners who charge only for the advice they give, most earn commissions from selling financial products – usually mutual funds, real estate or insurance. There are planners who earn both fees and commissions and others who are salaried employees of large financial institutions. You should watch for any potential conflicts of interest, but don't shun a commissioned planner simply because of the way he's paid. You should avoid the fee-only planner who will do a perfunctory job, just as you would shun a planner who is more interested in lining his pocket than creating the best plan for you.

Finding the right investment advisor

During a strong economy and healthy financial markets, when most people become involved in investing, it's hard for any investment advisor to look bad. During the years 1982 to 1987 almost everyone made money for clients just by riding the momentum of the stock and bond markets. But in today's skittish markets, choosing a good advisor is key to your investment success.

There are two different sorts of experts to whom you can turn: a stockbroker or an investment counsellor. A broker earns commissions from trading securities that you decide to buy or sell. Investors who have more than $100,000 to invest, but don't have the inclination or time to manage their investments, can turn to an investment counsellor. Unlike a broker, an investment counsellor has carte blanche to manage your portfolio, usually for a flat annual fee of about 1 percent of the value of your investments.

It can be very difficult for an individual to evaluate an investment broker or counsellor. The recommendations of friends or other financial advisors can steer you in the right direction, but you'll still have to decide if that person is suitable for you.

Decide whether you prefer a company with a few partners or a large brokerage or investment firm. Then consider the individual. Every broker or counsellor has a view of the market, a strategy and a style he adapts to each client. It's important that you feel comfortable with this style and with his or her personality. If you're not, you'll end up unhappy.

Ultimately, your broker's or counsellor's skill is weighed in dollars and cents. Ask your prospective advisor to lay his track record on the table. And once you've struck a deal, keep tabs on your portfolio's performance. Your yield will depend largely on your investment objectives, but there are bench marks. You could compare your returns with the ScotiaMcLeod Inc. bond index if you invest in debt instruments. If you invest in equities, there are a number of possible yardsticks. A diversified portfolio of domestic stocks could be compared with the Toronto Stock Exchange composite index. A portfolio of foreign stocks could be measured against a *Financial Times* index in Britain or the Nikkei index in Japan. Be sure to deduct your selling costs before calculating your yield. Of course, you could also compare your portfolio's performance with that of a mutual fund. If you and your advisor are not doing better than mutual fund managers, you might be better off in a fund.

A good working relationship with your broker takes time to build, but you should know within six months if it will work. If you're dissatisfied, don't put off discussing your problems. Talk to the broker or counsellor and, if necessary, switch to another.

A few final words

Once you've set your financial action plan in motion, be patient. Your financial destiny will unfold slowly, not overnight. It's a bit like watching grass grow, but give it time and you'll feel a momentum building. Finally, don't let yourself be confused by the complexities of the marketplace. Life insurance is a classic example. It's a tool, one simple product based on one simple premise: if you die, your beneficiaries receive money. Yet in Canada there are almost 163 companies selling close to 1,000 life insurance products.

You should understand what you're doing and buying. But you can take comfort in knowing that the simple product or the simple investment is often best.

CHAPTER 15

Three Personal Profiles

YOUR PERSONAL FINANCES are unique but many of the problems each of us encounters in our financial lives are similar to those of others. In the following profiles, you'll catch a glimpse of the techniques used by professional financial planners to solve some of those problems, and perhaps gain some insight into your own financial needs.

The financial plans described in these three profiles were prepared by professionals who were furnished with detailed lists of expenses, incomes, insurance, assets and liabilities before seeking solutions to the problems outlined at the beginning of each profile.

The uneasy success of the Coopers

The home of Michael and Libby Cooper exudes comfort and ease. There's a clutter of children's toys and knick-knacks recently brought back from a trip to India. A vase of freshly cut flowers sits by the fireplace. Carpet samples are stacked on the dining room table while the family tries to decide how to cover the floor of their renovated basement.

Despite an aura of financial satisfaction, when the talk turns to money, Michael sighs and Libby begins to fidget. Money shouldn't be a worry for this family. Over the past three years, Michael, thirty-six years old, has risen from salesman to director of marketing for a national packaging company. His salary has kept pace with his career, jumping from $43,000 in 1986 to $65,000 today. Libby is thirty-four and has just begun part-time work for a local community organization, where she earns about $5,000 a year.

Michael's most urgent worry is his life insurance. The Coopers' lives are devoted to their children: they believe strongly that Libby should stay at home until the kids have grown. Six-year-old John and three-year-old Emma are always impeccably dressed and the family's weekends are filled with theatre, museums, skiing and visits from family or friends. Michael would not want his death to force Libby back to work before the children are grown or to disrupt his family's lifestyle. Yet if Michael died, Libby would get only $62,500 from two whole life insurance policies Michael bought in 1972 and 1976.

Michael is convinced that he needs more insurance, so he's been dickering with his life insurance agent for six months. He's frustrated because the information sent to him has been vague and confusing. Finally, he told the agent he intended to cancel the policies and buy term insurance from another company unless he was given a good reason for keeping the policies he had. He was furious when his agent wrote: "You and Elizabeth have some very fine antique furniture. You know it doesn't have the shine of new furniture, but it does have its own unique qualities that could not be replaced. The same is true of your life insurance policies." That was all the explanation the agent gave. Michael wants to know how much insurance he needs. Should he cancel the whole life policies he has? Should he buy term insurance?

The family's insurance situation makes Michael anxious, but Libby sits quietly until the conversation turns to investments. Michael is pleased that he makes the maximum RRSP contribution every year, but Libby can't resist a derisive snort. Michael has a self-directed RRSP invested in common stocks and handled by an old friend of the family. The broker's letters are a chatty update of investment performance and chit-chat. His last letter admitted that "unfortunately, the equities came through once again with a resounding clunk. Even the one U.S. stock recently added to your portfolio fizzled. With performance like this, it's no wonder you don't turn up for tennis any more." Michael shrugs. The broker has managed his parents' investments for years and Michael doesn't want to rock the boat.

Michael is much more interested in a rental property he bought with his mother-in-law in a small community in eastern Ontario. They paid $37,000 for a semi-detached house in 1982 and it's now worth $110,000. The rent more than covers the cost of running the property and there is $6,000 worth of profit sitting in a bank account. The Coopers would like to buy another rental place, but they can't find a reasonably priced property.

These problems don't disturb the usual calm of their marriage, but dissatisfaction over the day-to-day handling of their money can be explosive. Libby's anger is evident as it's explained that she's always found it difficult to control her spending. Several years ago, Michael decided to give her $450 every two weeks for groceries for the family and gifts and clothes for her and the children. Libby usually runs out of money, making it impossible to save for expensive clothing purchases in fall or winter or for Christmas gifts. When she runs out of cash, the family meals are nourishing but simple. She has no access to any other money. Libby admits she can be a spend-thrift, but insists she's not given enough.

Libby and Michael have had years of emotional problems with money and, although they've finally settled on a system they agree seems to be working, Libby finds it demeaning. Michael calls her $450 allowance a salary for work she performs as a mother and wife. She finds this insulting, but doesn't know what to do. Talk about money inevitably degenerates into an argument, so it's avoided and money remains an irritant that subtly disrupts their marriage. There isn't a shortage of money; it's the handling of money that causes problems.

The Coopers' financial plan

To find a solution to their problems, the Coopers turned to JoAnne Anderson of MoneyPower Inc. in Mississauga, Ontario.

Michael and Libby Cooper have done well managing their money over the past few years. They have a home and portfolio of investments. Except for their mortgages, they're free of debt. Not only can they cover their expenses with their incomes, they can save $7,500 a year without a change in their lifestyle. Despite this, the Coopers feel dissatisfied. Money is a disruptive force within their marriage. This isn't uncommon. Money isn't just dollars and cents; it can be power, control or security, and can stir emotions of fear, shame and pride. If a husband and wife have different expectations for their money, there is the potential for conflict.

Rather than repeating past patterns, Libby and Michael need a fresh approach. Both need to understand their expectations and their financial situation. For the next six weeks, Libby should record every expenditure she makes so she can see how she's spending the money that flows through her hands. Is she buying the things she's expected to buy? Could she spend the money differ-

ently? Could her choice of purchases be altered? Once she has re-
corded the flow of cash, she'll know if she can change her spending
habits or if she needs more, or less, money. Once reality is documented, she can sit down with Michael and discuss the allowance –
it is an allowance, not a salary.

Libby and Michael should pick a time when they're both relaxed
and there won't be any interruptions or arguments. Instead of
launching into day-to-day money hassles, they should begin by discussing their goals. Each should list his or her most important goal
for the coming year, the next five years and the distant future. If
they understand their financial situation today and decide what
they want in the future, they'll be able to map a course of action. By
focussing on goals and how each can contribute to the attainment of
these goals, rather than on the difficulties of the past, the Coopers
may be able to break their financial impasse.

The Coopers' insurance needs

Michael's life insurance is an immediate concern. If Michael died,
Libby would need money to pay for Michael's funeral, the mortgages on the home and rental property and a cushion of $12,000 to
get her through the first few months after his death.

Finally, she would need money she can invest to create enough
income to raise the children. If Libby were on her own, Michael
feels her daily expenses would rise. She would dine out more,
which would create higher food and babysitting costs, and she
would have to hire people to help her maintain the house. Even so,
with Michael gone and the mortgages paid, the family's income requirements would probably drop by 25 percent. Based on their
budget today, Libby would need an annual income of $47,623 to
give her $34,289 after tax. Libby earns $5,000 a year. Without selling the house or cashing in RRSPs, Libby would have $14,500 in
cash and $55,000 in investments that could produce no more than
$7,000 a year.

This leaves a gap that can be filled with life insurance. At the
very least, Michael needs $550,000 in coverage to pay his last ex-
penses, pay off the mortgages and create a pool of money large
enough to support his family after his death. This wouldn't allow
for inflation protection or additional savings, but the RRSP reserves
would continue to grow tax-free and could be used if needed. Because the need for insurance on his life will decrease as the family

continues to build up its wealth and the mortgage is paid down, term insurance is more appropriate than whole life insurance.

Michael has two whole life policies in force now. Both have paid-up insurance options and special tax provisions in the policies that allow the cash to grow sheltered from tax. Also, when the death benefit is paid, it can be used to purchase an annuity, allowing Libby to pay the taxes on the capital gain over the life of the annuity and reduce her lifetime tax burden. Given this special tax treatment, the policies should be kept. Michael should buy enough term insurance, around $487,500, to cover the rest of the family's insurance needs.

Libby has a $10,000 whole life policy on her life and the dividends from the policy are used to purchase more paid-up insurance. If she were to die this year, the policy would pay $17,800. Since Michael could support the children simply from his income, this insurance is more than enough. However, like Michael's policy, Libby's insurance was issued before 1982 and has favourable tax treatment. She should keep it in force.

The Coopers' investments

When devising an effective investment strategy, the Coopers must consider their marginal tax rates – the rate of tax paid on the last dollar earned. Michael is in a high tax bracket, paying 46 percent of every extra dollar earned in tax. Libby, on the other hand, pays no tax. The marginal tax rate is important in calculating the after-tax rate of return on investments and the effect of additional tax deductions on overall tax liability.

For example, the Coopers own CSBs that pay 10.5 percent interest. With Michael reporting the interest, he'll pay 46 percent of the money he earns on these bonds in tax, leaving him with an after-tax return of just 5.67 percent. If Libby could claim the CSB interest, she wouldn't pay any tax until her annual income hits $6,000, leaving her with the full 10.5 percent return. However, she can't claim the CSB interest unless the bonds are bought with her money. For tax-effective investing, Libby should begin to save her salary and invest it while Michael pays the family's living expenses.

The impact of tax could also be reduced if Michael held his interest-bearing securities inside his RRSP and his stocks outside the RRSP. If he wants to retain his stocks, Michael could tell his broker to swap the securities so he could earn tax-free capital gains on the stock portfolio and shelter the interest he earns in his RRSP. In fact, Michael should take a harder look at his stock portfolio.

Michael's broker is a friend, and disrupting the relationship could cause some discomfort. But neither Michael nor Libby have any other pension plans and their future financial security depends not only on their contributions to an RRSP but on the performance of their stocks. Michael likes working and cannot envisage retiring, but he should take steps now to ensure that he can choose between working or retiring in the future. If he aims for financial independence when he turns sixty-five, he and Libby must save $8,800 a year, an extra $1,300 a year over the $7,500 he saves now, *and* earn an annual after-inflation return of 4.5 percent on his investments.

Recently, the performance of his RRSP has been poor. The market value of his RRSP exceeds the cost by only $435 in an $18,000 portfolio acquired over the past several years. Because funds in an RRSP are not taxed until withdrawn, it's an ideal place for interest-bearing investments. Michael could improve his performance dramatically, simply by taking the $18,000 and investing $2,000 in a three-year term deposit, $5,000 in a five-year term deposit, $4,000 in a bond fund, $4,000 in a mortgage fund and $3,000 in a strip bond.

Finally, Michael would like to buy another rental property. To do this, he would have to borrow heavily, an unwise strategy after several years of spiralling real estate prices in southern Ontario. Michael is wiser to put every cent he can into a spousal RRSP.

Finally, Libby and Michael haven't drawn up a will since 1977. Their lives have changed dramatically since then and recent changes to family law may also have an impact on the content of wills. They should see a lawyer as soon as possible.

This plan for the Coopers is not static. Family situations, economic conditions, tax laws and personal goals change. The Coopers should review their financial plan at least once a year, as well as when there is a major change in their lives.

The Levitches' dream of early retirement

The Levitches' house is small and tidy, not Spartan so much as comfortable in a practical way. A few books are stacked neatly on shelves while library books are scattered on the coffee table. Two timid pedigreed cats peek shyly around sofas. In front of the bay window, rows of vegetable and flower seedlings sprout, waiting for the warmth of spring. Richard and Marilyn Levitch are an unusual couple – they haven't any financial worries. They live a frugal life, untouched by consumerism. They both like reading, she likes to garden and he likes to go to movies. Together, they have one driving aspiration: to retire early.

It's a dream they're quite sure they can turn into reality. Marilyn, a forty-two-year-old Vancouver high school teacher, earns $34,970 a year. Richard, forty-three, earns $57,326 a year as a quality engineer with a multinational forest products company and around $5,000 a year as a freelance computer consultant. Richard likes his job and wouldn't mind working until he's fifty-five, although he would retire earlier if possible. Marilyn is more anxious. She'd retire tomorrow if she could.

Marilyn and Richard don't have children and, as they settle into their careers and middle age, their excess cash has begun to explode. By the summer of 1988 they had managed to save $110,000 and they decided to buy their first home, a $258,000 house in North Vancouver. Buying the house had not been the intent of this diligent saving, it just seemed a good way to invest the money. When Richard and Marilyn bought their house, they took out an open mortgage, knowing they would be able to pay it off very quickly. When Marilyn's father died later in the year, she received an inheritance of U.S.$20,000, which she used to pay down the mortgage. Richard's mother died during the winter, leaving him a monthly annuity of U.S.$700 that will last for seven years.

Although they feel comfortable with their money, they haven't been able to grasp the financial time frame. It appears the mortgage could be gone very quickly, but how quickly? And once the mortgage is paid, Richard and Marilyn could have close to $40,000 a year to invest. How do they invest this money and, if it's handled wisely, when can they retire?

At the moment, they have $15,000 in a joint savings account, $5,000 in CSBs, $17,000 in GICs in Richard's RRSP and $5,000 in GICs in Marilyn's RRSP. Richard dabbled in the stock market nearly a decade ago, but after making a good profit on a few stocks he became overconfident and lost the money on a sprinkling of small resource companies. The remnants of his stock portfolio are a gold mining company called Vedron Ltd. and an oil company called Chancellor Energy Resources Inc. He can't be bothered to sell the stocks and hasn't the interest nor the time to manage a portfolio of stocks and bonds.

However, he does have $56,000 invested in his employer's stock, which he acquired through the employee stock purchase plan. He purchased the stocks with an interest-free loan just after the stock market collapsed in 1987 and they've nearly doubled in value since then. There are rumours of a takeover, which could drive the shares even higher. He had bought the stocks as a retirement investment, not intending to sell them until he left the company. Should he keep them or should he sell them? Should he buy more?

The financial issues confronting the Levitches are quite straightforward:

- When will the mortgage be paid?
- If Richard works until he's fifty-five, when can Marilyn retire?
- If both Richard and Marilyn want to retire at the same time, when would it be possible financially?
- How should they invest their money once the mortgage is gone?

The Levitches' financial plan

The Levitches' financial plan was prepared by T.E. Financial Consultants Ltd. of Toronto.

The starting point for Marilyn's and Richard's retirement planning is to examine the wealth they've built already, as well as their income and living expenses. The Levitches' lifestyle leaves plenty of surplus cash that can be funnelled into saving for retirement. Together they earn $72,141 after tax, a yearly income boosted by U.S.$8,400, or $10,080, from Richard's inheritance. With only $39,800 in annual expenses, they have $42,421 to spend or save as they wish.

There are many possible retirement scenarios for the Levitches, but the first step in any of them is to pay off the mortgage. The Levitches have $15,000 sitting in a bank account earning 4.2 percent interest, while they're paying 10.5 percent interest on their mortgage. Although they feel comfortable having this cushion, they could obtain a personal line of credit to cover unexpected expenses instead. They would then take the cash in the savings account and pay down their mortgage. They'll still owe $102,000, but because of their unusual ability to save, the Levitches could pay off their mortgage within four years.

The planners looked at a series of projections, but isolated only two. In the first scenario, Marilyn can retire about six months after the mortgage is paid, when she's forty-six. Richard could then retire when he's fifty-five. Since she won't be fifty-five years old nor have the necessary ten years' membership in her pension plan, she would not be eligible for a pension but could roll the pension funds into her RRSP. Richard could take an early pension at age fifty-five, but it will be reduced by 4 percent for each year he retires before age sixty-two – or 28 percent. Although they will have to dip into their unsheltered investments to meet living expenses, the Levitches should leave their RRSPs untouched until they're seventy-one years old and then collapse the plans into RRIFs. This will allow their RRSP investments to continue to grow sheltered from tax.

In the second scenario, Marilyn and Richard retire together when he's fifty-two and she's fifty-one. Neither would be able to take a pension, since under the rules of their plans they must be at least fifty-five years old to do so. But both Richard and Marilyn could roll their funds into their RRSPs. Although the couple would have to dip into their capital, they should wait until age seventy-one to purchase RRIFs with their RRSPs. From age seventy-one to eighty-four, they could live on the income from their investments and pensions. At age eighty-four, they would again have to start cutting into their capital, but by then they would be past their life expectancies. With this strategy, there would be a much different flow of income and expenses than that depicted in the first scenario.

Retiring early will demand more than diligent saving by the Levitches. They'll have to structure their finances more efficiently. Marilyn and Richard have a net worth of $270,877, with the bulk of that wealth in their home, which is held in both their names, and their joint bank account. However, their remaining assets are split unevenly. Marilyn has only $5,000 in her RRSP, while Richard has $84,053 in RRSPs, CSBs, his pension plan and stock portfolio.

As a couple, they would be able to reduce their tax burden in retirement if they begin to build wealth in Marilyn's hands as well as in Richard's. All of Marilyn's net income should be used to pay down the mortgage, while Richard's income pays the living expenses. This should be carefully documented. Once the mortgage is paid, Richard can purchase Marilyn's interest in the home, thus putting investment funds into her hands. They should also build up Marilyn's RRSP by putting all of Richard's RRSP contributions into

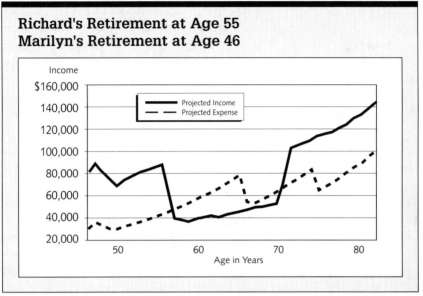

Richard's Retirement at Age 55
Marilyn's Retirement at Age 46

Income

—	Projected Income
– –	Projected Expense

Age in Years

CHART VII

a spousal plan for her. Marilyn would still make maximum contributions to her plan. If Marilyn and Richard can arrange their finances so they each have the same amount of income in retirement, their family tax burden will be reduced significantly.

The Levitches' insurance plans

If Marilyn retires at age forty-six, Richard's life and disability insurance becomes critical, since he will be responsible for funding their retirement. Richard has $100,000 worth of coverage from a private plan as well as $110,000 of group insurance.

But if Richard were to die, Marilyn would need closer to $395,000 from his insurance policies if she wanted to maintain her lifestyle and retire at age sixty. Richard needs another $185,000 in insurance. Marilyn has a $26,000 policy at work, $6,000 through Richard's employer and $100,000 in private coverage. This is adequate for now. Once the mortgage is paid or Marilyn retires, the insurance coverage should be reviewed. Richard has also opted to buy accidental death policies through his company plan – $250,000 on his life and $125,000 on Marilyn's. When Richard or Marilyn die, it is likely to be from natural causes, not by accident, making the policies unnecessary. The premiums would be best put toward basic insurance that will pay no matter what the cause of death.

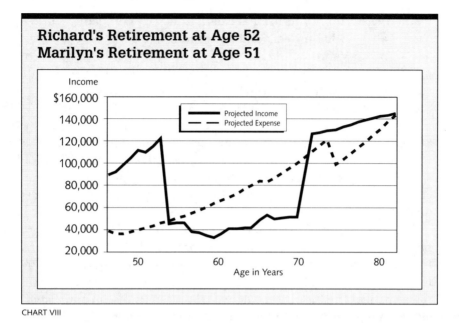

Richard's Retirement at Age 52
Marilyn's Retirement at Age 51

Income

Legend: — Projected Income / – – Projected Expense

Age in Years

CHART VIII

Both Marilyn and Richard are covered by disability insurance at work and may not be eligible to buy more insurance privately. However, they should look at the definition of total disability and the indexation of the benefits. There are private plans that could fill any gaps in the group plans. These plans are expensive but once Marilyn retires, Richard's coverage is critical.

The Levitches' investment strategy

Once the mortgage is paid, Marilyn and Richard should begin building an investment portfolio. Given their age and ability to tolerate risk, this portfolio should be invested 55 percent in equities and 45 percent in fixed-income securities. The RRSPs should be invested in GICs, term deposits, money market instruments, CSBs or government bonds.

Richard's decision to sell his company stock should rest on his view of the company's prospects – if the company is likely to continue growing and the stock price will probably continue to climb, there is little reason to sell. However, Richard should be aware that his interest-free loan from the company to buy the shares is gradually adding to his CNIL (cumulative net investment loss) account, restricting his ability to use his exemption. The company's outlook should also guide his decision to buy more shares.

As for the Vedron and Chancellor stocks, Richard can sell them now and use the loss to reduce his CNIL account or, since the stocks are now worth so little, he could keep them in the faint hope the companies will eventually turn around.

Once they both retire, the Levitches could have as much as $600,000 in investments, excluding their home. Since Richard does not want to be involved in managing these investments, he should split the management of these funds. He could put 30 percent or 35 percent in a mutual fund and the rest in the hands of an investment counsellor.

Finally, neither Marilyn nor Richard has a will. Both should prepare legally drafted wills as soon as possible. This will ensure that their wishes are carried out and their estate is distributed with the least possible taxation or disruption. Richard could consider creating a spousal trust for his estate with Marilyn as the income beneficiary, giving her the right to encroach upon capital. Because a trust is taxed as an individual, Marilyn's tax burden could be reduced by splitting her income into two streams – one taxed in the hands of the trust and the other in her hands.

Early retirement is Marilyn's and Richard's dream, but they should carefully consider the softer implications of leaving work early in life. Work doesn't just fill thirty-six or so hours a week. It can provide personal satisfaction and the friendship of colleagues. Marilyn likes to garden and enjoys reading, but she's contemplating thirty-five or forty years in retirement. Richard could live twenty-five or thirty years after he quits working. They intend to work hard to make retirement financially feasible. They should work equally hard to develop the interests, hobbies and friendships that will make retirement emotionally satisfying as well.

The unravelling of Mrs. Cole's bad advice

The voice on the other end of the telephone line was distinctly that of an older woman, her story spilling out a little more quickly than the receptionist could follow. The woman, Mrs. Jenny Cole, was a widow whose husband had died only a few months before. "I don't like to bother you, but I'm not sure just what I should do," she tried to explain. "My friends were only trying to help and they sent me to a financial planner who seems very nice. But, well, this just doesn't feel right."

Mrs. Cole is one of a million widows in Canada, a sixty-year-old woman suddenly faced with managing thousands of dollars and the loss of her most intimate and trusted companion. Although she was bereaved, she was not destitute. She owned a comfortable home in a small eastern Ontario town and her husband had left $50,000 in GICs and an $8,126 yearly annuity. She had also received more than $200,000 from his insurance policy. Intimidated by the task of investing the money, she was convinced by family and friends to see a financial planner.

After answering a multitude of questions, Mrs. Cole was advised not only to invest her nest egg in a portfolio of mutual funds, but to borrow $75,000 to boost her potential returns. Almost all of her money was then invested in the following mutual funds:
- $31,575 in Bolton Tremblay Taurus Fund,
- $36,276 in Bolton Tremblay International Fund,
- $9,367 in Mackenzie Financial Industrial Fund,
- $38,687 in Mackenzie Financial Industrial Dividend Fund,
- $3,009 in Mackenzie Financial Industrial American Fund,
- $3,648 in Mackenzie Financial Industrial Global Fund,
- $3,509 in Mackenzie Financial Industrial Growth Fund,
- $58,305 in United Financial American Fund,
- $60,897 in United Financial Accumulative Fund.

This left her with only $4,800 in her bank account, $50,000 in GICs, a $75,000 loan and a queasy feeling in the pit of her stomach. She had her daily living expenses to pay and was concerned that income from her investments would not sustain her lifestyle. She was taking $7,000 a year out of the mutual funds through a withdrawal plan, but this was more than her funds were earning. Despite the euphoria in the financial markets, she was worried that a downturn could have a painfully damaging effect on her financial well-being. On top of this, she was uncomfortable having a loan against her mutual funds and intended to make a $45,000 payment against the loan.

Mrs. Cole's financial plan
Mrs. Cole's financial plan was prepared in January 1987 by George Swan of Private Client Services, Bank of Montreal in Toronto.

Every investor has different goals for investments. A young couple hoping to soon buy their first home requires investments that can be turned into cash immediately. Individuals who are building up wealth for retirement need growth. Others who depend on income from their investments to meet their personal living costs need investments that provide a steady income and the assurance that their capital is safe.

Mrs. Cole had good reason to be worried about the portfolio that had been created for her. She had a net worth of $611,073, but $386,000, or 56 percent, was in her home, car and furniture. She had very little cash on hand and 83 percent of her investment portfolio was in growth-oriented mutual funds. It was a portfolio that didn't even provide the stream of income she needed to cover her daily needs.

When Mrs. Cole listed her living expenses, she discovered she required $33,564 a year. Yet her income from her pension, mutual funds, GICs and Canada Pension Plan benefits was only $18,394. Over the coming year, she wanted to buy a new car and a new furnace, and take a trip to Europe with her daughter. With less than 1 percent of her assets in cash, she wouldn't be able to meet these expenses.

In early 1987, when Mrs. Cole called Swan, he believed the stock market was more likely to decline than it was to rise over the next twelve to eighteen months. The future direction of interest rates was also unclear, although there seemed to be as many good reasons for interest rates to go down as for them to go up.

Mrs. Cole had been persuaded to invest in funds that didn't suit her need for income nor her ability to tolerate risk. Even though she was a retired widow whose financial circumstances could not justify risk, she had been counselled to invest the majority of her funds in risk-oriented investments. She had also been persuaded to borrow funds to purchase more risk-oriented investments. Since she wasn't receiving enough income from her mutual funds to support her annual living expenses, her investment advisors had established a plan for the automatic withdrawal of funds, gradually depleting her capital – a very dangerous move. Swan advised Mrs. Cole to systematically reduce the amount of risk and to increase the income-bearing investments within her portfolio. But, before making any changes to the portfolio, Mrs. Cole was advised to meet with an

investment broker to review the suggestions. He recommended the following strategy:
- Sell the Bolton Tremblay Taurus Fund and use the $31,575 to pay off part of the $75,000 loan.
- Transfer the $38,687 in the Industrial Dividend Fund to a mortgage or fixed-income mutual fund.
- Redeem the remainder of the Industrial mutual funds and re-invest the $19,533 in a fixed-income or mortgage fund.
- Redeem the United American and United Accumulative mutual funds and use $43,425 of the $119,202 to eliminate the remainder of the investment loan. Of the $75,777 remaining, $40,000 should be put into 90-day treasury bills. This would give Mrs. Cole a higher rate of interest than that of savings accounts and, if interest rates began to climb, she would have the flexibility to lock in higher rates in longer-term interest-bearing securities. The final $35,777 could be invested in another fixed-income mutual fund.
- Retain the Bolton Tremblay International Fund. It has a track record of superior performance and should provide enough growth to offset inflation. Any gains from this fund could be sheltered under the lifetime capital gains exemption.
- When the $50,000 in GICs matured in March 1987, Swan suggested that Mrs. Cole reinvest the money in interest-bearing securities.

This reorganization of Mrs. Cole's portfolio would reduce the growth-oriented equity portion of her portfolio to about 6 percent of her total assets, thus reducing her exposure to risk. Before making any changes to the portfolio, Mrs. Cole was advised to meet with a licensed investment broker to review these suggestions.

Along with her annuity and CPP pension, the new portfolio would provide a steady income stream, but at $26,985 a year it would still not be enough to cover her living expenses. Consequently, it was important that she establish a monthly budget to monitor her spending habits. This way she could identify and eliminate unnecessary expenses. It was also clear she would have to stagger the purchase of a car, furnace and her European vacation to prevent any major erosion of her investment capital.

The Future Value of a $1

YEARS	1%	2%	3%	4%	5%	6%	7%	8%	9%	10%
1	1.010	1.020	1.030	1.040	1.050	1.060	1.070	1.080	1.090	1.100
2	1.020	1.040	1.061	1.082	1.103	1.124	1.145	1.166	1.188	1.210
3	1.030	1.061	1.093	1.125	1.158	1.191	1.225	1.260	1.295	1.331
4	1.041	1.082	1.126	1.170	1.216	1.262	1.311	1.360	1.412	1.464
5	1.051	1.104	1.159	1.217	1.276	1.338	1.403	1.469	1.539	1.611
6	1.062	1.126	1.194	1.265	1.340	1.419	1.501	1.587	1.677	1.772
7	1.072	1.149	1.230	1.316	1.407	1.504	1.606	1.714	1.828	1.949
8	1.083	1.172	1.267	1.369	1.477	1.594	1.718	1.851	1.993	2.144
9	1.094	1.195	1.305	1.423	1.551	1.689	1.838	1.999	2.172	2.358
10	1.105	1.219	1.344	1.480	1.629	1.791	1.967	2.159	2.367	2.594
11	1.116	1.243	1.384	1.539	1.710	1.898	2.105	2.332	2.580	2.853
12	1.127	1.268	1.426	1.601	1.796	2.012	2.252	2.518	2.813	3.138
13	1.138	1.294	1.469	1.665	1.886	2.133	2.410	2.720	3.066	3.452
14	1.149	1.319	1.513	1.732	1.980	2.261	2.579	2.937	3.342	3.797
15	1.161	1.346	1.558	1.801	2.079	2.397	2.759	3.172	3.642	4.177
16	1.173	1.373	1.605	1.873	2.183	2.540	2.952	3.426	3.970	4.595
17	1.184	1.400	1.653	1.948	2.292	2.693	3.159	3.700	4.328	5.054
18	1.196	1.428	1.702	2.026	2.407	2.854	3.380	3.996	4.717	5.560
19	1.208	1.457	1.754	2.107	2.527	3.026	3.617	4.316	5.142	6.116
20	1.220	1.486	1.806	2.191	2.653	3.207	3.870	4.661	5.604	6.727
21	1.232	1.516	1.860	2.279	2.786	3.400	4.141	5.034	6.109	7.400
22	1.245	1.546	1.916	2.370	2.925	3.604	4.430	5.437	6.659	8.140
23	1.257	1.577	1.974	2.465	3.072	3.820	4.741	5.871	7.258	8.954
24	1.270	1.608	2.033	2.563	3.225	4.049	5.072	6.341	7.911	9.850
25	1.282	1.641	2.094	2.666	3.386	4.292	5.427	6.848	8.623	10.835
26	1.295	1.673	2.157	2.772	3.556	4.549	5.807	7.396	9.399	11.918
27	1.308	1.707	2.221	2.883	3.733	4.822	6.214	7.988	10.245	13.110
28	1.321	1.741	2.288	2.999	3.920	5.112	6.649	8.627	11.167	14.421
29	1.335	1.776	2.357	3.119	4.116	5.418	7.114	9.317	12.172	15.863
30	1.348	1.811	2.427	3.243	4.322	5.743	7.612	10.063	13.268	17.449
31	1.361	1.848	2.500	3.373	4.538	6.088	8.145	10.868	14.462	19.194
32	1.375	1.885	2.575	3.508	4.765	6.453	8.715	11.737	15.763	21.114
33	1.389	1.922	2.652	3.648	5.003	6.841	9.325	12.676	17.182	23.225
34	1.403	1.961	2.732	3.794	5.253	7.251	9.978	13.690	18.728	25.548
35	1.417	2.000	2.814	3.946	5.516	7.686	10.677	14.785	20.414	28.102
36	1.431	2.040	2.898	4.104	5.792	8.147	11.424	15.968	22.251	30.913
37	1.445	2.081	2.985	4.268	6.081	8.636	12.224	17.246	24.254	34.004
38	1.460	2.122	3.075	4.439	6.385	9.154	13.079	18.625	26.437	37.404
39	1.474	2.165	3.167	4.616	6.705	9.704	13.995	20.115	28.816	41.145
40	1.489	2.208	3.262	4.801	7.040	10.286	14.974	21.725	31.409	45.259

YEARS	11%	12%	13%	14%	15%	16%	17%	18%	19%	20%
1	1.110	1.120	1.130	1.140	1.150	1.160	1.170	1.180	1.190	1.200
2	1.232	1.254	1.277	1.300	1.323	1.346	1.369	1.392	1.416	1.440
3	1.368	1.405	1.443	1.482	1.521	1.561	1.602	1.643	1.685	1.728
4	1.518	1.574	1.630	1.689	1.749	1.811	1.874	1.939	2.005	2.074
5	1.685	1.762	1.842	1.925	2.011	2.100	2.192	2.288	2.386	2.488
6	1.870	1.974	2.082	2.195	2.313	2.436	2.565	2.700	2.840	2.986
7	2.076	2.211	2.353	2.502	2.660	2.826	3.001	3.185	3.379	3.583
8	2.305	2.476	2.658	2.853	3.059	3.278	3.511	3.759	4.021	4.300
9	2.558	2.773	3.004	3.252	3.518	3.803	4.108	4.435	4.785	5.160
10	2.839	3.106	3.395	3.707	4.046	4.411	4.807	5.234	5.695	6.192
11	3.152	3.479	3.836	4.226	4.652	5.117	5.624	6.176	6.777	7.430
12	3.498	3.896	4.335	4.818	5.350	5.936	6.580	7.288	8.064	8.916
13	3.883	4.363	4.898	5.492	6.153	6.886	7.699	8.599	9.596	10.699
14	4.310	4.887	5.535	6.261	7.076	7.988	9.007	10.147	11.420	12.839
15	4.785	5.474	6.254	7.138	8.137	9.266	10.539	11.974	13.590	15.407
16	5.311	6.130	7.067	8.137	9.358	10.748	12.330	14.129	16.172	18.488
17	5.895	6.866	7.986	9.276	10.761	12.468	14.426	16.672	19.244	22.186
18	6.544	7.690	9.024	10.575	12.375	14.463	16.879	19.673	22.901	26.623
19	7.263	8.613	10.197	12.056	14.232	16.777	19.748	23.214	27.252	31.948
20	8.062	9.646	11.523	13.743	16.367	19.461	23.106	27.393	32.429	38.338
21	8.949	10.804	13.021	15.668	18.822	22.574	27.034	32.324	38.591	46.005
22	9.934	12.100	14.714	17.861	21.645	26.186	31.629	38.142	45.923	55.206
23	11.026	13.552	16.627	20.362	24.891	30.376	37.006	45.008	54.649	66.247
24	12.239	15.179	18.788	23.212	28.625	35.236	43.297	53.109	65.032	79.497
25	13.585	17.000	21.231	26.462	32.919	40.874	50.658	62.669	77.388	95.396
26	15.080	19.040	23.991	30.167	37.857	47.414	59.270	73.949	92.092	114.475
27	16.739	21.325	27.109	34.390	43.535	55.000	69.345	87.260	109.589	137.371
28	18.580	23.884	30.633	39.204	50.066	63.800	81.134	102.967	130.411	164.845
29	20.624	26.750	34.616	44.693	57.575	74.009	94.927	121.501	155.189	197.814
30	22.892	29.960	39.116	50.950	66.212	85.850	111.065	143.371	184.675	237.376
31	25.410	33.555	44.201	58.083	76.144	99.586	129.946	169.177	219.764	284.852
32	28.206	37.582	49.947	66.215	87.565	115.520	152.036	199.629	261.519	341.822
33	31.308	42.092	56.440	75.485	100.700	134.003	177.883	235.563	311.207	410.186
34	34.752	47.143	63.777	86.053	115.805	155.443	208.123	277.964	370.337	492.224
35	38.575	52.800	72.069	98.100	133.176	180.314	243.503	327.997	440.701	590.668
36	42.818	59.136	81.437	111.834	153.152	209.164	284.899	387.037	524.434	708.802
37	47.528	66.232	92.024	127.491	176.125	242.631	333.332	456.703	624.076	850.562
38	52.756	74.180	103.987	145.340	202.543	281.452	389.998	538.910	742.651	1.020.675
39	58.559	83.081	117.506	165.687	232.925	326.484	456.298	635.914	883.754	1.224.810
40	65.001	93.051	132.782	188.884	267.864	378.721	533.869	750.378	1.051.668	1.469.772

The Future Value of $1 Invested Every Year

YEARS	1%	2%	3%	4%	5%	6%	7%	8%	9%	10%
1	1.010	1.020	1.030	1.040	1.050	1.060	1.070	1.080	1.090	1.100
2	2.030	2.060	2.091	2.122	2.153	2.184	2.215	2.246	2.278	2.310
3	3.060	3.122	3.184	3.246	3.310	3.375	3.440	3.506	3.573	3.641
4	4.101	4.204	4.309	4.416	4.526	4.637	4.751	4.867	4.985	5.105
5	5.152	5.308	5.468	5.633	5.802	5.975	6.153	6.336	6.523	6.716
6	6.214	6.434	6.662	6.898	7.142	7.394	7.654	7.923	8.200	8.487
7	7.286	7.583	7.892	8.214	8.549	8.897	9.260	9.637	10.028	10.436
8	8.369	8.755	9.159	9.583	10.027	10.491	10.978	11.488	12.021	12.579
9	9.462	9.950	10.464	11.006	11.578	12.181	12.816	13.487	14.193	14.937
10	10.567	11.169	11.808	12.486	13.207	13.972	14.784	15.645	16.560	17.531
11	11.683	12.412	13.192	14.026	14.917	15.870	16.888	17.977	19.141	20.384
12	12.809	13.680	14.618	15.627	16.713	17.882	19.141	20.495	21.953	23.523
13	13.947	14.974	16.086	17.292	18.599	20.015	21.550	23.215	25.019	26.975
14	15.097	16.293	17.599	19.024	20.579	22.276	24.129	26.152	28.361	30.772
15	16.258	17.639	19.157	20.825	22.657	24.673	26.888	29.324	32.003	34.950
16	17.430	19.012	20.762	22.698	24.840	27.213	29.840	32.750	35.974	39.545
17	18.615	20.412	22.414	24.645	27.132	29.906	32.999	36.450	40.301	44.599
18	19.811	21.841	24.117	26.671	29.539	32.760	36.379	40.446	45.018	50.159
19	21.019	23.297	25.870	28.778	32.066	35.786	39.995	44.762	50.160	56.275
20	22.239	24.783	27.676	30.969	34.719	38.993	43.865	49.423	55.765	63.002
21	23.472	26.299	29.537	33.248	37.505	42.392	48.006	54.457	61.873	70.403
22	24.716	27.845	31.453	35.618	40.430	45.996	52.436	59.893	68.532	78.543
23	25.973	29.422	33.426	38.083	43.502	49.816	57.177	65.765	75.790	87.497
24	27.243	31.030	35.459	40.646	46.727	53.865	62.249	72.106	83.701	97.347
25	28.526	32.671	37.553	43.312	50.113	58.156	67.676	78.954	92.324	108.182
26	29.821	34.344	39.710	46.084	53.669	62.706	73.484	86.351	101.723	120.100
27	31.129	36.051	41.931	48.968	57.403	67.528	79.698	94.339	111.968	133.210
28	32.450	37.792	44.219	51.966	61.323	72.640	86.347	102.966	123.135	147.631
29	33.785	39.568	46.575	55.085	65.439	78.058	93.461	112.283	135.308	163.494
30	35.133	41.379	49.003	58.328	69.761	83.802	101.073	122.346	148.575	180.943
31	36.494	43.227	51.503	61.701	74.299	89.890	109.218	133.214	163.037	200.138
32	37.869	45.112	54.078	65.210	79.064	96.343	117.933	144.951	178.800	221.252
33	39.258	47.034	56.730	68.858	84.067	103.184	127.259	157.627	195.982	244.477
34	40.660	48.994	59.462	72.652	89.320	110.435	137.237	171.317	214.711	270.024
35	42.077	50.994	62.276	76.598	94.836	118.121	147.913	186.102	235.125	298.127
36	43.508	53.034	65.174	80.702	100.628	126.268	159.337	202.070	257.376	329.039
37	44.953	55.115	68.159	84.970	106.710	134.904	171.561	219.316	281.630	363.043
38	46.412	57.237	71.234	89.409	113.095	144.058	184.640	237.941	308.066	400.448
39	47.886	59.402	74.401	94.026	119.800	153.762	198.635	258.057	336.882	441.593
40	49.375	61.610	77.663	98.827	126.840	164.048	213.610	279.781	368.292	486.852

YEARS	11%	12%	13%	14%	15%	16%	17%	18%	19%	20%
1	1.110	1.120	1.130	1.140	1.150	1.160	1.170	1.180	1.190	1.200
2	2.342	2.374	2.407	2.440	2.473	2.506	2.539	2.572	2.606	2.640
3	3.710	3.779	3.850	3.921	3.993	4.066	4.141	4.215	4.291	4.368
4	5.228	5.353	5.480	5.610	5.742	5.877	6.014	6.154	6.297	6.442
5	6.913	7.115	7.323	7.536	7.754	7.977	8.207	8.442	8.683	8.930
6	8.783	9.089	9.405	9.730	10.067	10.414	10.772	11.142	11.523	11.916
7	10.859	11.300	11.757	12.233	12.727	13.240	13.773	14.327	14.902	15.499
8	13.164	13.776	14.416	15.085	15.786	16.519	17.285	18.086	18.923	19.799
9	15.722	16.549	17.420	18.337	19.304	20.321	21.393	22.521	23.709	24.959
10	18.561	19.655	20.814	22.045	23.349	24.733	26.200	27.755	29.404	31.150
11	21.713	23.133	24.650	26.271	28.002	29.850	31.824	33.931	36.180	38.581
12	25.212	27.029	28.985	31.089	33.352	35.786	38.404	41.219	44.244	47.497
13	29.095	31.393	33.883	36.581	39.505	42.672	46.103	49.818	53.841	58.196
14	33.405	36.280	39.417	42.842	46.580	50.660	55.110	59.965	65.261	71.035
15	38.190	41.753	45.672	49.980	54.717	59.925	65.649	71.939	78.850	86.442
16	43.501	47.884	52.739	58.118	64.075	70.673	77.979	86.068	95.022	104.931
17	49.396	54.750	60.725	67.394	74.836	83.141	92.406	102.740	114.266	127.117
18	55.939	62.440	69.749	77.969	87.212	97.603	109.285	122.414	137.166	153.740
19	63.203	71.052	79.947	90.025	101.444	114.380	129.033	145.628	164.418	185.688
20	71.265	80.699	91.470	103.768	117.810	133.841	152.139	173.021	196.847	224.026
21	80.214	91.503	104.491	119.436	136.632	156.415	179.172	205.345	235.438	270.031
22	90.148	103.603	119.205	137.297	158.276	182.601	210.801	243.487	281.362	325.237
23	101.174	117.155	135.831	157.659	183.168	212.978	247.808	288.494	336.010	391.484
24	113.413	132.334	154.620	180.871	211.793	248.214	291.105	341.603	401.042	470.981
25	126.999	149.334	175.850	207.333	244.712	289.088	341.763	404.272	478.431	566.377
26	142.079	168.374	199.841	237.499	282.569	336.502	401.032	478.221	570.522	680.853
27	158.817	189.699	226.950	271.889	326.104	391.503	470.378	565.481	680.112	818.223
28	177.397	213.583	257.583	311.094	376.170	455.303	551.512	668.447	810.523	983.068
29	198.021	240.333	292.199	355.787	433.745	529.312	646.439	789.948	965.712	1.180.882
30	220.913	270.293	331.315	406.737	499.957	615.162	757.504	933.319	1.150.387	1.418.258
31	246.324	303.848	375.516	464.820	576.100	714.747	887.449	1.102.496	1.370.151	1.703.109
32	274.529	341.429	425.463	531.035	663.666	830.267	1.039.486	1.302.125	1.631.670	2.044.931
33	305.837	383.521	481.903	606.520	764.365	964.270	1.217.368	1.537.688	1.942.877	2.455.118
34	340.590	430.663	545.681	692.573	880.170	1.119.713	1.425.491	1.815.652	2.313.214	2.947.341
35	379.164	483.463	617.749	790.673	1.013.346	1.300.027	1.668.994	2.143.649	2.753.914	3.538.009
36	421.982	542.599	699.187	902.507	1.166.498	1.509.191	1.953.894	2.530.686	3.278.348	4.246.811
37	469.511	608.831	791.211	1.029.998	1.342.622	1.751.822	2.287.225	2.987.389	3.902.424	5.097.373
38	522.267	683.010	895.198	1.175.338	1.545.165	2.033.273	2.677.224	3.526.299	4.645.075	6.118.048
39	580.826	766.091	1.012.704	1.341.025	1.778.090	2.359.757	3.133.522	4.162.213	5.528.829	7.342.858
40	645.827	859.142	1.145.486	1.529.909	2.045.954	2.738.478	3.667.391	4.912.591	6.580.496	8.812.629

Index